CONSTITUENTS BEFORE ASSEMBLY

Under what circumstances do new constitutions improve a nation's level of democracy? Between 1974 and 2014, democracy increased in 77 countries following the adoption of a new constitution, but it decreased or stayed the same in 47 others. This book demonstrates that increased participation in the forming of constitutions positively impacts levels of democracy. It is discovered that the degree of citizen participation at the "convening stage" of constitution-making has a strong effect on levels of democracy. This finding defies the common theory that levels of democracy result from the content of constitutions, and instead lends support to "deliberative" theories of democracy. Patterns of constitutions are then compared, differentiating imposed and popular constitution-making processes, using case studies from Chile, Nigeria, Gambia, and Venezuela to illustrate the dynamics specific to imposed constitution-making, and case studies from Colombia, Ecuador, Egypt, and Tunisia to illustrate the specific dynamics of popular constitution-making.

Todd A. Eisenstadt is Professor of Government at American University. His democratization and rule of law scholarship includes his award-winning dissertation book *Courting Democracy in Mexico: Party Strategies and Electoral Institutions* (Cambridge, 2004). His research has been funded by Fulbright, the Ford and Mellon Foundations, and the National Science Foundation. He has held visiting appointments at El Colegio de México, Harvard University, the University of California, San Diego, and the Latin American Social Science Faculty (FLACSO) in Ecuador.

A. Carl LeVan is Associate Professor in the School of International Service at American University in Washington, DC. He is the author of *Dictators and Democracy in African Development: The Political Economy of Good Governance in Nigeria* (Cambridge, 2015) and co-editor of *African State Governance: Subnational Politics and National Power* (2015). Prior to receiving his Ph.D. in Political Science from the University of California – San Diego, he worked as a legislative director in the US Congress and later worked as a technical advisor to Nigeria's National Assembly.

Tofigh Maboudi is Assistant Professor in the Department of Political Science at Loyola University Chicago. His research on constitutional reform processes has appeared in the *American Political Science Review* and *Political Research Quarterly*. Prior to receiving his Ph.D. in Political Science from American University in Washington, DC, he worked as a foreign media consultant in Tehran, Iran, where he received his Master's degree in North American Studies. During his Ph.D. program, he received several awards including the American University's Award for Outstanding Scholarship at the Graduate Level.

Comparative Constitutional Law and Policy

SERIES EDITORS

Tom Ginsburg, *University of Chicago*
Zachary Elkins, *University of Texas at Austin*
Ran Hirschl, *University of Toronto*

Comparative constitutional law is an intellectually vibrant field that encompasses an increasingly broad array of approaches and methodologies. This series collects analytically innovative and empirically grounded work from scholars of comparative constitutionalism across academic disciplines. Books in the series include theoretically informed studies of single constitutional jurisdictions, comparative studies of constitutional law and institutions, and edited collections of original essays that respond to challenging theoretical and empirical questions in the field.

BOOKS IN THE SERIES

Constituents before Assembly: Participation, Deliberation, and Representation in the Crafting of New Constitutions Todd A. Eisenstadt, A. Carl LeVan, and Tofigh Maboudi

Buddhism, Politics and the Limits of Law: The Pyrrhic Constitutionalism of Sri Lanka Benjamin Schonthal

Assessing Constitutional Performance Tom Ginsburg and Aziz Huq

Engaging with Social Rights Brian Ray

Constitutional Courts as Mediators Julio Ríos-Figueroa

Perils of Judicial Self-Government in Transitional Societies David Kosař

Making We the People Chaihark Hahm and Sung Ho Kim

Radical Deprivation on Trial Cesar Rodríguez-Garavito and Diana Rodríguez-Franco

Unstable Constitutionalism edited by Mark Tushnet and Madhav Khosla

Constituents before Assembly

PARTICIPATION, DELIBERATION, AND REPRESENTATION IN THE CRAFTING OF NEW CONSTITUTIONS

TODD A. EISENSTADT

American University

A. CARL LEVAN

American University

TOFIGH MABOUDI

Loyola University Chicago

CAMBRIDGE
UNIVERSITY PRESS

CAMBRIDGE
UNIVERSITY PRESS

University Printing House, Cambridge CB2 8BS, United Kingdom

One Liberty Plaza, 20th Floor, New York, NY 10006, USA

477 Williamstown Road, Port Melbourne, VIC 3207, Australia

4843/24, 2nd Floor, Ansari Road, Daryaganj, Delhi – 110002, India

79 Anson Road, #06-04/06, Singapore 079906

Cambridge University Press is part of the University of Cambridge.

It furthers the University's mission by disseminating knowledge in the pursuit of education, learning, and research at the highest international levels of excellence.

www.cambridge.org
Information on this title: www.cambridge.org/9781107168220
DOI: 10.1017/9781316717080

First published 2017

Printed in the United States of America by Sheridan Books, Inc.

A catalogue record for this publication is available from the British Library.

ISBN 978-1-107-16822-0 Hardback

Eisenstadt dedicates this book to his daughters, Natalia and Paola, with great pride in how they are learning to negotiate adulthood with keen intellects, empathy, and strong constitutions.

LeVan dedicates this book to his friend and mentor, Rep. John Conyers, Jr., for his unwavering efforts to make unheard voices heard in the din of American democracy.

Maboudi dedicates this book to his parents, Abdul-Karim and Nosrat, for their sacrifice and foresight, and for founding his life's constitution.

Contents

Figures

Tables

Introducing Constitutions as Political Process

The "Last Word" or – More Likely – Just the Most Recent in Studies of Constitution-Making and Democracy?

From 1787 until well into the twentieth century, constitutions were understood as pacts around which societal expectations converged. They were largely viewed as the written record of elite settlements that reflected popular opinion to greater or lesser degrees, and as critical junctures – unusual moments that were the result of unique historical circumstances and contingencies. Liberals during decolonization and the subsequent wave of democratization challenged both dimensions of this view. Rather than symbolizing rare revolutionary events in the long arc of history, constitutions were simply tools and broad legal reforms within a political process better analyzed as continuous. And rather than representing elite pacts, novel participatory modes of constitution-making, such as constituent assemblies and the increased use of referendums, reinforced popular perceptions of constitutions as the cumulative result of new social contracts. As the Third Wave's democratizing momentum peaked in the 1990s, constitutional reforms emerged as precursors to "founding" elections, placing the people's consent at the center of regime transitions. This revised view thus implied that constitutions were no longer an elite affair. It inspired hopes that institutions could restrain rulers, and that popular participation would legitimize public authority – frequently if necessary.

This book explores the different roles constitutions play by focusing on the politics surrounding constitution-making. Since the 1970s, there has been a shift in norms for popular participation, and parallel shifts in international law, development aid plans, and ordinary citizens' rising expectations that their views must be taken into account. Still, translating public opinion into higher public law remains nearly as complicated as it was during the French Revolution. Popular participation can suffocate either dissent or rein in undemocratic arbitrary elite power. This book seeks to understand when constitutional processes improve such democratic connections between citizens and leaders, and when they do not.

New and developing democracies – here represented by cases from Latin America, Africa, and the Middle East – offer hard cases for the provision of public goods constitutions that improve fairness and equity and are actually implemented. Developed democracies fall short too, but in developing countries new to the art of promulgating democratic constitutions, these shortcomings are more transparent as they are less proficiently covered over. Hence, while our dataset includes all nations with new constitutions between 1974–2014, we place an emphasis in the empirical case chapters (mainly 4 and 5) on nations midway through the democratization process.

We seek a space where Madison's Dilemma, of how to empower citizens without overpowering political institutions with the tyranny that unruly majorities can bring, meets Hugo Chávez's shadow. Chávez, the late Venezuelan autocrat who was obsessed throughout his entire life with linking the Bolivarian Union of Nations via new trade agreements and political arrangements, sought to empower himself and his political allies with discretion, but in the garb of solomonic constitutional reform to consolidate democracy. Much has been said about "window dressing institutions" in the other great space where political factions negotiate and array their forces, the electoral space, in studies on "electoral engineering" and "sham elections." While "sham constitutions" require more set up and subtlety, and the phrase may ring too loudly, we do seek to question the longstanding stylization of constitutions as the "last word" (literally) on nations' quality of democracy.

The twenty-first century opened with democratic backsliding, semi-authoritarianism, and hybrid regimes. These new realities make it important – from empirical and normative perspectives – to consider the contexts and consequences of new constitutions. This new generation of constitutions also coincided with shifts in constitutionalism. Prevailing approaches to constitutions focus on content, the conditions influencing successful implementation, or their impact on subsequent institutional configurations, such as presidential or parliamentary government. By departing from these research areas, we aim to understand different types of constitution-making processes and to situate democratization research within emerging debates on constitutionalism, rather than the other way around.

One shift in constitutionalism is that rather than assuming constitutions amount to foundational documents, this volume explores how constitutions often came to be viewed as precursor "contracts" to founding elections. O'Donnell et al. (1986) portrayed constitutions as core elements of pacts during the Third Wave that would lock in place elite "buy in." This view of constitutions as contested expressions in ongoing historical and political processes seems more consistent with less teleological views of democracy as evidenced by the twenty-first-century reality of authoritarian reversion and hybrid regimes. For the tenth consecutive year in 2015, there were more declines than gains in civil and political rights worldwide. In 2013, 27 countries in fact showed significant declines (Puddington 2013). Indeed, considering constitutions as mere iterations in decades-long intra-elite bargaining processes becomes all the more important from empirical and normative perspectives. The Arab Spring – like Uganda's constitution-making process, which appeared to have all the hallmarks of participatory governance – has thus far yielded only limited symbolic societal gains. Institutional advances have proven ephemeral due to elite management of processes that aspired to elusive models of deliberative democracy. If we aim to understand these mixed successes and the record of social movements that seek to create space for new political actors or formalize populist passions within the architecture of government, we also need to reconsider the modalities of citizen-elite interactions. In other words, constitutions, and their negotiation, become frames through which we can observe and monitor changes in state–society relations.

To that end, another shift in constitutionalism entails an increased interest in the process of making constitutions, and not just their content. While acknowledging that what constitutions state in their clauses and amendments is important, since it allows us to explore law as interconnected sets of ideas and to assess compliance with the rules of the game, the chapters in this book are mostly about the politics surrounding constitutions. Several authors, including Brown (2008) and Elkins et al. (2009), have extensively addressed what constitutions promise and how this affects subsequent institutional configurations. This book seeks to part from these studies of the importance of what constitutions do and do not say, and of how such content or omissions are translated into practice. We seek rather to understand the role of citizens and the interest groups they form in the actual convocation of constituent assemblies and in the drafting of constitutions, as well as in their subsequent ratifications by deliberative bodies and by the public. In the process, we seek to highlight the relationship we start to establish in chapters 2 and 3 between constitutional processes, deliberation, and democracy.

Historically, there has been a presumption that constitution-making was largely an elite affair, or at least an undertaking that kept specialized legal experts at the center of the process. The American constitutional assembly in 1787 consisted of 55 men who claimed to represent the interests of a broader public through republicanism, but they deliberated in secret and rewrote their mandate to do more than merely revise the Articles of Confederation. Though Jeffersonian democrats envisioned an informed and participatory public eventually stepping into civic life, other delegates argued for a constitution that would entrench more Burkean notions of government. Hamilton explained, "There ought to be a principle in government capable of resisting the popular current" (Chernow 2004, 233). Other delegates similarly argued for a need to contain "the turbulence and follies of democracy" and "popular frenzy" (Wilentz 2005, 32). Gargarella (2010) associates this view with a "liberal" model that shaped constitutions in Latin America during the 1800s by attempting to limit executive power, generate competing authorities across branches of government, and balance the risks of tyranny (too much government) with the dangers of anarchy (too little government). It valued political moderation and moral neutrality to protect individual liberties. A conservative model of constitutions defended elites as guardians of virtue and the common good, while making liberty conditional on some other source of values – such as the Catholic Church. Gargarella concludes that these two ideal types generally prevailed over a more radical model of constitutionalism that identifies the origins of the common good in populist majorities. The suppression of the radical model limited the opportunities for participatory constitution-making.

Popular participation in constitution-making is relatively recent in much of the world. However, the Latin American and East European transitions in the 1970s and 1980s, and most recently, Tunisia's "democratization through constitutionalism," give new hope to democracy promoters seeking to establish democratic norms and democratic legal codes simultaneously. In fact, as we argue, Tunisia did have a longstanding tradition of interest groups representing labor and human rights. This trend in Tunisia stood in contrast to most nations of the Arab world, which, as late as the nineteenth century, were united by three overarching goals: strengthen the state in the face of internal rebellion, address fiscal crisis (often through representative assembly), and prevent external penetration through declarations of sovereignty (Brown 2002, 31–4). Since then, many countries arguably adopted constitutions based on Western models but which were often changed at the whim of rulers or ignored (Rosen 2006). Prior to the Iraq War, constitutional debates in the Muslim World often centered on how to reconcile democracy and Islam (Al-Hibri 1992). Socialist influences on Arab nationalism tempered critiques of secularism. Today, Muslim countries embrace a wide variety of interpretations of Islam's relationship to constitutional law. In Tunisia, U.S. Secretary of State Hillary Clinton noted that the Islamic party that emerged victorious from elections had also pledged to "embrace freedom of religion and full rights for women."[1]

---

[1] Keynote Address at the National Democratic Institute's 2011 Democracy Awards Dinner by Hillary Rodham Clinton, November 7, 2011. www.state.gov/secretary/rm/2011/11/176750.htm

But today's democratic reformers increasingly face pressures from explicitly Muslim social movements (Grote and Röder 2012; Feldman 2009).

How and whether participatory democratic culture really extends to making constitutions presented new challenges and higher stakes than simply electing a chief executive. Referendums seemed to merely reinforce the more ritualistic and shallow elements of democracy as Iraq descended into civil war, Venezuela dabbled with dictatorship, and Ugandans voted to sacrifice term limits for constitutional reforms. One study concludes that referendums "are blunt and clumsy instruments for endorsing complex proposals on the structures of the state and the formulations of fundamental rights. They are in any event *post facto* devices for testing support" (Haysom 2007, 105). In contemporary Latin America, for example, open budgeting and other experiments in direct democracy make the case for a broader conceptualization of participation that encompasses other modalities (Altman 2013; Masud and Lakin 2011). At worst, referendums may amplify electoral components of democracy at the expense of other modes of participation.

This book seeks to more directly address "the participation question," which is often addressed indirectly through other research questions. Institutionalists, for example, have explored important questions related to constitutional compliance by studying term limits. Executive power grabs in Africa have arguably failed where civil society has drawn upon constitutional language to defend contestation as a core democratic principle and alternation of power as an essential sign of democratic consolidation (Kramon and Posner 2011). Participation promotes compliance, though it clearly does not guarantee it. Elkins, Ginsburg, and Melton focus on the question of constitutional survival. They conclude that inclusive drafting increases the likelihood of constitutional endurance, and that it is also associated with constitutional rights and democratic institutions such as universal suffrage, the secret ballot, and a guaranteed role for the public input into amending the constitution in the future (Ginsburg 2012, 54–7). More inclusive processes enable the integration of new social forces conducive to constitutional survival because they "can promote a unifying identity and invite participants to invest in the bargain" (Elkins et al. 2009, 211).

While we seek to measure and quantify participation in constitution-making in this book, we got a visceral sense of the importance of participation and deliberation in drafting this manuscript. While any mistakes on the pages of this text are the full responsibility of the authors, we had extensive assistance in formulating the ideas and empirical cases presented here. Before elaborating the narrative of how the book evolved and those who helped us at each step along the way, we wish to express our special gratitude to eight individuals

whose generous critiques were especially valuable. Nathan Brown and Hélène
Landemore read and commented on the entire draft of the manuscript at
a book workshop generously supported by American University's School of
Public Affairs (SPA) and School of International Service (SIS) in June 2016.
In addition, the late Joel Barkan and Jonathan Hartlyn offered great encour-
agement early in the process, with Hartlyn mentoring us throughout, as did
Zachary Elkins, who shared data, encouraged us, and offered support. Ghazal
P. Nadi offered several rounds of attentive comments, Gabriel Negretto
pushed us on our working assumptions, and Rob Albro brought an original
anthropological approach to the cases.

   The gestation of this project informally started when Eisenstadt and LeVan
directed the American Political Science Association's (APSA) Africa Workshop
in Nairobi in 2011, where Karuti Kanyinga and Joesphine Ahikire were among
African and US-based political scientists who helped launch a debate about
the importance of Kenya's 2010 constitution. This excellent workshop with
generous funding from the Andrew W. Mellon Foundation was adroitly managed at APSA by Betsy Super and Helena Saele. Back at American University,
Eisenstadt and LeVan co-taught a seminar on participation and democratization in fall 2011. Here they sought to further discuss broad issues leading to
this text, and were joined by Maboudi, whose interest in understanding the
Arab Spring cases through his own dissertation and efforts in working with
Eisenstadt and LeVan to construct a worldwide dataset led to long summer
meetings about which variables to include, what they demonstrated, and how
to represent them operationally.

   Deans James Goldgeier (SIS) and Barbara Romzek (SPA) supported a
May 2013 conference on "The Gap from Parchment to Practice: Ambivalent
Effects of Constitutions in Democratizing Countries," as did a grant received
from the Latin American Studies Association and the Andrew W. Mellon
Foundation, which brought some of the very best scholars of these topics
to American University. Stefan Kramer of the American University Library
helped register our dataset, publicly available at http://doi.org/10.17606/
M63W25. We are in debt to the following participants in that conference, and
still regret we could not publish an edited volume with many of the valuable
contributions to that discussion (some of which have been published sepa-
rately): Rob Albro, Nelly Arenas, Diego Ayo, Ana Maria Bejarano, Ernesto
Calvo, Miguel Centellas, Michael Coppedge, Kristin Diwan, Zachary Elkins,
Jon Gould, Eric Hershberg, Miriam Kornblith, Katie Kuhn, Adrienne LeBas,
Jie Lu, Eleanor Marchant, Devra Moehler, Shaheen Mozaffar, Renata
Segura, Diane Singerman, Matthew Taylor, Susanna Wing, and Jennifer
Widner. Our then-chairs, Clarence Lusane and Candice Nelson, helped

us execute the conference, as did Nicole Siegel and Brittany Stewart. At the Latin American Studies Association (LASA), Milagros Pereyra-Rojas, Sandra Louise Klinzing, and Pilar Rodriguez managed the project as part of their Mellon-LASA program. Ryan Briggs, Yelena Osipova-Stocker, Jennifer Yelle, and Ghazal P. Nadi, now experienced young scholars, worked diligently to research, code, and construct the Constitutionalism and Democracy Dataset (CDD). American University PhD students Daniela Stevens and Barbara dos Santos also helped us prepare this manuscript for publication.

We also presented parts of the *American Political Science Review* (APSR) article (the basis of Chapter 2) and other parts of the manuscript at multiple meetings of the African Studies Association, American Political Science Association, the International Studies Association, and the Latin American Studies Association, where Catherine Boone, Archon Fung, Donald Horowitz, Jane Mansbridge, and Andrew Reynolds offered particularly helpful feedback. Additionally, we thank the following institutions that invited us to present our work, and the individuals who invited us and provided particularly extensive comments: the short-lived (but hopefully returning) American University SIS-SPA joint workshop (2013, Agustina Giraudy, Eric Hershberg, Matthew Taylor, Rachel Robinson, Matthew Wright, Antoine Yoshinaka), the American University Government Workshop (2016, Daniela Stevens, Ryan Moore), University of Vermont (2013, Ned McMahon), the George Washington University Comparative Politics Workshop (2014, Henry Hale, Katie Kuhn, Cynthia McClintock, Harris Mylonas), the Comparative Politics DC Regional Workshop (2015, Ernesto Calvo), Brown University's Center for Latin American Studies (2014, Richard Snyder), the University of Stockholm (2016, Maria-Therese Gustafsson), the American Bar Association (2016, Catherine Lena Kelly, Ginna Anderson), and the US Peace Institute (2016, Susan Stigant, Virginia Bouvier, Thomas Leo Scherer, Paul Johnson). At American University we also thank Romzek and associate deans Jessica Waters and Vicky Wilkins, who made possible the 2016 book workshop with an Excellence with Impact grant, as did Julie Taylor and Courtney Peterson at SIS and Lisa Manning at SPA. We also thank former *APSR* Editor John Ishiyama and Cambridge University Press Editor John Berger for their good humor and judgment, and four anonymous reviewers of the article and two anonymous reviewers of the book.

Finally, Eisenstadt was able to interview constitution-makers in Bolivia, with a 2012 travel grant from the American University Vice Provost for Research, and Ecuador (while traveling for another project funded by National Science Foundation grant SES-31258). Eisenstadt thanks Diego Ayo for helping him navigate La Paz and Bolivia, and The Latin American Social

Sciences Faculty (FLACSO) in Quito, where he taught a seminar to outstanding graduate students in the summer of 2012. LeVan journeyed to Nigeria, The Gambia, and Uganda with funds from an SIS Dean's Summer Research Award (2012) and an SIS Collaborative Research Award (2013). He is indebted to the Makerere Institute for Social Research for their advice and assistance. Maboudi received a Doctoral Research Award from American University Vice Provost for Research, Jonathan Tubman, and conducted research in Tunisia and Morocco in November 2014–January 2015. He extends his special thanks to Radwan Masmoudi, President of the Center for the Study of Islam and Democracy in Tunis, Baudouin Dupret, Director of Centre Jacques-Berque in Rabat, and John Davison (Director) and Yhtimad Bouziane (Associate Director) of the Tangier American Legation Institute for Moroccan Studies for their assistance.

On a personal note, Eisenstadt thanks his wonderful soon-to-be-adult daughters Natalia and Paola, who motivate him every day to try to undertake work that can help – in any small way – improve the world for them. LeVan wishes to thank Moni for her support and inspiration, and Thoreau and Emerson for their endlessly amusing playground adventures. Maboudi thanks his wife and intellectual companion, Ghazal, for her continuing support, patience, and constructive suggestions.

1

A Call to Pens (Even If Not Mightier than Swords): How Context and Process Prevail over Content in Constitutional Change

During the Arab Spring, four new constitutions appeared to plant the seeds of democracy in the Middle East: Morocco (2011), Egypt (2012 and 2014), and Tunisia (2014), but only in Tunisia did the seeds take hold. This result is especially surprising for the case of Egypt, where a highly mobilized citizenry in 2012 widely debated the constitution in city squares, public assemblies, and social media. The government established a Facebook page for the Constituent Assembly, where more than 68,000 Egyptians provided feedback on the draft constitution and offered 78,000 suggestions. Another 35,000 Egyptians delivered written feedback to Constituent Assembly members during workshops across the country. This constitution-making process might have been considered democratic, except that the participation was not effective: the new government, led by the Muslim Brotherhood's Freedom and Justice Party, imposed a constitution that generally ignored the views of participating groups and then cracked down on dissenters, constitutional and otherwise.

Egypt's truncated "top-down" process was followed by a more incremental and participatory "bottom-up" effort involving mostly secular groups and civil society. The constitutional drafting discussion commenced with seemingly democratic participation, and it concluded with a referendum (with low turnout), which failed to legitimize the outcome. Almost immediately after its promulgation, public pressure to revoke the constitution mounted. In response, the military removed President Mohammed Morsi and revoked the 2012 constitution, leaving thousands of protesters dead and the country divided. But, rather than starting from scratch, the military generals seized the opportunity in 2013 to direct and control yet another top-down constitutional process.

Tunisia's constitution-writing experience during the same period was much more successful in ushering in a more democratic era. The absence of powerful legacy institutions from the old regime – ones that could influence the constitution-making process (such as the military and the judiciary in Egypt) – paved the way for a successful transition that inspired other Arab Spring social movements. Citizen participation in constitution-making came later, and as a final means of overcoming elite differences. The by-laws of the National Constituent Assembly (NCA) did not oblige the drafter to seek the people's advice but emphasized process transparency. But as divisions among elites deepened, NCA representatives found citizen inclusion to be an effective means of bringing them together. Citizen participation was much lower than in Egypt but significantly more effective. Only about 5,000 Tunisians participated, providing fewer than 2,500 suggestions, although fewer than one-third of these public suggestions found their way into the final draft of the constitution. In Egypt, by contrast, the Constituent Assembly did not even have time to review the 113,000 suggestions they received. Despite terrorist attacks and political assassinations aimed at derailing the country's transition to democracy, the "bottom-up" process helped Tunisia succeed in its democratic institution-building, with a peaceful transition of power in 2014. Why did bottom-up constitutionalism in Egypt usher in the current era of human rights violations and illiberal politics, while in Tunisia it has enabled democracy to bloom?

This disjuncture between constitutional change and democratization in these countries illustrates broader global trends. Over the last four decades, the 119 countries that adopted new constitutions experienced inconsistent effects on democracy: out of 144 new constitutions promulgated between 1974 and 2014, the level of democracy increased in 77 cases but it decreased or stayed the same in 47 others (based on Polity IV scores). Not all constitutions necessarily intend to advance democracy, as the Egyptian case made clear. Some new constitutions have sought to reformulate underlying relations between citizens and their governments, while others have increased rulers' holds on power. The prevailing approaches to comparative constitutionalism have not fully grappled with this disjuncture. Social scientists have, for the most part, allowed legal scholars to dominate the discussion of constitutions and constitutionalism, meaning that these documents are often taken at their word. Scholarship has emphasized literalist *de jure* constitutional interpretation rather than contextualizing the *de facto* application of these documents, which is often incomplete or at the discretion of national rulers.

This may be the first book-length large-N study to emphasize the "low politics" process of constitution-writing rather than the "high politics" contents of the resulting document. As stated by Brown, "Much scholarly analysis of the process of writing a constitution [. . .] lays great stress on the distinction between normal politics and constitutional politics [. . .] some influential strains of the liberal constitutional tradition view a constitution that is merely the product of partisan horse trading, emotional appeals, and short-sighted calculations as liable to be both unstable and unjust" (Brown 2008, 675). Following Brown's distinction, we argue – contrary to these strains – that the process of writing constitutions is like any other political process, fraught with struggles between interest groups for power. Unlike legal scholars who may presume that writing a constitution is somehow "above politics," we as political scientists see process as a rare event that concentrates the attention and political energies of a nation. But, we argue, the promise of new constitutions inspires not only bold ideals of statehood, but also base instincts of politics.

This book shifts the focus from legal text to political context and generates a new argument centered on the politics of constitutional processes. We show how bottom-up pressure through deliberation can shape the form and content of constitutions and argue that when this does not happen, constitutions cannot readily improve a nation's level of democracy after promulgation. Participatory constitution-making can provide the necessary impetus for codifying foundational rules that contribute to democracy, as in Tunisia, and we rigorously demonstrate that it explains the divergent effects of constitutions on democratization globally. Yet Egypt reminds us that involvement from civil society and the general public can still give the executive, the military, or other powerful interest groups opportunities to impose a "top-down" constitutional process. Rather than interacting with popular pressures, participation here becomes merely a pressure valve. This "imposed" constitutionalism, we argue, diminishes a nation's level of democracy post-promulgation. It is also unfortunately all too common while the conditions enabling participation in Tunisia turn out to be rather rare.

We argue that in order to understand the true scope and impact of constitutions, it is vital to understand the process through which they are drafted, debated, and ratified. The elements and context of constitution-making processes are perhaps even more important than the written provisions that form the basis for legalistic analyses by constitutionalists and are the central causal variable in new institutional theories. We claim that participatory constitution-making – which we understand as transparent, substantive, and often direct citizen involvement – has a lasting and systematic effect on subsequent democratization. It gives people a stake in institutions. It enhances civic competence, which forms the basis for holding leaders accountable, making sure that they live up to their professed democratic ideals. In a way, it legitimizes citizen authorization, identifying an important procedural component of regime formation that enables a democracy to be better than the institutions themselves. And of course, being in the room allows this range of societal interests to participate in the drafting of language that will eventually be incorporated into the constitution, although, as we show in Chapter 3, the text is sometimes less important than the context when it comes to constitution-making.

Framing in Brown's terms, we part from the assumption that constitutional politics, like all politics, really, is also "normal politics" in the sense that all actors attempt to claim that they have put national interest above self-interest, putting principles above partisanship. This was increasingly evident as democratization's Third Wave cornerstone constitutions in Europe and Latin America gave way to the more mundane constitutional changes that have become routine. Instead of using the hagiography of sacred clauses and phrasing, we look to the role of interest groups and elites to explain constitution-making. Constitutions are power plays by governing elites under siege by social movements, political parties, or other domestic opponents, and they are influenced by contextual factors such as external shocks, economic crises, droughts, foreign invasions, or international pressures. We study the process of constitution-making in terms of whether and how opponents of the governing elites are able to participate, but within the context of the power of elites. This includes those that are directly in power, but it also refers to actors whose preferences are disproportionately valued due to their social standing and access to resources and political capital. We think of interest groups as actors with shared preferences who come together as cohesive and sustained coalitions. Unlike traditional pluralist models of interest groups from political science that imagined interest groups as modern "lobbyists," we have in mind a broader and more contemporary definition, encompassing coalitions among elites or among outsiders who challenge them. Sometimes they reflect combinations in between, as when elites leverage outside constituencies to enhance their influence and bargaining power.

Upon evaluating the relative power of elites, using the democratization literature pioneered by O'Donnell and Schmitter (1986), even though this is not primarily a book about democratization, we can better understand the role of the constitution (i.e. whether it is just a mechanism by elites to ratify their power or represents some sort of negotiation over a new elite settlement and pact with societal groups). Using direct empirical evidence from the coding of scores of cases over 40 years, we analyze degrees of participation in constitution-making by elites as well as non-elite groups, and then consider the implications of such participation. Another dimension of our analysis considers different *forms* of participation that lend themselves to greater or lesser public input. Following Landemore and Elster (2012), we consider three forms of participation: deliberation, aggregation, and bargaining, which we apply to eight case studies, and speculate about the effects of each form.

Yet neither the form nor level of participation is the whole story. We also argue that the timing of participation matters – and that it typically comes too late in the constitution-making process. Failure to incorporate substantive societal input early on amounts to an "original sin" that is difficult to rectify later through input. "Buy-in" at the front end by social movements and interest groups needs to complement widespread "bottom-up" ratification, through votes and plebiscites, which the constitution-makers need for public legitimation at the "back end." Bottom-up participation early on is difficult to achieve, not only because crafting a constitution is a complex process, but because the means by which people might participate is most uncertain at the front end. For illiberal regimes, postponing participation reduces political risk: it enables them to establish *status quo* positions that must be defeated while promising the right to reject them. For democratic reformers, like Egypt's in 2013, it increases the risk of authoritarian backsliding.

Using original variables to measure participation in constitution-making, our cross-national time-series analysis offers strong evidence that constitutions crafted with meaningful and transparent public involvement are more likely to contribute to democratization. This book shows that the level of participation systematically explains the observed disjuncture between constitutional change and democratization since 1974, using two different measures of democracy. Then, after disaggregating the constitution-making process into three sequential stages of convening, debating, and ratifying, we test levels of citizen participation during convening and later stages, and show that participation at this first stage has greater consequences for democratization than in subsequent stages. Our results hold across a broad range of controls, including variables measuring economic development, ethnic diversity, natural resources, and foreign aid that could interfere with the predicted relationships. The results also withstand robustness checks, as well as a probe for potential endogeneity since participatory constitution-making could simply be a function of prior democratic conditions – thus rendering our key causal claim prone to tautology. In a large number of cases, the impact of constitutional text significantly depends on the type of process that crafted it.

This is not formally a book about democratization, although much of the democratization literature, starting with O'Donnell and Schmitter (1986) and including Colomer (1994), Dahl (1971), and Przeworski (1991), is, in great measure, about how to get elites into the same room with other sectors in society in order to reach "social pacts," which can include, but are not limited to, constitutions. The Third Wave of democracies and democratization, starting in Portugal in 1973, ascribed greater agency to constitutions, imbuing them with powers to dispel the remaining ghosts of communism and communist parties in Eastern Europe, forges a way forward from "Dirty Wars" and attacks on leftists in Latin America, to moral cleansing and truth commissions, and, in South Africa, transition from nothing less than a racist and oppressive past to a more egalitarian future. The Arab Spring constitutions are just the most recent ones to place high expectations on new constitutions. Our framework here is to study the process of all new constitutions of the Third Wave era, the age when constitutional processes were inscribed with heightened expectations that they would usher in democracy. This era is an appropriate period to study because while some constitutions arose from the agency identified in the early democratization literature, others were the result of grassroots movements that corresponded with changing international norms of participation.

We formally address the strict micro-institutional lens of constitutional processes, although we do view that vantage as having implications for democratization, particularly as it relates to the roles of participation and deliberation in democracies. From this perspective, constitutions are indeed political, and thus subject to Brown's "political maneuvering." But even if these processes reflect politicians at their most base moments, they can still also depict idealistic aspirations and offer "high politics" opportunities for political participation and deliberation. In the section that follows, we elaborate on our basic model for how constitutional processes play out, and then more fully consider our "interest group" approach within the context of the broader literature.

As normatively concerned scholars persuaded by the evidence that democracy is better than other forms of governing large and heterogeneous groups of people, we advocate in the conclusion for more deliberation in constitutional processes. But most of this book is dedicated to showing that basic, empirically measurable participation by wide ranges of citizen interest groups improves levels of democracy in host countries. Ruling elites, those in power, or those with social standing and/or access to resources and political capital, are viewed in this study as the conveners of constitutional change. O'Donnell and Schmitter split regime incumbents – here elites – into "hardliners," who defended the *status quo* and sought to limit political uncertainty, and "softliners," who pressed for change in policies, but without changing those who were in power. "Pacts" or "elite settlements" were made between these factions about terms of a transition, which could occur when hardliners perceived that trying to keep power put them at greater risk than the assurances they would receive through compromise. Przeworski elaborated on this conceptual framework, dividing regime opposition, which threatened the hardliners and gained sympathy from the softliners. He divided the opposition between "reformers" and "radicals" (Przeworski 1991, 68–9).

In terms of constitutional processes, radicals were usually the initiators of social movements for dramatic change, fostering constitution-making under duress. Some of these cases of constitution-making, such as Colombia (1991), integrated deliberation by radical insurgents, political parties, and student demonstrators and moved them into the political process as reformers. Some, like Egypt (2012), did not achieve deliberation in participation, but merely aggregated citizen views and opinions (such as through social media) without managing to give citizens a sense of participation. As hinted already, constitutions came to serve different purposes in the latter two decades of our study than they did in the first two decades.

The shift from elitist "top-down" constitutional assemblies to more participatory constitution-making is historically recent but was scarcely noticed during the Third Wave, and especially since the mid-1990s. In the early nineteenth century, some two dozen nations of Spanish Latin America declared their independence and implemented enlightened, republican constitutions, emulating, in part, the top-down process first seen in the United States. The US Constitution, while far from perfect, offered a new model based on checks and balances and the rights of (at least some) citizens, although the process was a top-down one. The 1820s Latin American constitutions were "constitutions of tyranny" (Loveman 1993) as their parchments were enlightened and democratic, but they were observed only in the breach. They were used as baselines against which to issue decrees of rule by exception as *caudillos* (quintessential "strong men on horseback") who consolidated states out of colonies throughout the nineteenth century through coercion.

In 1917, Mexico adopted one of the most enlightened constitutions in the world – at least by early twentieth-century standards – only to "neutralize" the charter's progressive aspirations in favor of repressive informal practices that allowed the authoritarian ruling coalition to keep power until the country's political opening in the 1980s and 1990s (Eisenstadt 2004). Even in the 1990s, new constitutions like Argentina's, propagated in part to extend the terms of autocratic leaders, were commonplace. A similar set of challenges plagued post-colonial Africa, where the new independence-era rulers abandoned European institutional models and embraced American-style presidentialism (Akiba 2004). This lent itself to the executive excesses characterized by neopatrimonialism, where powerful presidents lacked restraint and violated the public trust (Bratton and van de Walle 1994). On both continents this occurred without either the republican institutions with liberal rights debated in the *Federalist Papers* or the principles enshrined in Washington's Farewell Address, in which he resoundingly endorsed the constitutional order even though he could have tossed the parchment aside and declared himself dictator (Lipset 1998).

After demonstrating the positive benefits of participation and establishing this constitution-making model's strong association with global trends since the 1990s, we devote extensive attention to two other questions generated by our findings: How do different types of constitution-making processes actually work? This is important because our statistical findings alone do not convey the causal story. In addition, how does a country end up with a process that is either elite-driven or highly participatory? After all, undemocratic countries might be stuck with exclusive and secretive processes while civic precedents make participation more likely in countries with democratic experience. To answer these questions, we run tests to account for the sources of "top-down" constitution-making associated with elite pacts compared to a "bottom-up" modality rooted in social movement theory and deliberative democracy. We then draw upon field research conducted on three continents, and extensive discussion of both conforming and confounding case studies.

This introductory chapter strives first to unify otherwise disparate academic literatures on democratization, constitutionalism, and recent democratic theory in order to assess the state of knowledge about the consequences of constitutional change. Democratization research advanced plausible theories about the benefits of participatory constitution-making but it has not rigorously tested them. Comparative constitutionalism has yielded conflicting conclusions about the effects of constitutional change on democracy. The literature review also briefly mentions research in democratic theory that can help explain how and why different modalities of making constitutions should have a lasting political impact. We conclude this chapter with an overview of the chapters that follow.

This book makes several critical contributions to our understanding of law, politics, and civic life around the world since the Third Wave began in the early 1970s. By showing that the modality of constitution-making matters much more than the mere promulgation of a new constitution, it offers an important corrective to the democratization literature. In contrast to the legal studies arguing that wording of constitutions shapes institutional outcomes, we show, perhaps for the first time, that arriving at this language via democratic process is also vital. Through one of the first large-scale empirical analyses of participatory constitution-making, we show that transparent, meaningful input during "constitutional moments" generates vital path-dependent benefits for democracy. Furthermore, by specifying that citizen participation during the earliest moments of constitution-making is the most important, we raise doubts about the lasting benefits of referendums – a hallmark of the

Third Wave and the preferred ratification device among democracy promoters. With Egypt's democracy in retreat, many of the Arab Spring's blossoms wilting, and a string of new constitutional coups in Africa, there is an urgent need to identify new factors contributing to such setbacks. Freedom House (2015) reports eight consecutive years of a global decline in democratic freedom. Our research hopes to generate important lessons for political reformers demonstrating that constitutional text offers a poor substitute for deliberation, and inadequate insurance against illiberal reversals.

LITERATURE REVIEW: ADDING POLITICAL EXPLANATIONS TO TRADITIONAL LEGAL ONES

Our literature review begins with a discussion about the consequences of constitutional change. Comparative constitutionalism has focused on constitutional endurance, compliance or content, and generally arrived at conflicting conclusions about the effects of constitutional change on democracy. This has left a large gap when it comes to broader comparative analyses of processes for changing constitutions – a surprising lacuna given new international norms of participation and increased use of various forms of direct democracy. Next, we examine how democratization research advanced plausible theories about the benefits of participatory constitution-making but did not rigorously test these. This is surprising since there is significant evidence that grassroots social movements, especially in Africa, the former Soviet Union, and parts of Latin America, contributed to democratization. This research gives us a basis for explaining how and why the modalities of making a constitution should have a lasting political impact. Throughout the book we contrast these "bottom-up" participatory theories with the aforementioned "top-down" tradition that highlights the role of elite "pacting," pioneered by O'Donnell and Schmitter (1986) and Przeworski (1991). That literature on democratic transitions during the early years of the Third Wave abruptly gave way to the "stop-and-go" hybrid regimes (straddling democracy and authoritarianism) adopted by many regimes over the last 20 years. Those non-transitions have generated a new generation of literature on why authoritarians wish to appear democratic but retain discretion and prerogatives (see for example Brownlee 2007; Levitsky and Way 2010; Hyde 2011; Svolik 2012). This newer research helps illuminate when popular participation is merely a ruse and when it is a force of change to be reckoned with.

To date, comparative constitutionalism and several significant, related literatures have addressed this fundamental question of whether and how constitutionalism affects democracy indirectly, incompletely, or through case studies that offer little basis for generalization. The limited treatment of this question by democratization researchers is surprising given the boom in transition studies in the 1990s, in the generation after O'Donnell and Schmitter. At the time, constitutional change and democratization were often mistakenly conflated, when in fact constitutional replacement occurred within a year of only 19 percent of the transitions to democracy and in 27 percent of the transitions to authoritarianism (Elkins et al. 2009). Various studies developed sound theoretical propositions regarding the broader political impact of participatory constitution-making, but these ideas were not fully tested.

In the most rigorous and systematic exploration of the political effects of new constitutions, an ongoing project by Elkins, Ginsburg, and Melton focuses on constitutional survival. Their study, testing 935 cases spanning two centuries, concludes that more participatory processes are conducive to constitutional survival because they "can promote a unifying identity and invite participants to invest in the bargain" (Elkins et al. 2009, 211). A related study reports that inclusive drafting increases the likelihood of constitutional endurance, and is associated with constitutional rights and democratic institutions such as universal suffrage, the secret ballot, and a guaranteed role for public input into amending constitutions (Ginsburg 2012, 54–7). These are seminal findings regarding endurance and content, but they leave unanswered the impact of processes on levels of democracy and *de facto* protections of rights – as opposed to the *de jure* protections mentioned in the text itself.

Widner's data-rich research measures participatory constitution-making, but like Elkins et al. it lacks a direct test of participation on the level of democracy. Her "Constitution Writing and Conflict Resolution" dataset covers 195 constitutions between 1975 and 2002 (Widner 2004).[1] Her results show that public consultation does not correlate with improved political rights protection (Widner 2008). This finding conflicts with an influential analysis of 12 countries by the International Institute for Democracy and Electoral Assistance (Samuels 2006), as well as 18 case studies of constitutional change in transitional states (Miller and Aucoin 2010). However, neither study systematically examines democratization or political rights as a dependent variable.

Carey (2009) conducts one of the few direct statistical tests measuring the impact of constitution-making on democracy. He finds that more "inclusive" constitutional drafting increases the level of democracy over the subsequent three years, as measured using Polity IV data on democracy and executive constraints. However, Carey concedes that his bivariate analysis is bound by

---

[1]   For reasons we explain in Chapter 2, our definition of a new constitution is narrower than hers, which is one important difference between our datasets.

data constraints, including the use of proportional representation as a proxy for the inclusiveness of institutional actors. These limitations deter him from using standard statistical models that would provide a stronger basis for broader generalization. In sum, to our knowledge, no study tackles the relationship between constitution-making processes and democratization using robust cross-national quantitative analysis.

The dearth of empirical studies of constitution-making processes and democratization is surprising. The dramatic rise of constitutional referendums during the Third Wave is one obvious sign of a dramatic increase in citizen participation. Between 1975 and 2000, one study estimates that 39 out of 58 electoral democracies had at least one referendum (Tierney 2012). There were more referendums (192) on new constitutions between 1974 and 2012 than over two previous centuries (117).[2] According to Wampler, "the direct incorporation of citizens into complex policy-making processes is the most significant innovation of the third wave" (Wampler 2012, 667). As expectations of and opportunities for citizen participation have expanded, so has the strength of international norms for citizens' right to participate in crafting the rules that will bind them or determine resource allocations. Many scholars argue that a legal standard guaranteeing a right to participation in international law now exists (Fox 2000; Miller and Aucoin 2010). In 2014 the International Monetary Fund instituted new transparency codes to this effect, and citizen participation is now integrated into the World Bank's Demand for Good Governance Project. Research on social service delivery similarly reports that participation generates a "virtuous cycle" that actually improves policy performance (Fox 2014). Evidence of this virtuous cycle shows that participation is more than merely a normative good: it actually improves the quality of public goods (Touchton and Wampler 2013). The United Nations argues for "inclusive, participatory and transparent constitution-making processes," citing various contemporary examples. According to the UN Secretary-General, participatory processes foster civic engagement and raise citizen expectations for government transparency (United Nations Secretary-General 2009, 4). Even without "uniform norms" for constitution-making, international law over the last half century has supported "a general requirement of public participation" extending to citizen involvement in "the actual process of drafting the constitution's final text" (Franck and Thiruvengadam 2010, 14).

Despite such "very strong recommendations for extensive popular participation" in constitution-making, Horowitz asserts "there is not even a scintilla

[2] This estimate is based on the data from the Centre for Research on Direct Democracy www.c2d.ch, which uses a looser definition of a new constitution than ours.

of evidence that it improves the durability or the democratic content of constitutions" (Diamond et al. 2014, 100).

This seems to be borne out in the rise of hybrid regimes over the last two decades, clothed in constitutions as "window-dressing" political documents more often than the earnestly stated aspirations of true democratizers. This originated in a prominent critique of the means and ends of the Third Wave of democratization, which recast transitions as long and ongoing processes rather than teleological progressions to a steady democratic equilibrium (Carothers 2002). Others argue that the timing of participation is what matters. Most prominently, Elster claims that "ratification by the citizens, following a national debate, is more important" than direct citizen input during the middle stages when the text itself is negotiated (Elster 2012, 169). Since few of the public's substantive ideas survive in the final draft, he suggests the public's role should therefore be "hourglass-shaped" because the anticipation of broad ratification influences (and presumably moderates) constituent assembly debate. Post-1980s democracy promotion seemed to reflect this logic but it focused on later stages rather than formative moments when political context can impede or enable constitutions' democratizing effects. We have had little evidence to assess whether there are particular points during constitution-making when participation generates substance and when it merely serves as a symbol for self-serving regimes.

Moreover, the democratization literature highlights or debates the benefits of participatory politics in various ways, yet these insights have remained largely disconnected from analyses of constitution-making. Lindberg (2009) for example argues that elections improve levels of democracy over time as the civic ritual of voting is repeated. Going to the ballot box places expectations on politicians and educates citizens and therefore becomes a means of developing a democratic political culture. Hyden argues that constitution-making is even more of a change agent for ordinary citizens than elections. He predicts that broad-based and participatory constitutional processes will give African countries "better prospects of succeeding with their regime transition than countries where such an exercise has not been carried out" (Hyden 2001, 216). Moehler (2008) arrives at a surprising finding in Uganda, where participation in constitution-making educated citizens about democracy but also made them skeptical (perhaps constructively so) about government. Wing's study argues that participatory constitution-writing helps nations avoid violent conflict, build democracy, and significantly foster legitimacy (Wing 2008). Though they do not test for it, Elkins et al. similarly observe that "sometimes, we suspect, the process of re-writing higher law can be therapeutic and empowering for citizens and leaders" (Elkins et al. 2009, 209). Justice Gilbert Mensah Quaye, who chaired The Gambia's Constitutional Review Commission, exemplifies this optimistic view. At the outset of his work in 1995, he predicted "people's participation would foster the creation of a politically mature citizenry with a comforting sense of dignity and pride that their views really matter and are respected" ("The Citizens and the Constitutional Review Commission" 1995).

There is also a well-developed debate within the democratization literature between elite versus grassroots drivers of regime change. The elite-oriented model draws upon the O'Donnell and Schmitter (1986a) research on "pacts" that was prominent in early Third Wave transitions in Southern Europe and parts of Latin America. These elite deals among different regime factions often lacked transparency, and they were sometimes not integrated into the constitution or other formal institutions. But they provided explicit guarantees to outgoing rulers and their allies – especially in the military. By reducing the uncertainty around what Hirschman (1970) famously called "exit," pacts helped keep transitions in Spain, Chile, and elsewhere on track. A generation of scholars such as Przeworski (1991), Higley and Gunther (1992), and Encarnación (2005) elaborated on the initial models pitting reformist regime "softliners" against the intransigent "hardliners."

These "top-down" models, as we refer to them, were swiftly challenged by democratic revolutions in Eastern Europe and the former Soviet Union, where grassroots pressures seemed to matter more (Ekiert and Kubik 1999; Bunce 2003). After the fall of the Berlin Wall in 1989, Boris Yeltsin standing on top of a tank in front of the Russian parliament renewed the image of what we characterize as "bottom-up" models of democratization. Africa's neo-patrimonial dictatorships soon crumbled too, as protest movements against economic liberalization were reborn as social movements for political liberalization (Bratton and Van de Walle 1997). In Latin America the Mothers of the Disappeared in Argentina and the pot-clankers in Chile also joined the social movement fray, as did the Catholic Church in Brazil and Central America and indigenous insurgents in Mexico, where some "bottom-up" movements turned violent (see for example Skidmore 1990; Eckstein 2001; Eisenstadt 2011). Altman (2011) makes a similar distinction between bottom-up and top-down forms of direct democracy; elites can initiate plebiscites, for example, even though we associate the latter with participation and civil society. Here we use the distinction in more general terms since our concept of top-down constitution-making largely excludes the public.

In some ways, constitutions were taken for granted in the 1990s, as legal scholars turned their attention to the text and questions of compliance, and a thriving "new institutionalist" literature focused on the effects of various formal configurations (March and Olsen 1996; Schmidt 2010), such as the debate about whether presidentialism or parliamentarism led to more stable and representative governments (Shugart and Carey 1992; Linz and Valenzuela 1994; Lijphart 1999). We seek to remedy this by exploring how both bottom-up and top-down theories of democratization generate relevant conceptual tools for understanding different modalities of constitutional change. Thus, even though our empirical findings strongly support direct citizen participation, we acknowledge the contributions of pacting research and seek to rehabilitate its ideas into a new generation of comparative constitutionalism.

These theories of democratization inform our juxtaposition of two differing visions of constitutional change: the top-down modality tells us that elite buy-in is necessary and agency remains theoretically relevant. Constitution-making requires legal expertise and a division of labor that entails some delegation; what matters are the risks of agency loss, and whether those elites will advance (and perhaps conceal) their own preferences. To help explain why incumbents would risk constitutions, we get some help from Ginsburg and Simpser's (2013, 5) discussion of the roles of constitutions in authoritarian regimes as "operating manuals, billboards, blueprints, and window dressing." As elaborated in Chapter 4, we believe that incumbents want to control challengers within their ruling coalition, signal their intentions to undertake reform (if they deem that necessary to stay in power), and, perhaps, bargain over terms of any transition of power they may anticipate. The democratization literature spoke of pressures for liberalization from reformers within the authoritarian coalition and from radicals outside it. Like the broader pacts they are often part of in democratic transitions, constitutions represent concrete bargains over the terms of regime continuance or change. Furthermore, it would seem that when incumbents have the luxury of choice, they opt for "imposed" deliberation from above, whereas when societal interest groups force their hands, and they understand this, they confront constitutional deliberation from below.

Our other vision of constitution-making, the bottom-up modality, shows us how social movements and interest groups may guard against elite manipulation, push for inclusion of marginalized constituencies or platforms, and occasionally assert popular sovereignty over constitution-making that deepens democracy. This tradition further reminds us that economic and social structures limit elites' decision-making latitude, making agency contingent upon context. Drawing upon this well-developed debate over whether pacting from above or popular pressures from below drive democratization, we adapt key concepts to explain the procedural options for constitution-making.

An important innovation in this regard is our adoption of developments from democratic theory, which evolved alongside the democratization debate, in order to account for the benefits of participation. When tumultuous social movements of the 1960s in Western Europe and the United States erupted, they challenged republican ideas of governance as well as modernization theory's pretentions that widespread participation (including the spread of the franchise) with insufficient institutionalization would lead to chaos (Huntington 1968). A new generation of democratic theorists and students of social movements rejected such ideas with a popular mantra "democracy is in the streets." Participatory models of democracy were born, arguing for direct citizen engagement to remedy defects of representation (Pateman 2012, 1970). These models challenged notions of trusteeship, delegation and elitism by implying that the people could not only be trusted – they were the best authors of their own freedom, to put it in Jeffersonian terms. Participatory democracy also took issue with systemic critiques of democracy that suggested it was irrational as a political system: because politicians sought to appeal to the "median voter," they had incentives to be deliberately vague. Voters therefore faced huge information costs, and the outcome of their behavior was merely a question of aggregation (thus making electoral laws – the mechanisms for translating votes to seats – a critical feature of a political system). Moreover, the low likelihood that voting would have an impact meant that citizens wouldn't bother doing so. Participatory models insisted that increased opportunities to vote were not only rational, they could remedy underlying defects of representation. A flourishing literature on referendums and opportunities for direct democracy seems to bear this out (LeDuc 2003; Tierney 2012). Deliberative models also worry about failures of representation, but assert that direct participation through public debate is more important than voting for deepening democracy (Dryzek 2000; Parkinson and Mansbridge 2012).

In sum, despite four decades of regime transformations to and from democracy, the emergence of strong international norms for participatory constitution-making, and a robust debate over elite versus grassroots drivers of democratization, we still have a weak empirical basis for assessing the value of direct citizen input into constitution-making. A participatory model highlights the benefits of referendums and other modalities for direct citizen input. A deliberative model goes a step further, emphasizing the importance of public debate and suggesting that participation must mean more than merely voting or delegating authority. In Chapter 2 we will formulate and test two hypotheses based on expectations generated by these models: a "participation" hypothesis predicts that higher levels of participation throughout the constitution-making process positively impacts democracy. Then an "origination" hypothesis predicts that participation at the earliest stage of the process is most critical. Since referendums are a primary feature of the final, ratification stage, the results

highlighting the disproportionately positive benefits of the earliest stage challenge key elements of participatory democracy – but not because elites must
be trusted. In Chapter 3 we debunk the other main theory, that the content of
constitutions matters more for democracy. Further, by demonstrating that the
transparent, participatory processes are not driven by a country's recent experience with democracy, we confront a potential endogeneity problem in our
theory. In Chapter 4 we imbue this important pattern with causal arguments
about why ruling elites would enter the uncertain terrain of constitution-making, which does sometimes (but not always) result in political opening that is,
almost by definition, against the interests of those in power when the new constitution is negotiated. Mirroring Chapter 4, we then explain in Chapter 5 why
some countries adopt constitution-making from below and how it works. In
particular, we argue that broad-based social mobilization is necessary but not
sufficient, highlighting the role of interest groups as mediators bridging the
gulf between popular participation and notions of elite trusteeship. Finally, we
demonstrate through our case studies in these chapters, how deliberation as a
form of participation is superior to either bargaining, which privileges elites,
or aggregation that reduces citizenship to the ballot.

OUTLINE OF THE BOOK

In Chapter 2, we describe extant datasets, our data collection strategy, and
the research design for testing the impact of participatory constitution-
making on democracy. We detail the construction of our Constitutionalism and
Democracy Dataset (CDD), which includes 144 constitutions in 119 countries
between 1974 and 2014 (at http://doi.org/10.17606/M63W25), and we explain
the construction of our *process* variable. Constitutions that are the product
of elite dominance, low transparency, and limited levels of public participation are coded as "imposed"; those crafted with significant public input are
labeled "popular," in a nod to Dahl's (1971) ideal-type notion of popular (but
implying agency by a broad range of actors); and constitution-making processes with both qualities are coded as "mixed." We describe our rationale for
breaking constitution-making into three sequential stages: convening, debate,
and ratification – each of which separately measures the level of participation.

We then sketch out a preliminary theory of participatory constitution-making,
elaborating on the principles from democratic theory discussed earlier. We
formulate and rigorously test the two hypotheses that result in the book's core
findings: a "participation" hypothesis predicts that higher levels of participation throughout the constitution-making process positively impact democracy.
The first stage of statistical tests regressing the *process* variable on two different

measures of democracy confirms the participation hypothesis. The results withstand robustness checks, and a further probe for potential endogeneity validates our claim that *process* does indeed distinctly measure participatory constitution-making. Next, an "origination" hypothesis predicts that participation at the earliest stage of the process is most critical. The second stage of tests confirms the origination hypothesis using the three stages of constitution-making as separate independent variables. Next, a separate series of tests demonstrates that contrary to much of the conventional wisdom from legal scholars, the democratic content of constitutions has little impact on the level of democracy itself. We use language from constitutions pertaining to the head of state's decree power, any restrictions on the right to vote, and provisions pertaining to a human rights commission. Adding these controls to our statistical models does not change our results, meaning that these "constitutional content" variables do not significantly impact the level of democracy. These results affirm findings from other studies suggesting that rulers often try to fool the international community by creating a veneer of democracy that exists in the text only (Negretto 2013). Finally, we run two stage-least squares tests using labor strikes as an instrumental variable. The results are similar to our initial Ordinary Least Squares (OLS) coefficients, indicating that *process* variable variant endogeneity is not determinant.

The results of our rigorous statistical tests of the participation and origination hypotheses offer an important corrective to the democratization literature since the modality of constitution-making matters. More generally, in contrast to the legal studies arguing that the particular wording of constitutions shapes institutional outcomes, we show, perhaps for the first time, that arriving at this language via democratic process is also vital. By conducting one of the first large-scale empirical analyses of participatory constitution-making, we show that transparent, meaningful input during "constitutional moments" generates vital path-dependent benefits for "back-end" democracy. Limitations on such participation at these early moments of constitutional convening amount to an "original sin" that is difficult to overcome through citizen participation, even in subsequent phases of constitution-making. Further, by specifying that citizen participation during convening is the most important, we raise doubts about the lasting benefits of referendums – the hallmark of the ratification stage during the Third Wave and a preferred device for democracy promoters. Voting via referendum and faith in constitutional text provide poor substitutes for deliberation and inadequate insurance against authoritarian retrenchment. This is an important lesson for political reformers who seek political insurance against illiberal reversals and authoritarian backsliding.

Chapter 3 provides additional evidence for our assertion in Chapter 2 that participation in the three stages of constitution-making is path dependent, meaning it is hard to correct for an "original sin" in the early stages of drafting that limits citizen input and asserts elite control. The chapter then confronts a potential endogeneity problem in our argument by identifying empirical linkages between prior political context and the type of constitution-making process that countries adopt. We do this first by demonstrating how prior regime type does *not* systematically shape the type of constitution-making process that a country adopts. This statistical finding is striking since 28 percent of the constitutions in our sample were drafted under democratic regimes, and 35 percent were drafted under personalist or single-party authoritarian regimes. The absence of a significant relationship between democracy and the adoption of popular process suggests that the actors make the process, and that effective participation during drafting occurs when there is a break with the previous regime – even if it was democratic. Second, using proxies, we test for "top-down" pressures and find that term limits and other types of executive constraints have an indeterminate impact. We attribute this to the possibility of checks and balances in democracies and autocracies alike (Gandhi 2008; LeVan 2015), which we illustrate through a brief analysis of Turkey. The strongest predictor of top-down constitution-making process is the political closeness of the political system, as measured using opposition vote share. Third and most importantly, statistical tests demonstrate how social movements and protests prior to constitution-making generate pressures for popular participation. However, we find differences between strikes and riots, since organized nonviolent protest generates more effective pressures for popular constitution-making than episodic and violent confrontations. These subtle conceptual distinctions between coercion and leverage demonstrate how broad participation can push elites to open the constitution-making process, and the findings further support recent research on contentious politics by underscoring the importance of targeted, nonviolent collective action (Teorell 2010; Chenoweth and Stephan 2014).

Chapter 3 also includes helpful descriptive information from the CDD about the 27 possible combinations of the three levels of participation at three different stages of our *participation* variable. After reporting the frequency of these different "pathways," we identify the three most important ones as imposed-imposed-imposed, mixed-mixed-mixed, and mixed-mixed-popular. We describe each pathway with reference to cases and seek to understand the political logic behind the most prominent modalities of constitution-making. We also graphically illustrate the association between these modalities of constitution-making and various regime types, including personalist, monarchical, and single-party. Figure 1.1 gives a sense of how these different pathways impact the overall level of democracy score. These descriptive statistics make clear that simply creating a new constitution, by itself, offers no guarantees.

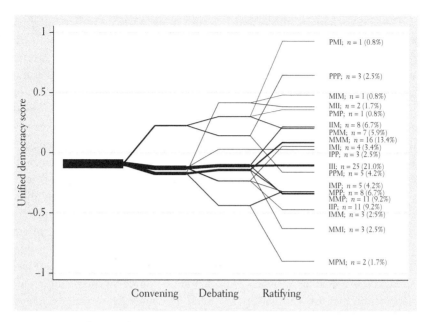

FIGURE 1.1. *Pathways of constitution-making and level of democracy since 1974*

Chapters 4 and 5 continue this case-based analysis by process tracing of two pairs of cases in each chapter, presenting a Janus-faced view of our argument that draws upon field research conducted on three continents. One goal of these chapters is to explain how bottom-up and top-down constitution-making actually works, and a mixed-methods approach helps identify complex relationships among variables not necessarily visible in regression analysis (Weller and Barnes 2014). For example, our cases address the issue of inclusion, which we do not explicitly control for in the quantitative analysis but is clearly important. A second goal is to account for how cases actually adopt a particular modality of constitution-making, thus complementing the statistical tests for endogeneity in Chapter 3 with a qualitative analysis. Despite our hopeful findings about the benefits of participatory constitutionalism, we find that the circumstances conducive to it are fairly unusual. A third goal is to delimit the scope of our theory – what it can and cannot explain – by analyzing conforming and non-conforming cases that potentially suggest equifinality (Lange 2009; Coppedge 2012). Participatory processes offer no guarantees, and elite-driven processes that we characterize as imposed sometimes do enhance democracy. Such top-down elite control is most frequent in cases of "authoritarian institutionalism," foreign occupation, or "pacted" constitution-making.

These two chapters also discuss each of our cases in terms of different forms – rather than levels – of participation. Here we again turn to political theory, drawing on the work of Landemore and Elster (2012), who consider three forms of participation. The first is deliberative, which emphasizes the centrality of "epistemic competence" (2012, 254) to democracy because it increases the flow of ideas and information, allows for separation of good arguments from bad, and facilitates the formation of a consensus regarding the best outcomes to problems like constitution-making (2012, 257). Deliberation emphasizes the non-coercive opportunities to change preferences (Dryzek 2000). Though deliberation is neither perfect nor strictly determinative of democracy, our case studies demonstrate how the other common forms of participation are normatively less desirable. The second form we consider is participation through mere aggregation, where "strength in numbers" drives non-elite participation, but where such participation is blunt (rather than subtly argued). Classic ideas from rational choice theory such as Arrow's Theorem and Condorcet cycling claimed for a long time that this can lead to irrational outcomes – for example, where the most popular preferences do not win because of the type of decision rules in use. Critics have since cast doubt on these logical proofs, since they depend on various assumptions such as non-repeating games, which are unreasonable representations of politics in the real world (Mackie 2003). The key point is that aggregation is largely in the aggregative view, relying on tools such as electoral rules and therefore leaving few opportunities to change opinion through deliberation and discussion. The third form of participation considered, which is less optimal than formal deliberation but normatively superior to sheer aggregation, is elite bargaining and pacting. This form of participation is perhaps most common, and, when analyzed through the lens of interest group politics, can be most readily understood as undergirding the process of constitution-making. This approach is the form of interest group politics popularized by O'Donnell and Schmitter and also by successors such as Higley and Gunther (1992) and Brownlee (2007). In Landemore and Elster's (2012) view, bargaining is an inferior form of participation because it leaves open the door for "strategic" communication, whereby actors are not sincere about their preferences. The costs of deception are high under conditions of repeated contact, as occurs within a constituent assembly, but bargaining lacks the epistemic benefits of deliberative forms. Interest groups do more than merely aggregate, since in our view they also amount to the collective actors who advance competing views about what belongs in the constitution. These three forms relate to the level of participation in our analysis in that the different forms play out in each stage (convene, debate, and ratify) but the unity of those forms matters the most in the first stage. They also establish a standard in our case studies for understanding the role of inferior forms such as aggregation or bargaining in processes that are either more or less participatory.

Chapter 4 explains the logic of top-down constitutionalism, drawing upon research that criticizes participatory models. A literature review underscores the value of "trusteeship," the benefits of some secrecy, and the importance of elite buy-in with new constitutions. For our case studies, we analyze the effects of constitutions imposed from above in Venezuela (1999) and The Gambia (1997). Both cases experienced a decline in post-promulgation democracy, as expected by our theory of participatory constitution-making. The second pair examines non-conforming cases of democratization following elite draft-ing processes in Chile (1980) and Nigeria (1999). This is important since our statistical results in Chapter 2 strongly suggested that countries generally fail to correct for "original sins" of imposed drafting from above at the early stage of constitution-making. According to one study, General Augusto Pinochet's acceptance of the 1988 referendum on his rule is one of only three times in the last century that a non-democratic regime accepted such a defeat at the ballot box (Altman 2011, 28). With a history of at least five coups and several failed transitions to democracy, the democratizing effects of Nigeria's 1999 constitution were also a surprise. This not only underscores the importance of the qualitative analysis, it also highlights our broader claim about how partic-ipatory constitutionalism requires more than merely voting.

Chapter 5 mirrors this analytical strategy organized around case studies that both challenge and support our overall statistical findings. We review litera-ture on social movements, interest groups, and populism in order to explain the basis for democratizing constitutionalism "from below." Then, once again building upon Chapter 3's tests treating *participation* as the dependent var-iable, case studies account for how countries may or may not adopt partici-patory constitution-making processes. We analyze two non-conforming cases to see how seemingly participatory processes in Ecuador (2008) and Egypt (2012) failed to generate democracy. Constitutionalism had some participatory qualities at the drafting stage, but these participatory promises were betrayed as the process continued, thus departing from the overall statistical pattern. The chapter considers Tunisia (2014), the birthplace of the Arab Spring, and Colombia (1991) as examples of successful constitution-making from below with lasting democratizing effects.

Table 1.1 summarizes our top-down and bottom-up cases with regards to changes in their democracy scores. The principal finding of these two "bookended" chapters is that constitution-making processes with lasting

TABLE 1.1. *Popular and imposed case studies*

		Outcome of interest	
		Democratic decline	Democratic increase
TYPE OF DRAFTING PROCESS	*Popular* Chapter 5	**Ecuador** (poly-poly-poly) • After 2008 constitution, slight decline from +6 to +5 • After 1998 constitution, slight decline from +8.6 to +7 **Egypt** (poly-poly-poly) • After 2012 constitution, declined from −2 to −4	**Tunisia** (poly-poly-poly) • Improved from −4 before 2011 to +4 (2011) to +7 (2014) **Colombia** (poly-poly-mixed) • Slight improvement from +8 before the 1991 constitution to +9 after
	Imposed Chapter 4	**Venezuela** (decree-mixed-poly) • After 1999 constitution, declined from +8 to +6.3 **The Gambia** (decree-decree-poly) • Declined from −2 before 1996 constitution to −5 after	**Chile** (decree-decree-decree) • After 1980 constitution, minor improvement from −7 to −6.6 **Nigeria** (decree-mixed-decree) • After 1999 constitution, improved from −4.3 to +4 • After 1989 constitution, slight improvement from −7 to −5

Shaded boxes are contrary to expectations.
Scores reflect Polity IV data before and after constitution.

democratizing effects can and do emerge across a broad of range of regimes and regions. These effects are independent of the preexisting democratic conditions or the precise legal language in the constitution itself, meaning that the parchment is less important than the process that generates it.

Chapter 6 then concludes by threading together our key findings and highlighting the implications for contemporary political reformers. By demonstrating that citizen engagement enhances post-promulgation democratization, we provide an empirical justification for emerging international norms of participation. While democratic experiments with direct democracy multiplied starting in the 1970s, we identify participatory constitution-making in particular as a prominent feature of the Third Wave, especially after the end of the Cold War in 1989. After finding that participation during drafting, the earliest stage of constitution-making, has path-dependent benefits, we argue that extensive participation during referendums is unlikely to correct for an "original sin" of limited citizen deliberation during drafting. One important implication is that democracy promotion needs to focus more on generating public "buy-in" at the front end of the constitution-making process, rather than concentrating on ratification at the "back end." Another important implication is that constitutions prior to the Third Wave may offer few relevant lessons for today's constitutionalists.

Since democratic text alone is a poor substitute for a democratic drafting process, this lends an air of urgency to our call for re-examining the contemporary wave of constitutional processes. Drawing on field research in Egypt, Morocco, and Tunisia, we further specify the role of top-down processes in provoking compromise among elites and facilitating political understandings that withstand the scrutiny of bottom-up movements. As Horowitz notes, participation cannot serve as a substitute for inclusion. In this regard we hope future research will guide constitutional architects to promote constructive deliberation that translates interest group preferences into democracy-enhancing legal provisions. Old models of interest aggregation and representation are being displaced by deliberative innovations, but democracy still involves both politicians and citizens.

CONCLUSION: THE CALL FOR CLOSER ATTENTION TO CONSTITUTIONAL PROCESS

The 144 new constitutions promulgated over the last 40 years coincided with a global wave of democratization but they did little to cause it. Unlike the Constitutional Convention in 1787 in Philadelphia, the dozens of "liberation" constitutions in Spanish America in the 1820s, or even Japan's 1947 constitution, many of the more recent constitutions were political instruments rather than historical ruptures. For example, Bolivian president Carlos Mesa sought a constituent assembly to break the political log jam that had limited his administration's government, but in retrospect he realized compromise was unavoidable. "I would have liked a 'founding moment' constitution in which we would have set important foundations for society which could endure change and provide a legal and social base for the political system. But we also had to be realistic."[3]

In the chapters that follow, we demonstrate persuasively that constitutions are only as good as the procedures that create them. But we also note how a broad range of regimes seek to manufacture "constitutional moments" in order to claim an exaggerated right to rule and to provide a veneer of conformity with recent international norms of participation. Process matters and it is largely a function of the degree and breadth of involvement by a wide range of societal interests. Constitution-making at the very beginning presages whether

[3]   Interview with Bolivia's former president, Carlos Mesa. La Paz, Bolivia. June 27, 2012.

a given constitution will improve democracy or betray it. Indeed, the Egyptian constitutional process of 2012 to 2014, which opened this chapter, offers a great case in point, as it was at different moments both a "bottom-up" social movement-demanded bid by religious groups, secular groups, and civil society to foment social change, and a top-down effort by the military and the Islamist incumbent authoritarians to "clamp down" on societal pressures. In the end, the Egyptian process exacerbated the existing political conflict and led to a military coup and a redrafting of a new, imposed constitution, although other Arab Spring constitutional processes, like that in Tunisia, have advanced with participatory inclusion. If democrats are not in the room from the beginning, they can do little to salvage the process later.

For scholars, this means that we need much more information about the contexts in which constitutions are made, including the conditions that enable or bar the entry of interests into deliberation. We also need to understand the particular features of constitutional moments as critical junctures that enable collective action. As for policy- makers and democracy-promoters, this means that they need to identify social movements and interest groups earlier, and be willing to expose processes that privilege elite opinion or that use expertise as a veil to marginalize bottom-up forces. Inclusion of such groups, from the very beginning, may be the ultimate difference between "dead letter" parchment and a living, democratic social contract.

2

Making the Constituents King: How Constituent Deliberation on New Constitutions Democratizes More than Mere Citizen Participation

INTRODUCTION

Following the Arab popular uprisings in the Middle East and North Africa, Moroccan King Mohammed VI proposed in March 2011 a constitutional change to address the public demand for an elected constituent assembly to write the country's highly anticipated new constitution. However, that very demand was the one that was rejected by the very same king. Moroccan constitutionalist Ma'ati Monjib used the king's rejection of a constituent assembly to call the government's motivation into question: "the king is not serious about democratic changes and the proposal to change the constitution is just to tame the protest waves."[1] King Mohammed appointed 17 constitutionalists – most of whom were advisors or became advisors after the constitutional process – to write a constitution consolidating his rule without any notable democratic changes in the kingdom's political institutions.

Interpreting the king's intentions in a manner similar to that of Monjib, the opposition allied with the independent civil society made only one demand: a publicly elected assembly write the constitution. The Moroccans' emphasis on the significance of the first phase of constitution-making to democratization is what this chapter is about. Why was this first phase of constitution making "input" so important to the Moroccan opposition? Why did they not wait to see what document emerged and then contest the actual document "output" later if they did not find it to their liking? Do different phases of constitution-making have different impacts on democratization? In summary, how important are constitutional processes for democratization anyway?

We answer this question in three steps. First, using an originally developed variable that quantifies the process of constitution-making, we test whether "process" has any impact on democracy. Second, we disaggregate our

---

[1] Interview with Ma'ati Monjib. Rabat, Morocco. November 19, 2014.

"process" variable into three stages – convening, debating, and ratification – and test whether each stage has a separate and statistically significant impact on democracy. And finally, we test whether the content of constitutions, rather than the process, drives our results.

This chapter proceeds as follows. First, we explain our database and how we define constitutional change and its impact on democracy. Then we talk about operationalizing our key independent variable, the "process" variable measuring levels of participation in the convening, debating, and ratification stages of constitution-making, and a range of other independent variables. This is followed by elaboration of our two hypotheses, a "participation" hypothesis and an "origination" hypothesis. And finally we run statistical models and discuss the results.

DESIGNING CONSTITUTIONALISM AND DEMOCRACY DATABASE

To generate our independent variables and include relevant controls, we constructed a "Constitutionalism and Democracy Dataset" (CDD) covering the 190 countries with available data between 1974 and 2014. The CDD builds on two extant datasets by Elkins et al. (2009) on the survival and legal scope of constitutions from the beginning of the twentieth century, and by Widner (2004) on the political processes yielding new constitutions and constitutional reforms since the 1970s. In this section we describe different approaches for measuring constitutional change and adopt a high threshold for coding a constitution as "new." Next, we break the constitution-making process into convening, debating, and ratification stages. We then describe how we measure levels of participation at each stage, which we can code as "imposed," "popular," or a mixture of the two. This generates a *process* variable measuring overall participation levels that can be disaggregated into each of the three stages.

What Counts as Constitutional Change?

Distinguishing "new" constitutions from amended older ones is not entirely straightforward. Zambia's shift from one-party rule to multi-party competition in 1991 or former President Hugo Chávez's (2009) reform of the Venezuelan constitution to allow himself additional terms are arguably the equivalent of new constitutions – even without wholesale redrafting and promulgation. Widner (2008) considers such cases "regime-changing amendments" amounting to new constitutions because they significantly impact civil and political liberties, ethnic or regional autonomy, or property rights. Banks and Wilson (2016) similarly include constitutional amendments that reorder prerogatives of different branches of government, such as switching from presidential to parliamentary executives. What counts with these approaches is the content of the constitutional changes. Alternatively, Cheibub et al. (2011) consider how reforms impact executive power and whether constitutional change took place outside of procedures specified in existing constitutions. This builds on Elkins et al.'s operational definition, that constitutional change adhering to existing amending procedures is coded as an amendment. Their extensive content analysis reports that replacements match parchment predecessors in 81 percent of the topics (Elkins et al. 2009, 55–9).

To reduce subjectivity in classification, the CDD applies a narrow definition of change counting only constitutions resulting from explicit promulgations. We identify these discrete political moments from the above datasets, secondary sources listed below, and from promulgation dates in constitutional texts. Applying these criteria between 1974 and 2014 the CDD identified 119 countries that implemented at least one new constitution[2] and approximately 71 countries that did not implement a new constitution (dataset available at http://doi.org/10.17606/M63W25). We start the dataset in 1974 to include the Third Wave (41 years in our dataset), encompassing transitions in the era of modern rights and constitutionalism, and because most needed data are available for this period.

Operationalizing Citizen Participation in Constitution-Making

After identifying the constitutions in our sample, constructing the *process* variable required breaking constitution-making into stages, with the ability to measure the level of participation separately for each one. Existing research often blends these stages with the degree of participation and the extent of inclusiveness. Widner (2004) measures the level of participation and representation in constitution-making by coding five process characteristics: type of deliberative body, method of selecting delegates, method of choosing delegates who draft initial texts, level of public consultation, and existence of a public referendum. Unfortunately this ambitious study did not gather enough information for a comprehensive set of cases. Carey (2009) focuses singularly on "constitutional moments," measuring inclusiveness with one variable that counts veto players and another indicating whether citizens voted on the constitution via referendum. Not only does this give us little leverage over discrete stages of the process, but veto players data exclude significant portions

---

[2] Insufficient information was available for four cases which implemented new constitutions fewer than three years ago. The CDD also does not include nations of fewer than 500,000 people.

of the developing world. Elkins et al. break the constitution-making process into stages of writing, deliberation, and approval. They reduce the deliberation stage to whether an elected body publicly debated the draft, while the basis for variation at the approval stage is whether a constitutional referendum took place (Elkins et al. 2009, 97–9). They operationalize inclusiveness using two proxies: a variable for whether constitutions were drafted during foreign occupations and another for whether a country was democratizing at the time.

Following the broad outlines of Elkins et al., we separate the constitution-making process into three stages of convening, debating, and ratification. However, since level of democracy is our dependent variable, using their democratization variable would generate obvious autocorrelation. More importantly, our *process* variable strives to directly measure level of participation rather than relying on proxies. To accomplish this, we gathered information on levels and modalities of citizen input or elite control over constitution-making at each of the three stages.[3] The convening stage includes activities in the constitution-making process related to selecting those actively and directly involved in crafting the constitution's content. We sought information about whether convening was done by a previously elected body or a newly elected body, whether those elections were free and fair, and whether there were otherwise systematic opportunities for direct involvement of ordinary citizens rather than delegating to experts. The debate stage explores how decisions were made about content and retentions and omissions from the text. This entailed negotiations and efforts to transform participants' preferences. The ratification stage entailed procedures for approving the constitution and making it binding for all citizens, including those who did not participate in its creation. If the constitution was approved through a national referendum, we also sought indications of doubts about the vote's credibility. We then used this information to construct the umbrella *process* variable, coding each stage of constitution-making with one of three ordered values measuring participation levels. First, "imposed" indicates elite control of a non-transparent process through a strong executive, a committee appointed by the executive with no meaningful external consultation, or a party acting as a central committee. At the convening stage, constitutions of the Dominican Republic (2010) and Morocco (2011) fit this mold since they were written behind closed doors with little public input. Drafters are often hastily appointed to preempt momentum for public input.

---

[3] Sources consulted include: Ellicott (2011), Hein Online (2012), Widner (2004), Institute for Democracy and Electoral Assistance's ConstitutionNet.org (accessed August 2013), Economist Intelligence Unit country reports, and the CIA *World Fact Book*. A few cases, such as The Gambia, Switzerland, and Afghanistan, required additional research from peer-reviewed area studies journals.

Constitutions with imposed qualities at the debate stage include Lesotho's (1993) and Nicaragua's (1974). Similarly, China's 1978 constitution was a product of the Communist Party's closed discussions, and even when a new process in 1982 was opened to elites, we found no evidence that their participation significantly altered content. Countries such as Morocco (2011), Burma (2008), and Nigeria (1999) did not even bother to submit constitutions to referendums for public approval, classifying their ratification stage as imposed.

Second, "mixed modalities" captures cases with overlap or tension between elite and bottom up influences, but we sought to avoid generating a residual category. Constitutions drafted with mixed modalities include Paraguay (1992), where drafters were elected but elites manipulated candidate selection or the electoral process. Similarly, Spain's constitution (1978) had strong democratic qualities but content was constrained by the elite pact shaping the transition. This also includes cases where a body previously elected for another purpose, such as a regular parliament, drafts a new constitution or appoints a committee. As Elkins put it, this generates the risk of "self-dealing." At the debate stage, we sought processes that were partially public but lacked readily identifiable divergences from elite preferences, as in Peru (1993), where an ad hoc subcommittee of the Democratic Constituent Congress passively received public input and communicated through regular radio broadcasts and press releases, but does not seem to have reckoned with public concerns about executive discretion following President Fujimori's *autogolpe* power grab. Burundi (1992) or Hungary (2011) epitomize mixed modalities at the ratification stage, where constitutions were approved by referendums – but were widely considered flawed.

Third, "popular" participation refers to extensive and meaningful opportunities for broad sections of the public to directly shape constitution-making processes. As in Mansbridge et al. (2012), experts and elites still played important roles. But the risks of delegated authority were minimized through transparency, and leverage that ordinary citizens institutionally held. At the convening stage, this occurred in cases such as Benin's Sovereign National Conference (1990) and Ecuador's recent (2008) constitution-making with extensive indigenous input. In some 10 cases meeting these criteria at the convening stage, a *specially elected* body drafted the constitution (usually via legislative self-dealing or unilateral executive appointments). At the debate stage, popular participation typically involved a legislature or constituent assembly. But unlike with mixed modalities, civil society and ordinary citizens visibly influenced debates, undermining experts' abilities to assert monopolies on constitutional wisdom, as in South Africa (1996). At the ratification stage, popular participation is fairly common for the reasons we identified earlier: free and fair national referendums on constitutions legitimize them and their creation. Table 2.1

TABLE 2.1. *Coding criteria*

	Stage of Process		
	Convening	Debating	Ratifying
Imposed	Strong executive OR exec-appointed committee OR party as central committee	Strong executive OR exec-appointed committee OR party as central committee. Debated in camera	No referendum OR decree by executive body
Mixed modalities	Strong elite influence AND existing legislature (OR specially elected body), but elites exercised some control over candidates/electoral process	Strong elite influence AND a debate in existing legislature (OR specially elected body) that was at least partially open, but that failed to overrule any elite preferences	Strong elite influence AND ratification by elected body OR ratification by a referendum with notable irregularities
Popular	Systematic civil society input OR strong transparency OR specially elected drafters "freely and fairly" elected	Public debate, with civil society, that visibly influenced draft content	Generally "free and fair" referendum

Level of participation

summarizes coding criteria and logical conditions. The CDD includes 140 cases at the convening stage (with four missing values) and 139 at the debating and ratifying stages (with five missing values in each).

A practical issue at each stage concerned conceptual connections between representation and participation: a process could theoretically have an unrepresentative small subset of interests that vigorously and visibly participated; it could also be broadly inclusive but entail little meaningful participation. Though we do not have a separate variable measuring representativeness, we believe our approach is nevertheless an improvement over the use of proxies by extant studies. Our coding strategy is also consistent with Mansbridge et al.'s approach judging exclusion on the strength of justifications offered as well as public acceptance of rationales. Moreover, our search for elite control substantially overlaps with representativeness. Finally, using public signals of exclusion to gauge process inclusiveness is consistent with practitioner real-world applications of concepts. For the Carter Center, for example, a participatory process "is one in which citizens are informed about the process and choices at stake, and are given a genuine opportunity to directly express their views to decision makers involved in the drafting and debating of the constitution" (Carter Center 2012, 5).

To characterize constitution-making processes, we assign *process* variable values on a scale ranging from 0 ("imposed" processes in all three stages) to 6 ("popular" processes in all three stages). The average score is 2.5, indicating a mixture of "imposed" and "mixed" modalities. For an average country with a process score of 2.5, the Polity IV score is 1.6 (on a scale of −10 for most autocratic to +10 for most democratic). However, if a country uses an all "imposed" process, its average Polity score is −3.2; and if it utilizes an all "popular" process, its average Polity IV score increases to +5.3. In other words, popular constitutional processes do correspond with higher levels of democracy. Additionally, over time there is a slight increase in process scores even without changes in Polity IV scores. That is, the number of countries using "popular" modalities increases as the process progresses. Figure 2.1 shows the number of cases since 1974 for each stage of constitution-making.

EMPIRICAL TESTS OF PARTICIPATORY
CONSTITUTION-MAKING ON DEMOCRACY

So does participatory constitution-making matter? And does it matter more at some stages of the process than at others? In this section we answer affirmatively to each question. Statistical tests of the participation hypothesis regress the *process* variable on the post-promulgation level of democracy, measured

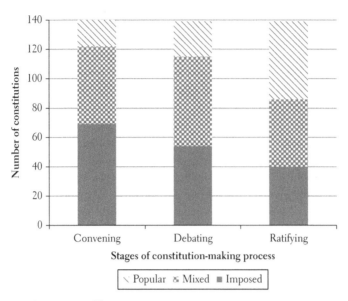

FIGURE 2.1. *Process variable*

at multiple intervals with the Unified Democracy Score (UDS) and Polity IV. Endogeneity tests with an additional instrumental variable (IV) further our claim that *process* does indeed measure participatory constitution-making specifically. Next, two sets of tests of the "origination" hypothesis demonstrate that the earliest stage, convening, has a greater impact on democratization than the debate stage or the modalities of ratification. Our results hold across a broad range of controls and robustness checks.

First Stage: Process Does Drive Democracy

In the first stage, we test the participation hypothesis, which states that high overall levels of participation throughout the constitution-making process positively impact levels of democracy. This builds on intuitions of the "bottom-up" literature discussed above, arguing that the grassroots basis for democratization has lasting benefits for democracy as well as for participatory models of democracy. To measure levels of democracy, we use the combined Polity IV score, a unified scale ranging from −10 (strongly autocratic) to +10 (strongly democratic). In a separate test, we use Pemstein et al.'s (2010) UDS. The UDS weights multiple democracy indices according to their reliability. The UDS ranges from −2.11 (lowest) to +2.26 (highest) and covers all countries from 1946 to 2012. Both dependent variables are measured as three year averages after the year of constitution promulgation (*t*) centered at year two (*t+1* to *t+3*), year five (*t+4* to *t+6*), and year nine (*t+8* to *t+10*), respectively. This provides a robustness check and shows the direction of change in democracy levels after constitutional promulgation, which is consistent for both measures of the democracy dependent variable. Hence, positive coefficients would support the participation hypothesis, stated as:

H 2.1: Higher overall levels of participatory constitution-making increase levels of democracy.

The statistical models also include variables measuring a variety of social, economic, and historical conditions that could account for the hypothesized relationship. First, the *ethnic* ratio variable controls for ethno-linguistic diversity using Alesina et al.'s (2003) data, with zero indicating ethnic homogeneity and one representing significant fractionalization. This is important because ethnicity could impede democratization by breeding parochialism (Horowitz 1985), advance democracy by enabling civil society mobilization (Bessinger 2008), or consistent with Widner (2008), not affect impacts of constitutional change on political rights. Second, Official Development Assistance (ODA) variable controls are used for net foreign aid assistance, since high participation is an international norm (Franck and Thiruvengadam 2010) and countries more dependent on foreign aid might have more participatory processes. Similarly, countries with more natural resources are considered less dependent on the international community for assistance and perhaps thus may incorporate fewer participatory processes. As such, we also control for natural resource rent. We use the World Bank's World Development Indicators (2013) of ODA as a percentage of gross national income, and natural resource rent as a percentage of GDP to control for foreign aid and natural resources, respectively. Each of our variables is measured as the average value for the three years before constitutional promulgation. Because modernization theory remains perhaps the most influential theory of democratization (Teorell 2010; Coppedge 2012), we also control for level of development with *GDP per capita*. Next, as larger countries may be less likely to democratize due to population density or other factors (Teorell 2010), we include the natural log of *population*. These last two variables come from the World Bank's World Development Indicators (2013). We also include year of constitution promulgation to control for trend as participatory constitution-making has emerged over time as a norm (Franck and Thiruvengadam 2010). Finally, we control for a nation's geographical region using data from Norris (2008).

The results in Table 2.2 show that *process* has a positive and significant impact on all Polity and UDS three-year post-promulgation averages, and the

TABLE 2.2. *Participation hypothesis and level of democracy*

Variables	Average Polity score			Average Unified Democracy score		
	t+1 to t+3	t+4 to t+6	t+8 to t+10	t+1 to t+3	t+4 to t+6	t+8 to t+10
Democracy_(t–3 to t–1)	–0.09	–0.02	0.03	–0.10	–0.07	–0.02
	(0.10)	(0.10)	(0.11)	(0.06)	(0.07)	(0.06)
Process	1.29***	1.73***	1.61***	0.14***	0.16***	0.17***
	(0.39)	(0.36)	(0.44)	(0.03)	(0.03)	(0.04)
Ethnic	–3.55	0.32	–1.34	0.39	0.26	–0.01
	(2.89)	(3.14)	(3.50)	(0.26)	(0.26)	(0.27)
ODA	–0.09*	–0.07	–0.09	–0.00	–0.01*	–0.01
	(0.05)	(0.05)	(0.06)	(0.01)	(0.00)	(0.01)
Natural resources	–0.05	–0.00	–0.04	–0.00	–0.00	–0.00
	(0.05)	(0.04)	(0.09)	(0.00)	(0.00)	(0.01)
GDP per capita	0.00	–0.00	–0.00	–0.00	–0.00	–0.00
	(0.00)	(0.00)	(0.00)	(0.00)	(0.00)	(0.00)
Population (log)	–0.24	–0.20	–0.60	–0.02	–0.05	–0.05
	(0.51)	(0.51)	(0.54)	(0.04)	(0.04)	(0.05)

	(1)	(2)	(3)	(4)	(5)	(6)
Promulgation year	0.02	0.05	0.05	0.00	-0.00	-0.01
	(0.07)	(0.09)	(0.13)	(0.01)	(0.01)	(0.01)
Africa	1.73	-1.21	-0.92	-0.22	-0.16	-0.15
	(1.74)	(1.65)	(1.99)	(0.14)	(0.15)	(0.17)
Asia	5.65***	4.95**	2.20	0.36*	0.45**	0.18
	(2.08)	(1.87)	(2.16)	(0.20)	(0.21)	(0.25)
Central Europe	-1.54	-2.11	-3.35	-0.10	-0.12	-0.14
	(2.04)	(1.96)	(2.81)	(0.18)	(0.17)	(0.21)
Middle East	-1.16	-0.66	-1.34	-0.40*	-0.28	-0.36
	(2.70)	(2.73)	(3.53)	(0.23)	(0.25)	(0.30)
Constant	-37.62	-97.74	-80.75	-3.30	3.06	16.20
	(142.75)	(167.85)	(263.11)	(16.69)	(16.95)	(26.83)
Observations	82	74	63	78	76	67
R-squared	0.32	0.41	0.39	0.40	0.42	0.41

Robust standard errors in parentheses.
*** $p < 0.01$, ** $p < 0.05$, * $p < 0.1$.

model explains a good deal of variance.[4] The results also show that not only is this impact significant, but that the coefficients increase slightly over time. While natural resource rent is not statistically significant, aid dependence has a significant and negative correlation with two democracy scores (Polity $t+1$ to $t+3$ and UDS $t+4$ to $t+6$ averages). In our Ordinary Least Squares (OLS) statistical tests, coefficients do not change significantly with changes in how democracy is measured. Of the dummies for region, only Asia has a positive and significant correlation with both Polity and UDS ($t+1$ to $t+3$ and $t+4$ to $t+6$ averages). The Middle East has a negative and significant correlation only with the UDS average of $t+1$ to $t+3$. This points to Middle East scholars' conclusions that in recent decades Arab states have grown rich in constitutions without necessarily growing richer in constitutionalism (Brown 2002).

Three caveats are in order. First, our case selection is non-random. The OLS regression for the above estimate of the effect of constitution-making process on change in democracy score is:

$$y_i = x_i \beta + \varepsilon_i \tag{2.1}$$

where y_i is the change in level of democracy of a country and x_i is the nature of its constitution-making process. Information is available about the nature of the constitution-making process only for countries choosing to write new constitutions. In other words, rather than forecasting outcomes for the universe of countries in our dataset, we must rely solely on a non-random subset of them. The "selection equation" for writing a new constitution might be:

$$U_i = \omega_i \gamma + u_i \tag{2.2}$$

where U_i represents the utility to country i of writing a new constitution and ω_i is a set of factors affecting a country's decision to adopt a new constitution, such as recent political independence. For example, democratizing countries might be more likely to adopt new constitutions than old democracies. To test for selection bias, we run a Heckman selection model (see Appendix A Table A.1). We used *new state* – a binary variable indicating whether the country is a newly formed state such as the post-Soviet states – as our variable in the selection equation. The unit of analysis in the Heckman model is country rather than constitution. We included the universe of countries regardless of constitution adoption. For countries adopting more than one constitution during the 1974–2014 time period, we included only the latest constitution. We could not reject the null hypothesis that there is no statistically significant difference between the coefficient of

---

[4] We also run our models with Freedom House's "Political Rights" and "Civil Liberties" and Cheibub's "Democracy–Dictatorship" measures. The process variable has a statistically positive correlation with these measures, too.

the Heckman selection model and the OLS model at a conventional level (ρ: 0.05). The model compares OLS coefficients with the Heckman corrections, showing that there is no statistically significant difference between coefficients of the two models. This is consistent with Elkins et al. (2009), who find constitutional replacement associated with regime change to be much less frequent than expected.

Next, we test for collinearity among independent variables. Collinearity could stem from the possibility that countries from certain regions utilize certain types of constitution-making process. Or that foreign aid dependence might have impacted whether particular constitutional processes involved citizen participation. We use two common indicators of collinearity – variance inflation factor (VIF) and tolerance – to detect potential collinearity. The mean VIF is 1.55, while the highest value of VIF and the lowest value of tolerance belong to the convening stage (VIF = 2.66 and tolerance = 0.38).[5] This indicates that collinearity is not an issue in our models.

Finally, we address the endogeneity problem since democratic, open societies are more likely to use popular means of creating constitutions. Tests for the correlation between democracy before and after promulgation show a significant correlation of 0.60 in Polity (−0.17 in UDS). However, as Figure 2.2 shows, the correlation between democracy before ($t-1$ to $t-3$) and after ($t+1$ to $t+3$) the constitution promulgation is not a determinant of the type of constitution-making process. Although imposed processes are more likely in non-democracies, the distribution of popular processes is fairly universal across levels of democracy. In fact, most cases that used popular process had a negative Polity score before the constitution promulgation year (only 40 percent had a positive score), but that significantly changed after the promulgation year, with 80 percent of those cases then having positive Polity scores.

Yet, to account for any potential impact of before-promulgation level of democracy we include lagged values of the dependent variables in our models. We also stratify our sample by regime type using Cheibub's Democracy–Dictatorship binary variable (see Appendix A Table A.2). Employing this solution diminishes our degrees of freedom, but the results do show that participatory constitution-making processes are even more effective in non-democracies than in democracies. This confirms our finding that popular processes significantly improve levels of democracy. We finally use an instrumental variable (IV) to test for endogeneity. We use the sum of major national strikes in the three years prior to promulgation as an instrumental estimator

---

[5] Individual VIFs measuring more than 10 and average VIFs of more than 6 indicate collinearity. Also, tolerance values close to zero (less than 0.1) can indicate potential collinearity.

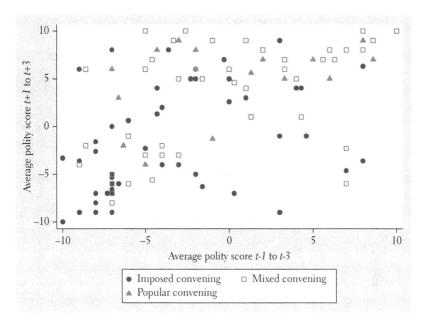

FIGURE 2.2. *Democracy before and after constitution promulgation based on convening stage*

for the *process* variable and run a two-stage least squares (2SLS) model, show-ing that strikes are as frequent in democracies as in non-democracies.[6] Labor movements play an important role in recent transitions, usually through strikes and other means of mobilization (Collier and Mahoney 1997). This indicates a close relationship among strikes, constitution-making, and dem-ocratic transitions over our study period. Citizens pressed challenges less as individuals than as groups (Diamond 1994). Labor unions played central roles in transitions since, through general strikes, they entered negotiations with authorities – negotiations often leading to more inclusion in political pro-cesses (Valenzuela 1989; Collier and Mahoney 1997). Hence, during times of transition, when constitutions are often crafted, strikes can impact democ-racy only through negotiating an inclusive political process. More strikes before constitution-making indicates higher levels of citizen mobilization and a greater chance of popular constitution-making. In other words, during

[6] Strikes are only 13 percent more likely in democracies than in non-democracies (Franklin 2013). In our dataset, the correlation between the *strikes* variable and Polity and UDS scores is 0.24 and 0.23, respectively. This is quite expected because the *strikes* variable affects these democracy measures through the *process* variable.

transitions strikes affect the type of convening process but affect democracy scores only through this convening process.

To test for endogeneity, then, we construct a *strikes* IV from Banks and Wilson's (2016) "general strikes" and run a 2SLS model using this variable. Since we are interested only in major national strikes, we use Banks and Wilson's "general strikes" including only strikes involving more than 1000 workers and more than one employer and targeted at national government policies or authorities. We incorporated this estimate for the IV, regressing it on our participation level *process* variable as the dependent variable in the first stage. Results from the first-stage of this 2SLS regression (reported in Appendix A Table A.3) show that the *strikes* independent variable estimate of the process variable (Polity IV) has a coefficient of 0.48 (and 0.46 for UDS) significant at 0.01 level. Thus, *strikes* have a positive correlation with *process*, indicating that the higher the number of strikes before constitution promulgation, the more popular the process. In the second stage of the 2SLS model we substituted our *process* variable for the fitted value of *strikes*, now as the independent variable, regressing it on the Polity IV and UDS variables (see Appendix A Table A.4). The results are similar to our initial OLS coefficients, indicating that *process* variable variant endogeneity is not a determinant. In other words, while strikes, a broader sign that civil society feels excluded from political processes (Parkinson and Mansbridge 2012), impacted the constitution-making process, this IV impacted broad democracy outcomes only through constitution writing. The democracy outcome was not severely impacted by endogenous variables.

Second Stage: Democratic Convening Matters for Democracy

We then test the "origination" hypothesis by using the stages of constitution-making as three separate independent variables (*convening*, *debate*, and *ratification*).[7] This is important because it explores whether the original sin of a non-democratic convening stage can be corrected by more participatory debate and ratification stages, and therefore improve post-promulgation levels of democracy. Each stage of the process was coded for level of participation, and participatory discussions may occur throughout. But we associate this hypothesis with deliberative democratic theory because meaningful public input at the earliest stage is least likely given the role of legal expertise that the literature associates with convening. The basic hypothesis is stated as:

---

[7] There is some correlation among the three-stage variables as decisions to use either process at different stages are not independent. Yet, our analysis indicates that collinearity is not an issue in our model (see Tables A.5 and A.6 in Appendix A).

H 2.2: Citizen involvement in the earliest "origination" stage of constitution-making (the convening stage) has a greater impact on democratic outcomes.

In our first tests of the convening stage, we run linear regression models showing that moving from an imposed convening process to a popular process increases the $t+1$ to $t+3$ average of Polity score by 11 percent (or an average of 2.19, holding other values constant, on the -10 to $+10$ continuum). For $t+4$ to $t+6$, the average Polity score increases by 16.2 percent, and for $t+8$ to $t+10$ it increases by 13.45 percent. Each country also experiences a nearly 8 percent increase in all three-year averages of post-promulgation UDS scores (between 0.30 and 0.36 units on average, holding other values constant, on the -2.11 to $+2.26$ index). Recall that only 18 cases used popular processes in the convening stage, while 24 and 53 cases had popular processes in the debate and ratification stages, respectively. Even given that fewer cases had popular convening than popular debate and ratification, the results from Table 2.3 show that only in the origination stage, convening, is the move from imposed to popular process statistically significant. This is a central finding of our study: that a popular process (i.e. involves wide sectors of society) matters in convening much more than in debate or ratification.

Admittedly, this finding is driven by few cases, which could raise suspicions that outlying observations might drive the results. To ease this concern, we conducted further statistical tests. First, after running all our models, we generated standardized residuals. All standardized residuals fall in the range of $+2.24$ and -1.71 indicating no outliers in our models.[8] Second, we estimated the model using only covariates without missing data to see if we observed the same effects in the larger model. Table A.7 in Appendix A shows that we do. Finally, we estimated the model using bootstrapped standard errors. As Table A.8 in Appendix A shows, the results also held up using bootstrapped standard errors. Together these tests show that our findings are not driven by outliers.

With regard to our controls, aid dependence (ODA) had a negatively significant correlation with each democracy measure (except for UDS $t+8$ to $t+10$). The natural log of population, *ethnic*, natural resource rents, and GDP per capita all showed negative but insignificant correlations with most measures of democracy. The promulgation year variable had a positive and insignificant correlation with all Polity scores and the $t+1$ to $t+3$ average score of the UDS, but its direction changes for $t+4$ to $t+6$ and $t+8$ to $t+10$ UDS averages.

An alternative explanation suggests that the content of constitutions, rather than the processes that designed it, has greater impact on the levels of democracy. Such ideas are evident in recent research exploring the "congruity"

---

[8] Standardized residuals greater than $+3.5$ or less than -3.5 are considered outliers.

of constitutional content (Galston 2011), the impact of particular provisions on broader democratic accountability (Fombad 2010), or on constitutional endurance (Ginsburg 2012). We control for democratic content of constitutions using three proxies from the Comparative Constitutions Project dataset (Elkins et al. 2009): whether the head of state has decree power (*HOS decree*), whether the constitution places any restriction on the right to vote (*Voter restriction*), and whether the constitution contains provisions for a human rights commission (*HR provision*). Table 2.4 shows the results with controls for the content of constitutions included as independent variables. While the results for process and other variables do not change significantly (except for *natural resources* becoming statistically significant) from Table 2.3 when these "democratic content" variables are added, these content variables do not show any significant correlation with levels of democracy. The results show that process has more significant and positive impacts on democracy than constitution content. This further confirms our broader point that strong empirical evidence exists that the process of constitution-making has vital implications for improving a country's level of democracy.

As with the findings regarding the *process* variable in our earlier statistical findings, the *convening* variable is robust in all cases when the *process* variable is disaggregated into three partials, while *debate* and *ratification* are not statistically significant. Hence we are able to rule out the broad "legalistic constitutionalism" hypothesis suggested in the literature review as a cause of democratic gains after some new constitutions. While we cannot definitively rule out changes in democracy levels brought by changes in political culture somehow set off by the constitutional process, our control variables related to political culture (regional dummies and ethnic division, for example) were not significant. A further argument against the agency of political culture in our model is that the results after *t+10* are quite similar to those at *t+ 1*. In other words, the passage of time has no effect on changing political culture. Rather, we strongly believe that the changes in levels of democracy we identify which we can trace back to the origination (convening) stage are due to the sorts of political institutions utilized by democratic reformer-driven processes as opposed to those managed by "window dresser" authoritarians. We offer contrasting ideal types using notorious authoritarian constitutional promulgations from Latin American history and a couple of participatory ones from the Arab Spring-era in the Middle East to illustrate our argument.

While not beyond critique (starting with Dahl 2002), modern democratic constitutionalism is said to have commenced with the US constitutional convention in 1787. This republican (if not fully democratic) precedent created an expectations gap between the hopes of liberation-era reformers of Spanish

TABLE 2.3: *Significance of convening, relative to debating and ratification*

Variables	Average Polity score			Average Unified Democracy score		
	$t+1$ to $t+3$	$t+4$ to $t+6$	$t+8$ to $t+10$	$t+1$ to $t+3$	$t+4$ to $t+6$	$t+8$ to $t+10$
Democracy_($t-3$ to $t-1$)	−0.05	−0.05	−0.00	−0.12*	−0.10	−0.05
	(0.10)	(0.11)	(0.11)	(0.07)	(0.07)	(0.07)
Convening	2.19**	3.24***	2.69*	0.30***	0.36***	0.35**
	(1.02)	(1.07)	(1.46)	(0.10)	(0.11)	(0.14)
Debating	1.26	0.37	1.21	0.03	−0.02	0.01
	(1.37)	(1.33)	(1.73)	(0.12)	(0.13)	(0.17)
Ratifying	−0.39	1.13	1.22	0.07	0.11	0.19**
	(1.00)	(0.98)	(1.10)	(0.08)	(0.09)	(0.09)
Ethnic	−2.44	−0.57	−1.39	0.31	0.18	−0.08
	(2.71)	(3.15)	(3.04)	(0.26)	(0.26)	(0.25)
ODA	−0.10*	−0.09*	−0.09*	−0.01*	−0.01**	−0.01
	(0.05)	(0.05)	(0.06)	(0.01)	(0.00)	(0.01)
Natural resources	−0.08	−0.02	−0.06	−0.00	−0.00	−0.01
	(0.05)	(0.04)	(0.08)	(0.00)	(0.00)	(0.01)

	(1)	(2)	(3)	(4)	(5)	(6)
GDP per capita	−0.00	−0.00	−0.00	−0.00	−0.00	−0.00
	(0.00)	(0.00)	(0.00)	(0.00)	(0.00)	(0.00)
Population (log)	−0.18	0.03	−0.47	−0.01	−0.03	−0.04
	(0.48)	(0.53)	(0.54)	(0.04)	(0.04)	(0.05)
Promulgation year	0.07	0.04	0.01	0.00	−0.00	−0.01
	(0.07)	(0.08)	(0.11)	(0.01)	(0.01)	(0.01)
Constant	−141.17	−86.59	31.12	−2.33	5.83	27.90
	(147.01)	(161.08)	(218.90)	(15.69)	(15.10)	(20.68)
Observations	82	74	63	78	76	67
R-squared	0.25	0.32	0.36	0.32	0.35	0.40

Robust standard errors in parentheses.
*** $p < 0.01$, ** $p < 0.05$, * $p < 0.1$.

TABLE 2.4. *Impact of process and content of constitutions on democracy*

	Average Polity score			Average Unified Democracy score		
Variables	t+1 to t+3	t+4 to t+6	t+8 to t+10	t+1 to t+3	t+4 to t+6	t+8 to t+10
Democracy_(t−3 to t−1)	0.04	0.04	0.07	−0.06	−0.04	−0.02
	(0.11)	(0.11)	(0.11)	(0.08)	(0.09)	(0.08)
Convening	2.17*	3.17**	2.12	0.36***	0.36***	0.29*
	(1.16)	(1.22)	(1.36)	(0.12)	(0.12)	(0.16)
Debating	0.93	0.53	1.76	−0.00	0.03	0.12
	(1.20)	(1.29)	(1.37)	(0.13)	(0.13)	(0.17)
Ratifying	−0.19	1.60	0.88	0.04	0.08	0.11
	(1.11)	(1.06)	(1.19)	(0.10)	(0.11)	(0.11)
Ethnic	−4.06	−3.44	−4.11	−0.10	−0.15	−0.31
	(3.38)	(3.52)	(3.64)	(0.35)	(0.35)	(0.34)
Natural resources	−0.14***	−0.09**	−0.15***	−0.01***	−0.01***	−0.02***
	(0.05)	(0.04)	(0.05)	(0.00)	(0.00)	(0.01)
GDP per capita	0.00	0.00	0.00	0.00	0.00	0.00**
	(0.00)	(0.00)	(0.00)	(0.00)	(0.00)	(0.00)
Population (log)	0.78	0.81	0.15	0.07	0.06	0.01
	(0.64)	(0.61)	(0.55)	(0.06)	(0.06)	(0.06)

Promulgation year	0.11	0.04	−0.01	−0.00	−0.00	−0.02
	(0.11)	(0.11)	(0.16)	(0.01)	(0.01)	(0.01)
HOS decree	0.01	0.01	0.00	0.00	−0.00	−0.00
	(0.02)	(0.02)	(0.02)	(0.00)	(0.00)	(0.00)
Voter restriction	−4.09	−0.65	−2.40	−0.41	−0.34	−0.50
	(2.48)	(2.28)	(2.05)	(0.26)	(0.30)	(0.31)
HR provision	−0.03	−0.01	0.03	−0.00	0.00	0.00
	(0.03)	(0.03)	(0.03)	(0.00)	(0.00)	(0.00)
Constant	−217.46	−89.66	24.47	2.17	7.14	33.71
	(225.42)	(225.35)	(308.63)	(21.89)	(21.95)	(28.49)
Observations	71	74	67	78	77	70
R-squared	0.41	0.43	0.51	0.45	0.47	0.58

Robust standard errors in parentheses.
*** $p < 0.01$, ** $p < 0.05$, * $p < 0.1$.

America in the 1820s for enlightened post-monarchical rule, and their fears of anarchy, famously articulated by The Liberator himself, Simón Bólivar ("America is ungovernable; those who served the revolution have plowed the sea," as quoted in Liss and Liss [1972]). Their solution then (and followed by 35 dataset constitutions such as Kenya [2010], Niger [2010], and Venezuela [1999]) was to enact "dead letter" republican parchments, but with no implementation whatsoever, or, to our direct argument, no societal participation, to keep nineteenth-century authoritarians from making "regimes of exception" the rule (Loveman 1993). Similarly, in twentieth-century Brazil, authoritarians used constitutional processes as an "escape valve" for social tensions, but not as a means of constructing democracy (Veja 1980; Linz and Stepan 1991); and in twentieth-century Mexico, ruling party autocrats implemented one of the most progressive constitutions in the world (Hansen 1971, 90) but established metaconstitutional practices (Garrido 1989) and informal bargaining tables (Eisenstadt 2004; Eisenstadt 2003, 2006) to circumvent *de jure* dictates in favor of *de facto* elite practices. Indeed, Negretto's (2013, 10) analysis of 194 post-independence constitutions in 18 Latin American nations shows that the pluralism of institutions in new constitutions depends on "whether the party that controls or is likely to control the presidency has unilateral power or requires the support of other parties to approve reforms." In other words, from the top-down, authoritarians and "hybrid regime" leaders sometimes must break political log jams by calling for new constitutions, but this has nothing to do with democracy and everything to do with consolidating authority.

If these "stage-managed" and unimplemented Latin American constitutions, mostly negotiated by military elites, dominant-party leaders, and other authoritarians (at least prior to the 1980s Third Wave opening), demonstrate the pattern of "top-down" origination yielding little democracy, Benin (1990) and Greece (1975) (with +13 and +12.6 points increase in Polity score, respectively) embody the other extreme, with popular participatory process yielding more democratic outcomes. In the most recent constitution in the world, Tunisia (as with 12 cases in our dataset, including Colombia [1991], Portugal [1976], and Uganda [1995]) opened the constitutional process in the hope of strengthening democratic institutions or building new ones. Tunisian constitutionalist, Secretary General of the Tunisian National Constituent Assembly's Constitution Drafting Committee, made the point:

> Right after the revolution, our main concern was how to avoid a return to the authoritarian rule. As such we decided to open the [constitutional] process from its initial stages because only an open, participatory process can secure a democratic transition.[9]

---

[9] Interview with Habib Khedher. Tunis, Tunisia. January 22, 2015.

A popular process not only guarantees a democratic transition by including all groups, but also by checking the majority. "Bottom-up" processes only balance power when opened at origination, however, because a closed process in the convening stage, no matter how popular it becomes later on, only includes certain groups and excludes others from participation in the first place.

Looking back at Figure 2.2 above, the real benefits of popular processes tend to be for countries with Polity scores at $t-1$ to $t-3$ which range from about -4 to about 2. Countries, like Colombia (1991), which already has a high democracy score ($+8$ on -10 to $+10$ scale), had the least changes among countries using popular process (Colombia's post-constitutional democracy score shifted to $+9$). But for countries like Lithuania with a Polity score of -2.6 at $t-1$ to $t-3$, employing a popular process has the most significant impact, as the country's democracy score shifted to $+10$ at $t+1$ to $t+3$. For the countries on the same pre-constitutional democracy level, mixed processes, also, seem to be beneficial, but to a lesser degree. Czech Republic (1993) shifts from $+8$ to $+10$ on democracy scale after using a mixed constitutional process, and Brazil (1988) moves from $+7$ to $+8$. And when Chad in 1996 used a mixed process, its democracy score improved from -4 to -2 after the constitution promulgation. Among the three types of constitutional processes, imposed processes seem to have the least effect on changing a country on the democracy scale. Algeria (1976), Chile (1980), China (1982), Oman (1996), and Congo-Brazzaville (2006) are among the non-democracies which their negative democracy score does not change following their imposed constitutional processes. The main conclusion to be drawn here is that while popular (and to a lesser degree, mixed) processes are most beneficial for countries in transition toward democracy, imposed processes, which are mostly employed in non-democracies, tend to have no effect on improving the level of democracy.

Caveats on Formal Constitutional Powers: Rule via Metaconstitutionalism in Mexico

The significant finding that convening broader groups of people produces more democratic constitutions is conditional. The condition is that the constitution be implemented, as nearly all Third Wave constitutions (those since 1973 that form part of our statistical sample) have been. Needless to say, this is a self-evident caveat, although that has not always been the case. Before norms of democracy were widely understood through the media and academic literature – even in authoritarian regimes – constitutions were often ignored *de facto* in day-to-day governance, even if they were obeyed to the letter (*de jure*) in formal terms. Perhaps the best case of a constitution that was literally adhered to but ignored in the bigger picture was Mexico's democratic 1917 constitution, which justified authoritarian rule in that country until about 1990. That case is discussed in this section as a powerful illustrative warning to constitutional formalists who fail to consider the informal processes and contexts, flagged by Brown (2008) and cited in our introduction. While those "low politics" informal processes may be less explicitly evident now than they were in the vulgar manipulation of constitutional politics by Mexico's authoritarian leaders for decades, those informal processes still matter, and are, as shown in the following three chapters, determinant in the quality of popular participation possible in constitution-writing processes.

Of the great social revolutions of the twentieth century – in China, Cuba, Mexico, Nicaragua, Russia – Mexico's produced one of the most progressive constitutions. The Constitution of 1917 may be one of the best examples of a democratic rights-promoting constitution, codifying some of the world's most substantial land reforms and workplace rights of the time (Hansen 1971, 121–2). It was the result of the Congress of Queretaro, convened by moderates from Mexico's north who were part of the victorious social and military movement. As Gargarella (2010) points out, they swiftly took control of the process and there were few opportunities for citizen participation. This was made easier by *campesino* apathy about the process itself: despite their bloody revolutionary victory, Emiliano Zapata and Francisco "Pancho" Villa famously abandoned the presidential chair in Mexico City and expressed disinterest in promulgating laws and constitutions.

The result was a mixed constitution-making process that sought to avoid a reversion to the revolution's violence by encoding land rights and political reform, but omitting those with the leverage to enforce such progress. Consistent with our Chapter 3 finding that democratic constitutional content has little to do with democratic practice, the moderates, under Venustiniano Carranza and an emerging new northern Mexico-based political elite, seized control of the process, allowing the revolution to gradually transit government back into authoritarianism, despite the popular aspirations of the document itself. Implementation of that constitution happened only in the breach for the next seven decades, essentially until the Third Wave reached Mexico's shores.

During that time, Mexico's informal party structure of the ruling Party of the Institutional Revolution (PRI, initials after the Spanish), which first emerged in 1929, was constructed alongside the powerfully constituted executive branch. It was not until electoral competition empowered opposition legislators 60 years later in the 1990s to call into question the cozy and sycophantic arrangement between the ruling party and the state that the constitution could be separated from the ruling party to allow for the actual democratic conditions needed for the 1917 constitution to be effective. The document was enacted only in the breach, and scholars over the next several generations defined the term "metaconstitutional powers" as those conceived by the president and ruling party to override the constitution.

Indeed, the Mexican constitution of 1917 promised separation of powers, strong federalism, and independent elections but delivered only strong presidentialism – with executive control over the legislative branch, the "hiring and firing" of subnational leaders, and the rigging of elections for the ruling PRI, from that party's inception in 1929 until the mid-1990s. National opposition victories in 2000 and 2006 sealed the end of the PRI's dominion of informal institutions, re-orienting radically the context (and implementation) of that constitution without substantial changes in the text. The fact that Mexico held presidential elections rigged by the ruling PRI, and that the president acted as *de facto* head of this party (Weldon 1997) gave the president a range of *de facto* or "metaconstitutional" powers, to use Carpizo's (1978) term. Garrido codified nine "metaconstitutional" powers (1989, 422–5) of the president, including: "establish himself as ultimate authority on electoral matters," "designate successor of his presidency," "designate state governors, members of the PRI majorities in Congress, and most state representatives and mayors," "remove governors, mayors, and legislators at the federal and state levels," and "hold sway over municipal governments, overriding local government autonomy as set forth in Article 115 of the Constitution." While we mention in Chapter 3 that the democratic nature of the constitution's content was not statistically significant, meaning that democratic content might not matter, Mexico's constitution was drafted at least somewhat from below, and the Queretaro Constitutional Assembly of victor-named delegates occurred just months after the near-decade of vicious fighting ceased. But its implementation was usurped by these informal metaconstitutional powers.

As long as Mexico's president, as head of the PRI party, could rely on his metaconstitutional powers, the executive was all-powerful (Eisenstadt 2004). Party discipline was strong because there was no re-election and party politicians had to look to the PRI's leadership to see where their next job would be. A successful and disciplined PRI legislator might aspire to a mayoral position in his/her home state, a high-ranking post in the party bureaucracy, an executive post position (assistant secretary or even secretary, after thriving for a few rounds), or even that most coveted of posts – just short of the all-powerful presidency itself – a governorship. No re-election, combined with the *dedazo* (Spanish term for "fingering") by the president of his successor, along with the protection of the president from criminal investigations or prosecutions, made the chief executive almost invincible.

All of these powers were informal; that is, they were not written in the constitution. When the PRI lost power, so did the office of the president. Indeed, with the increasingly plural Congress and with the opponent National Action Party (PAN, initials after the Spanish) victory in 2000, the regimented and efficient – but authoritarian – system, whereby the president passed on his position to a successor, and essentially conducted the transfer of power right on down the line to his network and its representatives at the most local levels, fell apart. The PRI returned to power in 2012, but the metaconstitutional powers of the PRI had been dismantled, and the PRI was just another political party (albeit an extremely powerful one), which – mostly – adhered to the democratic constitution.

Mexico's great social upheaval from 1907 to 1915, culminating perhaps in the biggest loss of life worldwide between the turn of the century and World War I, did not produce a constitution commensurate with all the sacrifices that had been made, because the radicals were not interested in constitutions and instead ceded control of the process to an alliance of the reformers and the softliners, who, over time, were able to reinvent themselves as hardliners. Perhaps this was consistent with thinking by Lenin, who led the other contemporary social revolution, that revolutionary social movements without a "vanguard party" to direct the revolution and steer its interests are useless. Certainly, this was true in Mexico, where the constitution became relevant only during the CDD time frame and in other cases from our dataset, such as Ecuador and Egypt, detailed in Chapter 5. In this case, a victorious revolutionary social movement was unable to institutionalize itself into a constituent assembly and hence there were no political parties or other organized interests to defend Mexico's revolutionary peasants. In the successful cases of "bottom-up" constitution-making presented later in Chapter 5, Colombia and Tunisia, interest groups did lead constituent assemblies, from the O'Donnell, Schmitter, and Przeworski "reformer" group, rather than from among the radicals (such as Mexico's revolutionaries).

Why did tumultuous social revolution in Mexico fail, through its constitution, to help produce a more robust democracy? One important difference with the modern cases of successful popular constitution-making concerns the level and inclusiveness of the mobilization. As we showed in Chapter 1, what matters for improving levels of democracy is representation by a broad range of societal groups in the convening stage. Tunisia's National Dialogue Quartet protected broad representation in its constitution-making, while some of the principal victors of the Mexican Revolution abandoned the constituent assembly – not because they had to but apparently because they didn't see it as important. This opening enabled the northern moderates to co-opt the process and for hardliners to begin deconstructing democracy through metaconstitutional powers, rebuilding a decentralized system of *caudillo* power beneath the PRI's democratic veneer. Another important difference concerns strategy: Like the French Revolution, Mexico's bloodshed destroyed the old order but impeded democratic institution-building. It took decades for challenges to the metaconstitutional powers to succeed, by which time global norms of participation had shifted, elevating constitutions as both symbols and instruments of grassroots democracy.

IMPLICATIONS AND CONCLUSIONS

By demonstrating the central importance of the convening stage in contemporary cases of constitution-drafting (since the Third Wave began in 1973), our results refute elitist Burkean notions of constitution-making via trusteeship. Our statistical results demonstrate first, that constitutional change contributes to improvements in democracy in only half of all cases of constitutional promulgation during the Third Wave. This is important because despite democratic backsliding worldwide over the last several years, we have learned little about conditions under which new constitutions effectively deepen democracy. Second, tests of our "participation" hypothesis demonstrate that increased public participation throughout the constitution-making process overall significantly contributes to levels of democracy at all three-year average intervals after promulgation. This offers empirical support for emerging international norms of participatory governance and for participatory models of democracy. Moreover, it shows that participatory procedure, rather than particular language in the draft, matters.

Third, the results from our "origination" hypothesis generated the unexpected finding that convening, which occurs earlier in constitution-making, has the greatest impact on subsequent levels of democracy. This is an important caveat to would-be constitutional engineers about the "original sin" of the convening stage so clearly demonstrated here. More broadly, to the extent our tests capture the essence of deliberative democracy, our results suggest that the model may be both more beneficial and more feasible than its critics contend. "The preconditions of free and equal discussion are much the same as the preconditions of free and equal voting," argues Mackie (2003, 387). Moreover, democracy promotion has often emphasized – even romanticized – referendums, which often take place only in the final stages of ratification. Indeed, democracy levels improved only in 45 percent of cases that incorporated broad consultation at debate and ratification stages, but not at the initial, convening stage. By contrast, 82 percent of the cases in our data that used popular convening, regardless of popular participation in later stages, show such improvement.

The few nations that do integrate popular "bottom-up" participation from constitutional process inception tend to involve more serious democrats. Late entrants to popular participation (73 in our sample), seeking to remedy their "original sin" of neglecting popular participation early on, are more likely to fail. Contrary to Elster's "hourglass shaped" process amplifying the importance of approval procedures, our findings show that direct citizen input early on might not matter much for the constitution's content, but it matters a great deal more than referendums for the kind of democracy that emerges. Since the components of a constitution-making process are "tightly coupled" in Mansbridge et al.'s terms, our evidence suggests that direct citizen participation early on increases the likelihood of positive spillovers later.

Extant single-country studies have exposed the vulnerability of constitutional processes to elite manipulation. While we have made important strides by identifying the overwhelming importance of participatory convening, constitutional processes in specific cases at particular moments need to be further examined cross-sectionally and longitudinally. If the citizen engagement that brought down dictators has a mixed effect on the quality of constitutions and their enduring effects on political culture and rule compliance, this could influence both donor priorities and which processes of constitution-making are deemed most effective.

Our findings offer conclusions useful to scholars and analysts seeking to understand the political effects of constitutions. They may also be used to improve levels of democracy using statistical analysis of the CDD in nations implementing new constitutions, as well as in carefully selected ethnographies of constitution-founding moments. We argue that the degree of participation by citizens is crucial to understanding whether constitutional change improves levels of democracy. Further research should merge procedural and substantive concerns by addressing not only whether and how citizens participate in convening, debate, and ratification, but also how substantial this participation is in terms of proposing concrete language that otherwise would not have made the draft. The strong call for greater participation emerging from this chapter should be joined by a call for "quality participation" rather than just populism. Several different measures of democracy (including Polity, UDS, and Freedom House) demonstrate that participatory constitution-building improves levels of democracy, but we still need to know which components of democracy are actually improved. Along the same lines, it would probably be useful to further disaggregate participation as a causal variable by separately measuring inclusion. Such an approach might help resolve the paradox presented by Horowitz, who argues that Indonesia's constitution-making process was "representative and inclusive, but it was certainly not participatory" (Horowitz 2013, 12).

Recall from Chapter 1 that we are dividing participation into three modalities: deliberation, which is the strongest form of non-elite participation; mere aggregation ("strength in numbers"), the weakest form of non-elite participation; and elite bargaining and pacting, the most common form of non-elite participation (through interest groups). While we did not in this chapter formally test the quality or modality of participation utilized in each case, we will in Chapter 3 empirically test effects of "top-down" constitutionalism (usually undertaken via the pacting model), and "bottom-up" constitutionalism (usually undertaken via the aggregation model, where social movements and opposition parties try to take from the ruling elites via numbers what they cannot claim through social networks or resources). In Chapters 4 and 5 we explore these three modalities of participation, demonstrating, true to Landemore and Elster (2012), that deliberation produces better democracy later. Unfortunately, we were unable to code each case in sufficient detail to sort each one into these three modalities. We offer case applications of these concepts later, but must leave the statistical demonstration that deliberation leads to improved democracy to future research.

Contemporary constitution-making has differed in important ways from earlier eras, through involvement of competing donors, assumptions about the virtues of participation, and beliefs that human agency can prevail over adverse historical or geographical conditions. Constitutional changes during the Third Wave have had a mixed impact on democracy, and our analysis offers a compelling explanation for this ambiguity by demonstrating the systematic benefits of direct citizen involvement, thus offering a compelling rationale for legal theories and prevailing international norms. New knowledge of the relationship between constitution-making and democracy will help scholars, analysts, and policy-makers focus attention on both process and substantive content, and to reconsider those elements of the process most conducive to realizing democrats' aspirations.

As the Moroccan constitutionalist stated, in the opening of this chapter, and as we tried to show statistically, one crucial element of the process of constitution-making is the nature of its "origination" stage. The Moroccan king seems to have had an intuitive sense of what we found empirically and presented in this chapter: that constitutional processes are most beneficial for democratization if the process is opened up to all early on. King Mohammed revealed in his rejection of a constituent assembly that he did not want democracy to flourish. Opening the constitutional process in the first stage was the only demand of the February 20 Youth Movement, which launched the Moroccan uprisings of 2011. And yet, Mohammed VI rejected precisely this same demand and instead offered other symbolic political changes, possibly fearing that a participatory constitutional process might spiral into a democratization of the kingdom that would diminish his control.

The February 20 Movement still considers the constitution illegitimate because it was not written by people's representatives and claims that such an illegitimate constitution cannot bind the state to respect human rights. In Chapter 3, we focus on this element of constitutional processes in detail. We ask whether the process of constitution-making has any impact on a state's provision of services to the public. We also test whether constitutional processes impact voter turnout in national elections and respect for human rights after constitutional promulgation. Then we illustrate the pathways of constitutional deliberation, like Morocco's, that do not improve levels of democracy, and compare these to other pathways of constitutional deliberation that do improve levels of democracy. After presenting these pathways, we discuss, in Chapters 4 and 5, cases of constitutional deliberation "from above" (convening by elites) and "from below" (convening under pressure from civil society and social movements).

3

Parchment Politics: The Importance of Context and Conditions to the Drafting of Constitutions

In the previous chapter we offered a new measure of constitution-making processes (i.e. *process* variable) to capture the degrees of openness of the process
at three different stages of constitution-making: convening, debating, and ratification. Constitution-making processes are so dynamic that they beg for elaboration beyond the definition of our measures and the coding rules, which
we extensively did in Chapter 2. The primary actors (or veto players) differ
significantly in various constitution-making settings. Actors involved in different constitution-making processes can include elected constituent assemblies,
legislative committees or commissions, national conferences or transitional
legislative bodies, elite roundtables, the executive, advisory bodies, and the
general public (Widner 2007).

But constitutional reform processes are usually contested and in many
cases the involvement of actors changes throughout the process. In Kenya for
example, the complicated constitutional process started in 2000 with more
than 600 delegates and two constitutional bodies (the Constitution of Kenya
Review Commission and National Constitutional Conference) drafting the
constitution with direct public input (Bannon 2007). The process was suspended for almost four years (from 2005 to 2009) following political conflicts
over the constitution and the 2008 elections. In 2009, another constitutional
body, the Committee of Experts, in consultation with the Parliamentary
Select Committee took up the mission to significantly modify the earlier draft
and write the constitution, which was eventually approved by a public referendum in August 2010. Even modes of constitution-making sometimes change
throughout the process. The Rules of Procedure of the Tunisian National
Constituent Assembly, adopted on January 20, 2012, did not require citizen
participation for the constitutional process. While the provisions of the Rules
of the Procedure emphasized transparency, they did not oblige the constitutional committees to open up the process in any way to the public for broader

forms of participation. Yet, this seemingly delegative model was opened up due to public pressure for an inclusive process and severe elite fragmentation within the constituent assembly, and we ultimately code it as popular.

In this chapter we begin by describing changing actors and other important characteristics of constitution-making as a contested political process. We review existing literature on the types of actors and modalities, and succinctly analyze summary statistics from the Constitutionalism and Democracy Dataset (CDD), the dataset we introduced in Chapter 2. We also briefly discuss Iceland as a case where a participatory process ironically did not produce a constitution at all, and recall the Chapter 2 discussion of revolutionary-era Mexico, where many of the upheaval's victors ultimately did not participate in crafting the constitution, disengaging them from the broader processes to socially enforce the political rights they had fought for. The parchment meant little without peasant participation. Next, the chapter seeks to establish the causes of imposed "top-down" convening, as well as the drivers of "bottom-up" popular convening. We theorize about anticipated differences between these two modalities of constitution-making, and then establish strong statistical correlations between regime characteristics and types of drafting processes, showing very stark differences between top-down and bottom-up approaches. By turning the *process* variable into a dependent variable, we thus confront an endogeneity problem inherent in our theory of participatory constitutionalism thus far: do more democratic countries and more liberal political contexts simply produce more popular processes? The evidence suggests that pressures "from below" – and labor strikes in particular – have a significant popular effect on subsequent constitution-making. Next, we provide information from the CDD about how often the modalities of the process change.

The chapter concludes by describing the criteria for the paired case comparisons we develop further in the following two chapters. Based on our analysis here, Chapters 4 and 5 will consider top-down and bottom-up ideal types of constitution-making processes, respectively, drawing on field research from Africa, South America, and the Middle East. We will address the "mixed" intermediate category of constitution-making, with both popular and imposed qualities, in the book's conclusion along with potentially ambiguous outcomes. Popular constitutionalism may be the best guarantor of a democratizing constitution, but the conditions that enable it are hardly common.

CONSTITUTION-MAKING PROCESSES: MODES AND ACTORS

The dynamics of constitution-making processes, as depicted in examples from cases such as Kenya and Tunisia, make understanding constitutional processes and their modes and actors important for our knowledge of the democratizing effects of constitutions. Among Ginsburg et al.'s (2009) categorization of constitution-making models, covering 460 constitutions adopted between 1792 and 2005, they identify 18 constitution-making models (Ginsburg et al. 2009, 205). Among these, the "constituent legislature" model ranked first with 89 constitutions (19 percent of their sample) being drafted by a constituent legislature. Constituent legislatures together with the executives were responsible for drafting another 78 constitutions (17 percent of the sample). The executive with public referendum was the third model with 57 constitutions (12 percent) being drafted via this process. In sum, they find that the major actors in constitution-making processes are the constituent assemblies, executives, ordinary legislatures, and the public by means of plebiscites. In at least 95 percent of the cases, one of these four players is part of the constitutional reform process (Ginsburg et al. 2009, 205).

As Ginsburg et al. (2009) admit, these categories do not tell us anything about the depth and quality of different players' involvement. For example, they show that the executives have been involved in constitution-making in 250 cases (54 percent of their sample), but we do not know if this involvement was on relatively equal terms with other interests – or if a president was dominating the process on behalf of elite cronies. In other words, for our purposes, this accounting does not reveal much about whether these were "bottom-up" or "top-down" constitutions. Similarly, their study shows that referendums have been used to ratify 108 constitutions (23 percent of their sample), but they do not recognize the public's involvement beyond referendums. But as we showed in the previous chapter, public participation in the first stage (i.e. convening) is what matters most for democracy and not the later participation in the final stage of ratification. This limitation in their study rises from the proxy they use for identifying the 18 different models of constitution-making. Ginsburg et al. (2009) identify these models from analyzing the content of constitutions. However, in many cases, the constitution is silent on the actors involved in drafting it, specifically the general public's involvement in convening and debating stages.

Their approach therefore is unable to generate insights about participation prior to ratification. This is an important limitation since the involvement of citizens in constitutional reform processes over the last few decades has shifted from a mere vote on the whole package via plebiscites to more deliberative engagement by seeking individuals' suggestions for the constitution. In the case of Tunisia, for example, the main drafting body was a constituent assembly. This quasi-legislative body was directly elected by the public and enabled citizens to provide significant input on the content of the constitution through a broad participatory process. This "bottom-up" constitution-making process, analyzed in detail in Chapter 5, was in fact one of the most successful participatory processes in recent years, and it resulted in significant improvements in the country's level of democracy. Countries have even embarked on the most innovative means such as crowdsourcing or "bringing the constitution online" for public input (Maboudi and Nadi 2016). The use of social media as a tool for public engagement in constitutional reforms, which started in Iceland in 2010 and was followed by Egypt in 2012, has several advantages to the traditional means of collecting public input through national dialogue meetings and conferences. Online deliberation significantly lowers the financial burdens of public deliberation. It also removes geographical obstacles, which is a main cause in low public turnout in official constitutional conferences, and brings a diverse group of citizens into deliberation (Fishkin 2009, 80).

Public deliberation, whether online or on-site, has some downsides to it. Adding more veto players decreases the possibility of reaching consensus (Tsebelis 2002), which is specifically important for a peaceful transition in ethnically divided societies (Ghai 2005). For instance, the Kenyan participatory process in 2000–2005 resulted in an incoherent and inconsistent text that led to more violence in the country (Bannon 2007). These considerations convinced several scholars, such as Elster (2012), to suggest that the optimal model of constitution-making should be hourglass-shaped with citizens being involved at both ends of electing the constitution designers and ratifying the constitution through referendums, but completely excluded from the actual writing of the constitution. However, more idealistic scholars, like Vivien Hart (2003), believe that citizens should be involved throughout the entire process because only such participation creates a sense of ownership among the public and legitimizes the constitution.

Based on empirical evidence from the previous chapter, we believe that the ideal type of "bottom-up" constitution encompasses citizen input early on in the constitutional reform process. In this model of constitution-making the civil society plays a crucial role by organizing public pressure for an inclusive process. Tunisia is exemplary in this case, where public protests and demonstrations, organized mostly by civil society organizations from the Tunisian General Labor Union to the Tunisian Human Rights League, were the key to the successful participatory process in the country. This is evident from the 2014 Nobel Peace Prize, which was awarded to the Tunisian National Dialogue Quartet, a group of four civil society organizations.[1] Understanding

---

[1]   See Chapter 5 for more on the role of civil society in the constitutional reform processes.

the risks of participation in the initial stage of constitution-making, the king of Morocco, on the other hand, was ready to accept any demand from the revolutionary February 20 Movement except for an elected constituent assembly in charge of writing the constitution.

Even so, bottom-up processes may go wrong. On the one hand there are cases such as Egypt and Ecuador, discussed in greater detail in Chapter 5, which constitute outliers in the CDD because participation failed to advance democracy. On the other hand, there are several important cases that did not produce a constitution at all and thus are missing from the CDD. Iceland presents one important example, further discussed in Chapter 6, where a far-reaching democratic and participatory process failed to produce a constitution due to several flaws and weaknesses in the design of the process itself (Landemore 2017). Iceland's extensive use of the Internet appears to illustrate a fetishization of online participation, similar to Egypt's, rather than our more Tocquevillian model. We return to these distinctions in the book's conclusion, noting the appeal of online participation to deliberative democrats but arguing that technology should not be equated with polyarchy.

In the next section, popular use of violence turns out to be one important distinction in the CDD between an unsuccessful and successful democratizing constitution. Taking a step backward from our statistical analysis in Chapter 2, we examine what causes popular and imposed constitution-making processes in the first place. By treating our primary independent variable, *process*, as a dependent variable, we empirically identify when top-down and bottom-up pressures are more likely to result in imposed or popular processes.

DRIVERS OF POPULAR CONSTITUTIONALISM

Empirical tests in Chapter 2 established a robust correlation between popular constitution-making and subsequent levels of democracy. We also demonstrated that popular participation at the convening stage had especially strong effects. The discussion above provided some theoretical and historical basis for such participation, and outlined significant contemporary forms of citizen input shaping governance and constitution-making. In this section we seek to account for the sources of elite-driven constitutionalism or effective popular participation by testing for the impact of prior political contexts on convening, which we previously identified as the earliest moments of constitution-making. Empirical tests of a "bottom-up" hypothesis establish a strong statistical connection between pre-constitutional protests and successful incorporation of popular processes. Specifically, we find that peaceful, targeted pressure by

civil society, labor, and other grassroots actors is associated with more participatory constitution-making. A "top-down" hypothesis then proxies for elite
control of politics in three different ways, reporting that neither regime type
nor strong executives in the pre-constitutional political context systematically
explains whether a country will adopt what Chapter 2 described as imposed
constitution-making. Elites are best positioned to dominate constitutional
drafting when the process emerges from more closed political systems, where
the opposition has little access to political competition.

The division of constitution-making into mass- and elite-led processes
is consistent with Haggard and Kaufman's (2016) findings that related, but
separate, processes of democratization may be led by masses or elites. Mass-led
democratizations through mobilizations seem driven, according to Haggard
and Kaufman's assessment of their 1980–2008 cases, by the inclusionary
or exclusionary nature of authoritarian regimes. Elite-driven democratic
transitions, according to Haggard and Kaufman, are best explained by "the
role international forces have played and to elite calculations and intra-elite
conflicts" (Haggard and Kaufman 2016, 4). We have endeavored to treat
constitution-making and democratization as distinct, but sought to extend
theoretical models explaining democratization to address constitution-making,
as few theories explain the politics of constitution-making, while an entire
literature exists seeking to explain the causes of democratization. This new
work on democratization is rigorous and contemporary, but also helps
refocus the literature on democratic transitions back on the O'Donnell
and Schmitter's (1986) framework, which prominently considered elite-pacted
transitions (top-down), as well as those prominently involving opposition-led
movements (bottom-up).

These two sets of results – for top-down and bottom-up constitutional
processes – are important to our overall argument because they address a
potential endogeneity problem by persuasively showing that adoption of a
constitution-making process is rooted in political context, and that shifts to
popular modalities are rooted in prior participatory disruptions of elite control. To this end, our dependent variable in the tests of the bottom-up and
top-down hypotheses is our original *process* variable. As explained in Chapter 2,
this variable ranges from 1 (most imposed) to 6 (most popular) and the average score is 2.5, indicating a mixed modality. Since the values of the dependent variable are irrelevant except for having a hierarchical order, we treat
them as ordered categories rather than continuous (Lederman et al. 2005).
As such, we use an ordered probit model to estimate the effect of top-down
and bottom-up pressures on the nature of constitution-making processes.
Below we explain the hypotheses and the variables we use to test them.

We start here with the bottom-up processes and will then introduce the top-down hypotheses.

Bottom-up Hypothesis

Our main predictors for the bottom-up hypothesis are the broad social pressures with the capacity to limit elite control and with the effect of increasing public participation in constitutional processes. These pressures are "contentious" in the sense that they collectively articulate claims, making procedural and/or substantive demands on the incumbent regime and other organized interests (Tilly and Tarrow 2007). They arise from changes in the opportunity structure from the emergence of new centers of power, elite instability, or violence that stimulates counter-mobilization from social movements and other actors (McAdam et al. 2009). In this sense, we have in mind disruptions to everyday politics that may or may not successfully increase popular control over a process as complex as making a new constitution. Our expected threshold for a successful bottom-up process is therefore quite high; elites do not simply cave in the face of most protest. It further entails different types of collective political action.

To this end we operationalize bottom-up processes through three variables representing different types of collective action: strikes, demonstrations, and riots. While strikes represent an organized pressure that is usually targeted at specific grievances of the working class in society, demonstrations show a broader dissatisfaction with government policies among the general public. Both strikes and demonstrations are usually peaceful. Chenoweth and Stephan's (2011) analysis of 323 protest campaigns over the last century suggests that such nonviolent "civil resistance" is more likely to succeed than armed rebellions because it attracts a larger and more diverse base of support, deploying flexible tactics and stimulating elite defections from the regime (Chenoweth and Stephan 2014). By contrast, riots represent the violent expression of dissatisfaction against the government. As with armed rebellions, this violence not only alienates potential supporters, it may drive challengers to seek external support against the regime that paradoxically de-legitimizes their claims. It may also simply be ineffective, which is a key finding of a recent study of the Arab Spring, where the "popular mob is more often met by violence than by visionary reforms" (Brownlee et al. 2015, 7). After all, the authors point out, peaceful protests in Bahrain and Syria quickly faded. Thus, each of these three predictors measures a distinct bottom-up pressure (i.e. peaceful vs. violent, and targeted vs. general pressures). Framing our tests in terms of contentious political forces also makes sense in terms of the theories of participatory democracy that anchor Chapter 2. Deliberative democracy theory appreciates that protest is a sign of institutional failure, whereby the "level of civility may need to go down in order for inclusion to go up" (Mansbridge et al. 2012, 18–19). Deliberative theorists such as Mansbridge concede that protest can be counterproductive, but insist that it contributes to deliberation when it equalizes representation or pushes relevant information into the public sphere. As such, we raise the following hypothesis:

> **H 3.1 – *Protest Hypothesis*:** As public protests increase prior to the constitution-making process in a given country, the constitutional process is more likely to be popular.

For all three predictors we use Banks and Wilson's (2016) Cross-National Time-Series Database. Their *General Strikes* variable measures "any strike of 1,000 or more industrial or service workers that involves more than one employer and that is aimed at national government policies or authority." Their *Demonstrations* variable is a measure for "any peaceful public gathering of at least 100 people for the primary purpose of displaying or voicing their opposition to government policies or authority, excluding demonstrations of a distinctly anti-foreign nature." And finally, we use their *Riots* variable for its measure of "any violent demonstration or clash of more than 100 citizens involving the use of physical force." For all these three variables we use an average of three years before the promulgation year. That is,

$$\overline{Xi} = \frac{Xi_{t-1} + Xi_{t-2} + Xi_{t-3}}{3} \tag{3.1}$$

where Xi represents the three main predictors (Strikes, Demonstrations, and Riots) and t is the promulgation year. If Hypothesis 3.1 holds true, then we expect the coefficients of our predictors to have a positive sign, meaning that higher degrees of bottom-up pressure will increase the likelihood of employing a popular constitution-making process. The results would be especially persuasive if nonviolent protest is more effective than riots. This would align with Mansbridge et al.'s functional claim that institutions enable deliberation when they produce preferences and decisions informed by facts and reason, promote mutual respect of citizens, and promote inclusion. Violence interferes with these conditions, and thus differentiates between the "popular mob" and the participatory politics associated with polyarchy.

Top-down Hypotheses

In Chapter 2, we defined imposed constitution-making as a process whereby elites maintain significant control over a non-transparent process. Elites explicitly internalize the costs of excluding the public through institutions such as a strong executive, a committee appointed by the executive with no meaningful external consultation, or a party acting as a central committee. The key point is that elites collude to limit the influence of citizens and interest groups that enjoy some autonomy from regime meddling. In subsequent chapters, we will further distinguish this sort of elite control from the use of expertise during the process or temporary delegation of authority, both of which are a part of our notion of constitution-making from below.

In order to evaluate the effects of top-down pressures on constitution-making processes, we test three hypotheses. First, a "political closeness" hypothesis states that political closing before the constitution increases the likelihood of imposed constitutional processes. Second, an "executive constraint" hypothesis states that weak political and legal constraints on the executive are more likely to lead to imposed constitution-making. And third, a "regime type" hypothesis states that different regime types are associated with different attitudes toward participatory constitution-making. The logic here is that certain types of non-democratic regimes may feel less threatened by participation, or more vulnerable to popular pressures for it. More importantly, tests of the regime type hypothesis in particular help resolve the endogeneity problem identified in the previous chapter, since more democratic regimes might be more likely to adopt constitution-making processes with more "democratic" qualities, including openness and inclusiveness.

Our first hypothesis tests whether political openness/closeness has any effect on constitutional processes. Regimes that are politically more closed to the opposition should be more likely to use imposed processes. If they do allow the opposition to participate, these regimes use all possible means to ensure such participation is not a threat to the status quo. We expect these regimes to supervise the constitutional process extensively in order to limit the risks. Assessing the level of openness for competition is important because an effectively organized opposition party can possibly challenge the incumbent's constitutional preferences. More generally, parties play an important aggregation function in political systems by lowering the costs of participation for citizens and providing information shortcuts about complex issues – such as crafting a constitution. In this sense, our tests for openness/closeness capture the ability of an institution mediating between elites and citizens, a function we elaborate on through the "transitology" literature and pacts in Chapter 4, which we juxtapose with research on social movements and participatory democracy in Chapter 5. For sure, political competition in closed polities can sometimes yield undesired outcomes for incumbents if they lose control of liberalizing reforms, a path famously illustrated through *abertura* by Brazil's military regimes (Stepan 1988). But our hypothesis expects closed political systems to regularly yield imposed processes. "A central task for modern constitutionalism," says one study on the role of parties, "is to seek to preserve and sustain ground rules of political competition that enable parties to compete for political power" (Pildes 2011, 262). Closed political systems give incumbents an important upper hand in limiting public input into the rules governing competition.

We operationalize the openness/closeness of the political system to the opposition using party coalition and vote share of opposition political parties. For party coalition, we use the *Party Competition* variable, based on Banks and Wilson's (2016) "Party Coalition" variable, which ranges from 0 (closed political system with no coalition and no opposition party existing) to 3 (open political system with multiple parties including opposition parties with no coalition), with a mean of 2.0 and a standard deviation of 1.05. For an average country with a mean *Party Competition* of 2.0, the *process* variable is 2.51 (on a scale of 0 to 6) indicating a mixed constitutional process. For a country with the lowest *Party Competition* score (0), the *process* variable is 1.69, indicating an imposed constitutional process; and for a country with the highest *Party Competition* score (3), the *process* variable is 3.22, which again indicates a mixed constitutional process. To estimate the vote share of opposition political parties, we use the "Vote Share of Opposition Parties" variable from the Database of Political Institutions (DPI), which ranges from 0 to 100 percent of the votes (Keefer 2005), but in our dataset it varies from 0 to 61.2 percent with a mean of 8 percent and standard deviation of 16 percent. For both variables we used three-year averages before constitution promulgation. That is,

$$\overline{PC} = \frac{PC_{t-1} + PC_{t-2} + PC_{t-3}}{3} \tag{3.2}$$

and

$$\overline{OVS} = \frac{OVS_{t-1} + OVS_{t-2} + OVS_{t-3}}{3} \tag{3.3}$$

where PC and OVS are estimates of *Party Competition* and *Opposition Vote Share*, respectively. If our Political Closeness Hypothesis holds, then we expect the coefficients of *Party Competition* and *Opposition Vote Share* variables to have a positive sign, meaning that the more the political system is open to the opposition (higher values of PC and OVS), the higher is the probability of popular (bottom-up) processes. The hypothesis is stated as follows:

> **H 3.2 – *Political Closeness Hypothesis*:** The more a political system is closed to the opposition, the more it is likely to use an imposed constitutional process.

Our second top-down hypothesis tests whether strong executives are drivers of coordinated elite control over constitution-making. This hypothesis builds on the "top-down" literature discussed above, in particular O'Donnell's (2007) "horizontal accountability" as a necessary means to balance the strong "vertical accountability" of executive dominance. In other words, it tests whether more limits on executive discretion lead to more popular processes. This is the case in several Middle Eastern and Latin American states, where strong executives strictly control their constitutional processes in order to avoid liberal constitutions that might result in more executive power limits. Zimbabwe's two constitutional reform processes provide good contrasting examples: its first attempt at reforms took place in 2000, as labor, the international community, and opposition parties successfully began to open up a political environment dominated by the ruling party and its allied interest groups, notably veterans from the liberation war against white minority rule (Lebas 2011). The defeat of those reforms stunned the regime, leading to a closing of the political system by the heavy-handed dictator, Robert Mugabe, whose second attempt at reforming the constitutions sailed through by a 94.5 percent vote in 2013. Those reforms specifically abolished the office of the prime minister, an office that had generated some horizontal accountability through an elite pact in 2008 (Raftopoulos 2013; LeVan 2011a). Throughout both processes, the regime tolerated a measure of competition, but the political system was more closed the second time around.

For constraints on the executive branch, we use term limits on the executive and checks and balances. For both estimates, we use variables from DPI (Keefer 2005). "Finite term" is a binary variable determining whether the executive has a term limit (1) or not (0). It has a mean of 0.59 and standard deviation of 0.47, which indicates that most of our cases have term limits on the executive. The other predictor, the *checks* variable, measures the level of checks and balances in both presidential and parliamentary systems and ranges from 1 (lowest) to 18 (highest), but in our dataset varies from 0 to 5.67, with a mean of 1.70 and standard deviation of 1.15, indicating a low level of checks and balances for the majority of our cases.[2] For these two predictors we use an average of three years before the promulgation year:

$$\overline{FT} = \frac{FT_{t-1} + FT_{t-2} + FT_{t-3}}{3} \qquad (3.4)$$

and

$$\overline{CB} = \frac{CB_{t-1} + CB_{t-2} + CB_{t-3}}{3} \qquad (3.5)$$

where FT and CB are estimates of *Finite Term* and *Checks* variables, respectively. If we find support for our Executive Constraint Hypothesis, *Finite Term* and *Checks* variables should have positive and significant coefficients. That is, more constraints on the executive (higher values of FT and CB) increase the probability of popular processes.

> **H 3.3 – *Executive Constraint Hypothesis*:** The fewer constraints on the executive in a given country, the more likely that country uses an imposed constitutional process.

Our third top-down hypothesis broadly tests the idea that the existing rules of governance are more important than the qualities of the ruler in determining the type of constitution-making process. This "regime type" hypothesis therefore tests not only whether democratic countries are more likely to permit participatory constitution-making, but also whether certain types of non-democracies are more likely to insist on closed processes controlled by elites. "When the military transformed themselves into civilian administrators," said a senior legal scholar in The Gambia, "their attitude towards political rights started to be different." His point was that the type of regime shaped constitutionalism, even though the individuals were the same.[3] To test such conjectures, we use six binary variables based on Geddes et al.'s (2014) regime type categories as the basis for our analysis, but combine some of the categories to create seven categories for Democracy, Personal,[4] Single Party, Military, Monarchy, Mixed Non-Democracy, and Other types. The first five categories are original in Geddes et al.'s dataset. We combined all mixed types of

---

[2]   Eighty of our cases have a very low score of "1" for checks and balances.
[3]   Interview (name withheld). Banjul, The Gambia. July 1, 2013.
[4]   Geddes et al. (2014, p. 6) define personal regimes as "regimes led by dictators with wide personal discretion over policy making (such as those in Libya under Qaddhafi and Yemen under Saleh)."

non-democracies, such as military and personal or single party and personal, and created the Mixed Non-Democracy category. And "Other" types, which we drop in our analysis, include foreign occupation, warlords, and provisional.

The relationship between regime type and modalities of constitutional change could play out in several ways. Personalist regimes are organized around a cult of leadership (Guliyev 2011), and, like classic "sultanistic" regimes, they lack a coherent ideology (Linz 2000). Instead they often rely on populist techniques, such as leveraging outsider status to come to power – often through elections – by attacking status quo institutions. After circumventing parties and directly appealing to the public, populists face strong incentives to rewrite the constitution or convoke a constitutional assembly since they believe they can dominate such processes (Levitsky and Loxton 2013). In such cases, we expect the ruler to be able to simply delegate the constitution-making process to cronies and enforce loyalty to his or her preferences. One might expect monarchies to similarly be able to simply delegate constitution-making to cronies. But since the basis of their legitimacy in tradition helps to insulate these regimes from succession crises (Brownlee 2011), constitutional change may be able to coexist with stable royal authority. Indeed, regimes with hereditary succession consistently survive longer than other types of personalist regimes (Kailitz 2013; Brownlee et al. 2015). Even with the Crown Prince Salman leading calls for dialogue and reform in Bahrain during the Arab Spring, and the ruling family split between "hardliners," the royal basis for institutional power was preserved, prevailing over calls for constitutional change (Mecham 2014). In the language of Ginsburg and Simpser (2013), it's reasonable to expect that both monarchies and other personalized regimes would adopt "billboard" constitutional processes. They differ from other non-democratic regimes that must play to public demands. This can shape leaders' accountability by generating "audience costs" should the ruler deviate too starkly from the public's expectations (Weeks 2008). Party-based dictatorships enjoy the advantage of an institutional mechanism for conflict resolution, managing elite recruitment, and articulating an ideological basis for power (Geddes 2003). In the context of constitutional reform, hegemonic parties are equipped to conceal disagreements among elites or enforce conformity. They can also create an illusion of public access, as the case study of Uganda will later demonstrate through President Yoweri Museveni's ability to stage manage a prolonged process with thousands of public comments. Finally, in military dictatorships, the regime typically lacks an institutional basis for legitimacy and faces conflicting impulses about the role of civilians (LeVan 2015). In this context, making a new constitution could help to improve public perceptions of the regime.

These regimes need constitutions as "blueprints" that capture societal aspirations. Our third hypothesis is stated as:

H 3.4 – *Regime Type Hypothesis*: Non-democratic regimes are more likely to use imposed constitutional processes than democracies.

As Figure 3.1 illustrates, democratic regimes, compared to other regime types, have the highest utilization of popular (23 percent) and mixed (54 percent) processes in the convening stage of constitution-making. Monarchies, on the other hand, have the lowest share of popular (0 percent) and mixed (12.5 percent) convening modalities and the largest share of imposed (87.5 percent) modalities among all regime types.

Yet, despite this pattern of modalities of convening stage, the democratic consequences of constitutions written under these regime types is surprisingly different. Figure 3.2 shows that while constitutions in 73 percent of the democratic regimes yield to more democratic opening, 89 percent of constitutions promulgated under military rule result in democratic improvement. Or, while 16 percent of constitutions promulgated under democratic regimes resulted in democratic decline, there is not a single constitution under monarchies that resulted in such decline. Yet, we should also notice that 71 percent

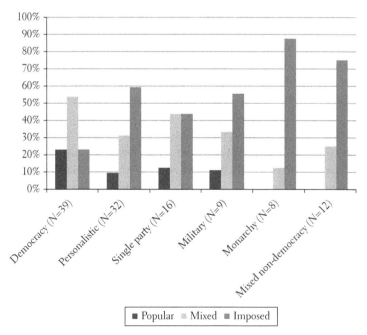

FIGURE 3.1. *Regime types and modalities of convening stage*

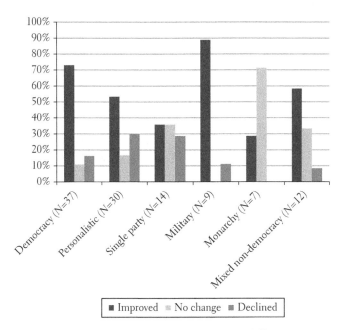

FIGURE 3.2. *Democratizing effects of constitutions under different regimes*

of constitutions promulgated under monarchies had no impact, whatsoever, on democracy. A large share of personalist regimes (59 percent) also use an imposed process at the convening stage (Figure 3.1), which is consistent with the literature's expectations that these rulers believe they can rewrite the rules of the game, but here we see that their populist governance techniques often backfire. Unlike party-based regimes with an institutional basis of governance, personalist rules lack intermediate aggregators of information, limiting the predictability of the political environment (Gandhi 2008); it is not unusual for them to overestimate their ability to limit the liberalizing effects of constitutional change.

Support for the regime type hypothesis would appear as a positive and significant correlation between democracy and the *process* variable, while the other five regime type categories would have a negative and significant impact on the dependent variable. However, if we reject the regime type hypothesis, then this would support our theory since it would mean that participatory constitution-making originates outside of the regime itself, at least in part.

Chapter 2 demonstrated that what matters in process is the first of the three stages (convening as opposed to debate or ratification). Here we hypothesize about the causes of imposed versus popular constitutional processes, and in Chapters 4 and 5 we offer case studies to demonstrate how "top-down" convening varies greatly from "bottom-up" convening. The point of this chapter is to show that those patterns mostly hold across regime types, and that there are causes of "top-down" imposed constitutional processes, and separate causes of "bottom-up" popular constitutions. As further discussed in Chapter 5, the successful cases of "bottom-up" popular deliberation, i.e. those that do improve levels of democracy post-promulgation and thus are – from a normative standpoint – those to emulate, share two pre-conditions. First, these regimes feature a lack of consensus among incumbent elites, leading to a constituent assembly as a regime "reboot," or a power vacuum among these elites precluding them from moving forward without a constitutional process. Second, these regimes possess a pre-existing array of interest groups with mobilization capacity and a strong interest in constitutional change.

STATISTICAL TESTS AND ANALYSIS

How can we identify indicators of elite division or weakness and the preexistence of social movements and interest groups seeking constitutional change? Our tests to identify the sources of bottom-up and top-down processes use an ordered probit model with *process* as the dependent variable. We use the same control variables as we did in Chapter 2. We control for ethnolinguistic divisions in the society, dependence on foreign aid, and natural resources by using the same measures as in the previous chapter. We also control for level of development with GDP per capita, because modernization theory expects public participation and political inclusion to be a function of a country's wealth (Lipset 1959). In particular, modernization theory posits that economic development displaces old cleavages and identities, opening up new avenues for public engagement and new expectations for citizen autonomy (Welzel 2013). It has also emphasized the role of literacy in driving political change as citizens became capable of "empathy" and are better cognitively equipped to evaluate government performance (Lerner 1954). However, recent evidence from the Arab Spring suggests that popular mobilization across the Middle East occurred not because of cognitive changes or shifts in values, but because higher levels of economic development empowered oppositions with more resources (Brownlee et al. 2015). Modernization theory clearly remains one of the most enduring ideas in comparative politics and an important control (Coppedge 2012). Finally, we control for population, using the natural log of population, because larger countries may be less likely to democratize due to low population density or other factors (Teorell 2010). These last two variables come from the World Bank's World Development Indicators (2013). The statistical results are displayed in Table 3.1.

TABLE 3.1. *"Popular" and "imposed" constitutional processes*

	Variables	Ordered probit (process)
Pressure from below	Strikes	0.48**
		(0.20)
	Demonstrations	0.04
		(0.06)
	Riots	−0.02
		(0.08)
Closeness of the political system	Party competition	−0.15
		(0.17)
	Opposition vote share	0.04**
		(0.01)
Executive constraints	Executive finite term	0.19
		(0.39)
	Checks on executive	−0.10
		(0.18)
Regime type	Democracy	0.79
		(0.70)
	Personal	0.10
		(0.62)
	Single party	−0.23
		(0.64)
	Military	0.28
		(0.86)
	Monarchy	−1.84
		(1.32)
	Mixed non-democratic	−0.14
		(0.82)
Control variables	Ethnic	0.65
		(0.77)
	ODA	0.03
		(0.02)
	Natural resources	−0.01
		(0.01)
	GDP per capita	−0.00
		(0.00)

(*continued*)

TABLE 3.1 *(continued)*

Variables	Ordered probit (process)
Population (log)	−0.17
	(0.15)
Promulgation year	0.01
	(0.02)
Observations	60

**Standard errors in parentheses.

The results in Table 3.1 show that *Strikes* has a positive and significant impact on the overall constitutional *Process*, meaning that constitutions promulgated after a few years of organized strikes are more likely to be written via participatory and inclusive processes. This corroborates our hypothesis that "bottom-up" pressure increases the likelihood of inclusive and participatory constitutional processes. The results indicate that while "peaceful" bottom-up pressures through *Strikes* have a positive impact on the outcome, "violent" pressures tend to have a negative impact (*Demonstrations* is positive but not significant). In other words, while constitutions drafted following peaceful pressure are more participatory and inclusive, those crafted following violent pressure from the public are more imposed.

The results suggest that the nature of bottom-up pressures has an impact on decisions for constitutional processes. Strikes, in fact, represent all types of targeted, organized, and peaceful civilian pressure. This type of bottom-up pressure has more significant impact on constitutional design that results in more open and inclusive processes. Demonstrations or other types of peaceful but not specifically targeted public pressure can also produce positive results, although these are not statistically significant. However, violent pressures usually do not successfully open up the process for public participation. On the contrary, violent bottom-up pressure produces negative results and leads to more imposed constitutional processes. This is consistent with Chenoweth and Stephan's (2011) findings attesting to the efficacy of nonviolent protest or "civil resistance," as well as Mansbridge et al.'s expectations that deliberative institutions enable well-reasoned exchanges and a mutual respect among citizens. In the context of constitution-making, violent tactics appear to undermine any constructive basis for the exchange of ideas between elites and activists. Violence may further give the regime the sort of pretext it needs to curtail or delegitimize public participation as a destabilizing process.

Sierra Leone's 1991 constitution is instructive here: President Joseph Momoh formed a National Constitutional Review Commission (NCRC), which recommended shifting to a multi-party system and solicited public comments for four months. When a group of expatriates based in neighboring Liberia, who considered themselves a "provisional ruling council," launched a border war in March 1991, the NCRC reacted by shifting position and not allowing a public review of the draft constitution. The constitution was submitted to the House of Representatives in June, passed by referendum in August, and promulgated in October 1991 (Ellicott 2011; Thompson 1997).

The results in Table 3.1 also show that while *Party Competition* has a negative and insignificant correlation with constitutional processes, *Opposition Vote Share* has a positive and statistically significant impact on constitution-making processes, meaning that the more the opposition is powerful (in winning votes), the more popular constitutional processes would be, and vice versa. This corroborates our Political Closeness Hypothesis. It means that a "top-down" political structure in which opposition parties are not allowed to participate (or are only permitted a small vote share) tend to have more imposed constitutional processes.

The results, however, are inconsistent for our Executive Constraint Hypothesis. While *Finite Term* has a positive correlation with constitutional process, *Checks* has a negative correlation, and both coefficients are statistically insignificant. Therefore, there is not enough evidence to support our second hypothesis that fewer constraints on the executive lead to more imposed constitutional processes. That is, strong executives are not the only drivers of illiberal constitutions. The reason, we believe, is that constraints on the executive do not necessarily mean the political system is more open and democratic. On the contrary, countries with very low democratic scores may also have executive constraints. An example in our dataset is Turkey in 1982, which according to Polity had an average democracy score of −0.3 (on a −10 to +10 scale) for three years before constitution promulgation, but scored 5.6 in checks and balances (highest in our dataset) and had term limit on the executive. Moreover, constraints on the executive can also mean that the executive is subordinate to a single ruling party or other non-democratic institutions, which also justifies the negative direction of the *Checks* variable.

Our Regime Type Hypothesis produced mixed results as well. While democratic, personalist authoritarian, and military authoritarian regimes have positive relationships with constitution-making processes, monarchies, single party authoritarians, and mixed non-democracies have a negative correlation with the type of constitution-making process. The relationship is statistically insignificant for all regime types. These results do not corroborate our third hypothesis, meaning that regime types are not determinative of the type of constitutional processes. This confirms our argument in Chapter 2 that regime type is not a significant predictor of constitutional processes. Finally, none of our control variables are statistically significant. In sum, while we find some evidence for our Closeness of Political System Hypothesis, we cannot confirm the other "top-down" (i.e. Executive Constraint and Regime Type) hypotheses.

These results are consistent with another large N study of constitutional change, Negretto's (2013) analysis of 194 post-independence constitutions in 18 Latin American nations. Consistent with our finding that the more multipartisan the debate stage, the more popular the result, he shows that the pluralism of institutions in new constitutions depends on "whether the party that controls or is likely to control the presidency has unilateral power or requires the support of other parties to approve reforms" (Negretto 2013, 10). The fact that non-democratic regimes commence constitutional reforms in a imposed manner is also not a surprise. This confirms our point from Chapter 2 that authoritarians and "hybrid regime" leaders can call for new constitutions to break political stalemates, but, as will be elaborated extensively in the next chapter, this may be more about consolidating authority than about opening it up to citizen input.

While the CDD does not extend back before 1974, Negretto compiles data from 1900 to 2008, and notes a change in the implementation of new constitutions after 1978. To Negretto, "The number and scope of constitutional changes in Latin America since 1978 reflect the need to adjust preexisting rules to the new conditions of democratic competition that have arisen following decades of dictatorship and frustrated transitions to democracy" (Negretto 2013, 237). While we cannot definitively confirm Negretto's pattern for the rest of the world, we would concur with his assessment, and do know that while constitutional promulgations did promote higher levels of democracy at the commencement of our sample in 1974, this was diminishingly true over time. Indeed, Freedom House (2015) recently reported the ninth consecutive year of democracy's backsliding around the world, a trend consistent with our research. Figure 3.3 shows a constant downward slope in the plot of levels of democratization fostered by new constitutions over time. This indicates to us that while more constitutions during the Third Wave (1974 to about 1995) did improve levels of democracy, as they replaced Latin America's military regimes with democratic ones, and Eastern Europe's communist party authoritarianism with democratic governance, the last 20 years have witnessed far fewer consistent democratic gains from constitutional promulgation. Africa largely shares this experience well, since constitutional reform "has only led to

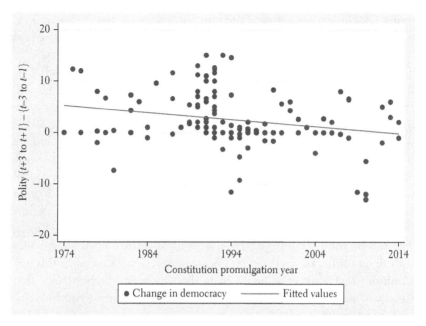

FIGURE 3.3. *Impact of constitutions on change in level of democracy over time*
Note:
Change in democracy score = (o) if Polity's score of three-year average after the promulgation minus Polity's score of three-year average before the promulgation = (o)
Change in democracy score = (+) if Polity's score of three-year average after the promulgation minus Polity's score of three-year average before the promulgation = (+)
Change in democracy score = (−) if Polity's score of three-year average after the promulgation minus Polity's score of three-year average before the promulgation = (−)

genuine political change in countries where domestic and international actors were willing to mobilize in order to ensure that the rules were respected" (Cheeseman 2015, 231).

Process Variable Pathways

The *process* variable used as the independent variable in Chapter 2 and as the dependent variable in the above tests breaks constitution-making into three stages with three possible values for the level of participation at each stage. We have conducted tests based on overall levels of participation and tests that focus only on the first stage of the process, convening. This produces 27 possible pathways of constitution-making processes, and we recorded 21 in the CDD.[5] Here we outline the principal pathways and outline our criteria for subsequent case study analyses. For the ease of argument we call imposed processes "I," mixed processes "M," and popular processes "P." The most recurring pathway in our dataset is I-I-I (i.e. imposed in all three stages). Twenty-six constitutional reform processes, or 19 percent of cases in our dataset, were imposed in all three stages. Many authoritarian states in Asia, Africa, Latin America, and the Middle East have used this path to write their constitutions in the last four decades. Notable examples include Saudi Arabia (1992), where the royal family drafted a constitution mainly to coordinate state actions and update the succession rules, Chile (1980), where General Augusto Pinochet shared veto authority with the military services, and Zimbabwe (1979), where Robert Mugabe and his rebels emerged from the bush to establish the hegemonic party that remains in power today. The second most recurring pathway is M-M-M (mixed in all three stages) with 16 constitutions, or 12 percent of our cases, being drafted in this way. Countries that have used this path to draft their constitutions vary from European democracies such as Finland (2000) to African authoritarians such as Mozambique (1990). The third most recurring pathway is M-M-P (i.e. mixed in the convening and debating stages, and popular in the ratification stage). Notable examples include the Brazilian constitution-making process (1988) and the constitutional reform process in Iraq (2005).

These three pathways vary across different regime types and do not correlate with any specific regime type.[6] As we demonstrated above, about 63 percent of the constitutions in our dataset were drafted under three regime types (Democracy, Personalist, and Single Party). In addition, Figure 3.4 shows that the three most recurring pathways combined comprise 47 percent of constitutions drafted under personalist and single party authoritarian rules, and 38 percent of constitution in democratic regimes.[7] This confirms the above statistical results by showing that the type of regime is not a determinant of the process of constitution-making. More broadly, the level of democracy in a given political regime does not determine its pathway of constitution-making. On the contrary, the breadth and scope of civil society mobilization, especially in the form of constitutional movements, and the degree of openness of the

---

[5] See Appendix B for the list of different pathways of constitution-making.
[6] For the list of constitutions that used these three pathways see Appendix C.
[7] In Figure 3.4 Pathways with frequencies lower than 5 percent are dropped; regime types are based on Geddes et al. (2014) categories; and for Change in Democracy Score we used Unified Democracy Score (UDS) of three years after the constitution promulgation minus the same score for three years before the constitution promulgation.

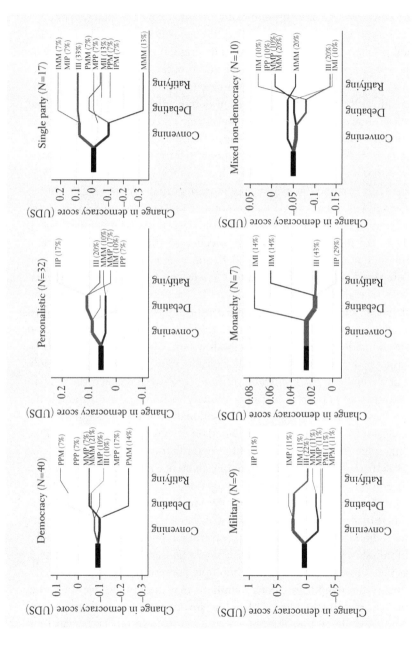

FIGURE 3.4. *Pathways of constitution-making processes based on regime types*

77

political system to the opposition are stronger and more significant determinants of constitutional pathways.

The pathways of constitution-making are in themselves path-dependent. As we showed in Chapter 2, excluding the opposition, civil society, and the general public in the first stage is like an "original sin," one that cannot be compensated for no matter how much the process will open in the subsequent stages. If a constitutional reform process is initiated undemocratically, it is significantly more likely to result in democratic decline. This "original sin" thesis, however, does not mean that if a given country starts the process in an imposed manner it cannot include other players, including its citizens, in the later stages. In fact, 40 constitutional reform processes in our dataset (28 percent of our sample) start with a decree process in the convening stage, but gradually become inclusive in the debating or ratification stages. On the contrary, all cases that started with a popular process remained inclusive in the debating and ratification stages. The only exception is Guatemala (1985), which started the process with direct election of the National Constituent Assembly (ANC) by the public. The debating stage was also participatory and the European Union and United States Agency for International Development financed several NGOs to consult and educate the indigenous population about the constitution. Even before the constitutional process, Sweden hosted peace talks between different Guatemalan groups to negotiate the Accord on Constitutional Reforms and the Electoral System, which opened the path for the constitutional reforms (Brett and Delgado 2005, 15). However, the military junta which led the political transition (1982–1985) dictated the content of constitutional reforms concerning military institutions, even though the military was not directly involved in the National Constituent Assembly (Brett and Delgado 2005, 10). As such, and based on our coding rules, we coded the debating stage "mixed" in this constitutional reform process. And finally the constitution was ratified without a public referendum, which, based on our coding criteria, makes the ratification stage "decree."

In the two chapters that follow we offer ideal-type cases of these pathways into our broad bottom-up and top-down characterizations of constitution-making. The ideal type of bottom-up constitution-making should be popular at all three stages, just as the top-down would be imposed at all three stages. But as noted in the above, there are multiple pathways to each in the CDD. Our theory throughout this book maintains that the overall level of participation and early higher levels of public involvement are both important. We thus elaborate on how the bottom-up and top-down processes work, and specify how interactions between elites and citizens play out. In Chapter 4, we elaborate more extensively on constitutions as pacts, using the terminology of

O'Donnell and Schmitter (1986) and Przeworski (1991). These were essentially pacts from above, where constitutions were expressions of elite settlements that originated in elite-controlled transformations. In cases such as Mexico (1929) and Colombia and Venezuela (1957–8) the situation is described as "less sudden than an elite settlement, this process is a series of deliberate, tactical decisions by rival elites that have the cumulative effect, over perhaps a generation, of creating elite consensual unity" (Higley and Gunther 1992, xi). In top-down processes, elites are *the* actors responsible for drafting the text with no or minimal input from the public.

In the CDD, such top-down processes emerge in at least three important circumstances: foreign occupation, authoritarian institutionalism, and elite pacts. First, pacted constitutions are drafted behind closed doors, but may be politically inclusive. Classical examples include the Spanish Constitution of 1978 and the Portuguese Constitution of 1976. These are constitutions that are implemented as part of broader "elite settlements," such as that in Mexico in the 1920s and 1930s, when the aforementioned "metaconstitutional" powers were inaugurated with the formation of the National Revolutionary Party (1929), which was later renamed the Party of the Institutional Revolution. A second circumstance where top-down processes emerge is under "authoritarian institutionalism," whereby constitutions are drafted by a ruler's decree. Egypt's military constitution (2014), Morocco's monarchic constitution (2011), and China's party constitution (1982) all provide examples. Despite the differences in regime types, these constitutions share important commonalities. For example, the executive is usually a (if not *the*) principal actor in writing the constitution. Also, the public is not involved in the first and second stages (i.e. convening and debating) of the constitutional process. And in most of these cases, a public referendum is used to legitimize the constitution, despite the decidedly undemocratic character of the earlier stages of the process. Finally, some top-down constitutions are drafted by a decree of a foreign military in occupied states. The occupier's involvement in drafting varies from Japan's 1946 Constitution, in which a group of American bureaucrats drafted the basic law of the country in a little over a week (Moore and Robinson 2004), to Iraq's 2005 (Benomar 2004) and Afghanistan's 2004 (McCool 2004) constitutions, which were more consultative but still favored groups that allied with the US coalition. These "Occupation Constitutions" (Ginsburg et al. 2008) often lack public legitimacy (Chesterman 2004). Feldman argues that today new constitutions must be "understood as locally produced to acquire legitimacy" (2004, 948). Yet, "local ownership" contradicts the circumstances under which these "occupation constitutions" are drafted since a foreign military power controls the impetus for the constitutional process (Chesterman 2004).

Two pairs of case studies then form the core analysis of Chapter 4, where we examine top-down processes. We select democratizing and non-democratizing instances of imposed constitutions, following the logic outlined in the book's introduction: two cases that conform to our statistical expectations and our theory, along with two confounding cases that do not. This analysis explains why countries adopt top-down processes as well as why these imposed constitutions might have democratizing effects anyway. Constitutions promulgated in Venezuela (1999) and The Gambia (1996) reveal the inner workings of imposed processes, and persuasively demonstrate why the gamble to change the constitution paid off for the respective rulers. By contrast, constitutions imposed in Chile (1980) and Nigeria (1999) represent outliers in our statistical tests since they did have subsequent democratizing effects, despite top-down constitution-making controlled by elites.

Chapter 5 turns to bottom-up constitution-making processes. In particular, we introduce interest groups, such as social movements and opposition parties that mediate demands through softliners and reformers, and different organizational actors who can serve as intermediaries between citizens and elites. We argue that pro-regime societal interests (who must be willing to legitimize whoever calls the constituent assembly to begin with) can help steer constitutions in directions their constituencies seek, and likely improve levels of democracy afterwards, in cases where there is a leadership vacuum among the incumbent executive's government and where these interests can agitate effectively for change. These interest group intermediaries help to induce effective participatory processes where they can accomplish aggregation without agency loss; that is, where citizens' control is rendered efficient but not compromised. This is important in order to respond to skeptics of deliberative democracy. "Although the romantic vision of the individual citizen as the vehicle of democratic self-governance still has powerful emotional and symbolic resonance," writes one such scholar, "the reality is that in any large state, the most enduring and powerful vehicle for organizing citizens into effective participants in politics is the political party" (Pildes 2011, 254). Deliberative participation is more than merely aggregation, and while parties remain important, they hardly capture the critical diversity of intermediary actors who can channel constructive citizen engagement. Nor does such participation preclude the use of experts or a division of labor during drafting; parties are only one such an intermediary that can facilitate these functions. The key feature of bottom-up processes is the inability of elites to dominate the process, and the best check against elite control is the participatory ingredients of polyarchy in the earliest stages. Our argument, based on our findings, is therefore not asserting that participatory constitution-making should exclude elites.

Tunisia offers important lessons in this regard. Freedom House, in its 2015 report *Discarding Democracy: Return to the Iron Fist*, singled it out for bucking the global trend toward authoritarianism: "The one notable exception was Tunisia, 'which became the first Arab country to achieve the status of Free since Lebanon was gripped by civil war 40 years ago.'" Based on our field research, we attribute this to the early and deep public participation in its constitutional project, which provided political insurance against illiberal reversals. Adopting a case selection strategy that mirrors Chapter 4, we analyze Tunisia alongside Colombia as two bottom-up cases that led to democracy, contrasting them with Ecuador and Egypt as cases where participatory processes failed to deepen democracy. Just as Tunisia offers hope for the future, and clarifies the causal mechanisms of participatory processes, the non-conforming cases provide powerful cautionary tales. In Ecuador, populism's subversion of intermediary institutions undermined the long-term democratizing effects of its participatory constitution, while in Egypt the Facebook revolution was more pyrrhic than foundational, and repression defeated the rebellious democrats. "In the end, technology is merely a tool, open to both noble and nefarious purposes" (Diamond 2016, 134). Citizen control over constitutional crafting separated the democratizing cases from the unsuccessful experiments in participation.

We have established that imposed constitutions tend to occur in cases of foreign occupation, authoritarian institutionalization, and elite pacts, and that popular constitutions tend to be drafted where there are extensive social movements or other regime opposition. However, in addition to considering likely conditions under which imposed and popular constitutions occur, we consider, in Chapters 4 and 5, the modalities of participation under which constitutional processes transpire. Recall from Chapter 1 that we identified three forms: participation through mere aggregation, where "strength in numbers" drives non-elite participation, but where such participation is blunt, deliberative participation where ideas are debated and interest group positions fully represented, and elite bargaining and pacting, which usually involve some interest group participation, but not as much as deliberation requires. As we will see in the following chapters, elite bargaining and pacting are more common in imposed constitutions (which tend not to improve levels of democracy), whereas aggregation is common in popular processes with less incumbent elite support, and deliberation is likely where popular processes possess more incumbent elite support.

CONCLUSION

Crafting a new constitution is rarely a linear process. As a broad range of actors compete for influence and leverage, the process itself typically changes. This chapter summarized common patterns of those changes in the CDD, our dataset covering constitutions between 1974 and 2014. Our *process* variable has 21 out of the 27 possible "pathways" of constitution-making, with overall "imposed" values at each of the three stages (convening, debating, and ratification) representing 19 percent of the cases in our dataset, and "mixed" values representing the second most common (11 percent) of our cases. We provided further evidence of the claim we made in Chapter 2: that this three-stage process has strong characteristics of path dependence, making it hard to correct the "original sin" of convening modalities that limit citizen input and assert elite control at the convening stage.

By focusing attention on the sources of the *process* variable itself, the chapter also confronted the potential for endogeneity in our argument about participatory constitution-making, identifying several important insights about how prior political context shapes the process. First, like Negretto (2013), we find that regimes increasingly attempt to modify constitutions in order to create a veneer of conformity with new international democratic norms. New constitutions and the surging use of multiparty elections after 1989 are both signs of these norms. There is a vast literature analyzing how rulers manipulated elections over the last few decades, for example through "electoral authoritarianism" (Schedler 2006). But until now there have been few systematic analyses documenting rulers' corresponding efforts to stage manage constitutionalism. Our evidence suggests that, like flawed elections, illiberal efforts to coopt constitution-making are an increasingly common characteristic of the late Third Wave.

Second, only 28 percent of the constitutions in our sample were drafted under democratic regimes, while 35 percent were drafted under personalist or single party authoritarian regimes. However, our statistical tests demonstrated that regime type is not a significant predictor of the constitution-making process. The absence of a significant relationship between democracy and the adoption of a popular process is especially compelling because it suggests that the actors make the process, and that effective participation during convening occurs when there is a break with the previous regime – even if it was democratic. Our additional tests for top-down pressures through term limits and other types of executive constraints were indeterminate. We believe this is because checks on executives frequently operate in democratic and non-democratic regimes alike (Frantz and Ezrow 2011; LeVan 2015) – a claim we illustrated by reference to Turkey. The strongest predictor of a top-down constitution-making process is the political closeness of the political system, which we measured using opposition vote share. If the political system is closed, then popular process participants face an uphill struggle, regardless of the regime. These results hold across our controls for population size and level of development.

Third, the findings relating to bottom-up processes are especially important. They emphasize differences between strikes and violent riots, supporting new research on contentious politics by underscoring the importance of targeted, nonviolent collective action. They also potentially push deliberative demo-cratic theory on important conceptual terms. According to Landemore, for example, communication becomes a form of cooperation where persuasion lacks the presumptions of force or leverage (Landemore 2012). Classic works emphasize deliberation as non-coercive opportunities to change preferences rather than the capacity or will to impose them (Dryzek 2000). We did not test for the *regime's* use of violence, and some scholars argue that governments successfully deployed repression against Arab Spring protests; "clubs were trumps" as Brownlee et al. (2015) put it. But our test results point to subtle distinctions between coercion and leverage, with popular constitution-making emerging from broad participation that pushes elites to open the process and is sustained enough to hold them accountable for diverging from popular expectations.

If such pressures were evident in the Tunisian process, we also noted how it contrasts with Mexico's experience in important ways, even though constitution-making in both countries can fairly be characterized as bottom-up. In the case of Tunisia, the process was relatively peaceful other than the self-immolation of the vendor Mohamed Bouazizi and a few skirmishes. The outcome of its broad, inclusive process orchestrated by the Nobel Prize winning "Quartet" of drafters was the only democracy in the Arab world. By contrast, estimates of casualties in the Mexican Revolution range from 300,000 to 2.1 million (McCaa 2003). In addition, Pancho Villa and the *campesino* victors won the social revolution but essentially abandoned the political project, seeing land, rather than the constitution, as the metaphor and the meaning of their triumph over elite *caudillo* power. Thus, not only do the differing outcomes support Chenoweth and Stephan's claims about the hazards of violence for democrats, the cases point to a boundary of our claims: popular constitution-making is largely a feature of the Third Wave – and one that is being eroded by autocrats and dubious democrats keen on protecting their power.

4

The Logic of "Top-Down" Elite Constitutionalism: How Imposed Processes May (But Usually Do Not) Produce Better Democracy

In an ideal image of democracy, constitutions are viewed as "focal points" around which societal actors' expectations converge on the roles they expect elites to play in governing (Ellickson 1991). Many constitutions in the early years of the Third Wave of democratizations reinforced this view as they helped democratic phoenixes arise from the ashes of authoritarianism in Eastern Europe's communist regimes, Latin America's military juntas, and Africa's Cold War "Big Men." However, democrats and dictators alike learned as the Third Wave advanced, clouding the stylized Greek-inspired image of democracy, that even though such phoenixes could create dramatic ruptures with the past, they frequently yielded only fluid continuities, resurrecting authoritarian atavisms. In this less idealized image of democracy at the turn of the twenty-first century, Latin American presidents engaged in "re-constitution,"[1] paving the way to re-election rather than re-founding legal bases for their regimes in democratic control. As noted in Chapter 2, Negretto's analysis of 194 post-independence constitutions in 18 Latin American nations shows that the pluralism of institutions in new constitutions depends on "whether the party that controls or is likely to control the presidency has unilateral power or requires the support of other parties to approve reforms" (Negretto 2013, 10). Middle-Eastern and African presidents similarly sought to instrumentalize constitutionalism, successfully extending terms in office in Uganda, Gabon, and Chad, and unsuccessfully attempting to do so in Nigeria, Zambia, and Burkina Faso. Constitutions around the world have thus often served as resources for incumbents to pursue narrow self-interest, diverging from their functions as focal points and often resurrecting old illiberal impulses.

---

[1] See for example the 1994 Peru constitution, the 1993 Argentine constitution, the 2014 debate about reforming Ecuador's constitution, efforts to amend Venezuela's 1999 constitution in 2009, and Bolivia's new constitution in 2009, which cynics do argue had much to do with the re-election of President Evo Morales.

The booming literature on "hybrid regimes" is a reflection of this ambiguous relationship between institutionalization and authoritarianism (Morlino 2009; Levitsky and Way 2010).

Our statistical analysis in Chapter 2 offered strong empirical evidence that the type of constitution-making process matters, and that the more deliberative the process early on, the more likely the new constitution will reinforce rather than undermine democracy. Specifically, we found that the *process* variable positively impacts post-promulgation democracy, as do its disaggregated partials, with the *convening* variable appearing as robust in all cases, while *debate* and *ratification* are not statistically significant. We were therefore able to rule out the broad "legalistic constitutionalism" hypothesis that attributes post-promulgation democratic gains to the constitution's text. Similarly, tests in Chapter 3 failed to link either term limits or executive constraints to popular processes. Even regime types, other than monarchies, lack a strong statistical relationship to subsequent modalities of constitution-making, which we interpreted as persuasive evidence that the drivers of participatory constitutionalism are not endogenous. Instead, they originate in prior political conditions – notably strikes and other nonviolent contentious strategies. However, since these findings collectively lend themselves to normatively "good" implications of participatory constitution-making, it is important to not leave unanswered questions about how elite-driven processes that appear normatively "bad" might enhance democracy anyway. More importantly, characteristics of participatory constitution-making such as direct, substantive, and transparent citizen input are similar to key features of democracy. This raises the possibility of tautology as well as a larger issue of potential endogeneity in our analysis: aren't more democratic countries simply more likely to adopt more "democratic" constitution-making processes that enhance subsequent levels of democracy?

This chapter explains the logic and consequences of pacted constitutions "from above," and works in tandem with Chapter 5's account of participatory constitutions "from below" to address these issues and clarify the causal mechanisms at work. Thus the constitution-making examined here contrasts with the "bottom-up" constitutional deliberation envisioned by political theorists and social movement scholars. Pacted constitutions may be imposed by a general, a president or a small group as in Venezuela, or may result from a more plural group of elites, as in Chile, Spain, or Nigeria. Such cases raise an additional question of inclusion, since elites could represent a broad range of preferences yet limit public input or transparency. This was implicit in our quantitative analysis; here we more directly acknowledge its importance, explaining why incumbents may encourage constitutional change and why elite agreements lacking the qualities of deliberative politics sometimes deepen democracy anyway.

Our starting point is the well-developed research on pacting in the democratization literature, innovated by O'Donnell and Schmitter (1986) and the generation of literature they pioneered. This helps us to understand how constitutional negotiation "focal points" can set in motion democratic transitions despite elites' instrumental approaches to constitutions, as in Brazil (1985) or Chile (1988), or validate – and perpetuate – authoritarians, such as in Peru (1993) and Venezuela (1999). Authoritarians and hybrid regime leaders sometimes seek to break political stalemates with new constitutions, but this may have as much to do with keeping their authority as democratizing it. While seeking to distribute risk or enhance their legitimacy, elites can lose control of the process or misjudge the larger consequences of seemingly minor concessions. There are also, however, good reasons to believe that participatory constitution-making increases the likelihood that the worst of populism will prevail, as some of the constitutionalist literature claims. Rather than questioning the veil that America's founders hid behind in July 1787 as Dahl and others do (Dahl 2002; Wilentz 2005), this political theory tradition claims that elitism is merely a by-product of expertise. Like Burke's notion of "trusteeship," this view advocates a measure of insulation from public scrutiny as necessary for nobler minds to craft constitutional language on its merits rather its popularity. This would seem to be especially important in the early convening stage of constitution-making, yet our results so far say otherwise.

Next, we ask why a country adopts a top-down or a bottom-up constitution-making process in the first place. Two pairs of case studies in this chapter complement the tests in Chapter 3: the first considers the path of "window-dressing" constitutions imposed from above in Venezuela (1999) and The Gambia (1997), which both experienced a decline of democracy, as expected by our theory of deliberative constitution-making. The second pair follows the less-expected results of elite drafting processes in Chile (1980) and Nigeria (1999), which both saw democracy improve. This is important, since our statistical results in Chapter 2 as well as Chapter 3's analysis of pathways (changes in the actors or modalities in constitution-making process midstream) strongly suggested that countries generally fail to correct for "original sins" of imposed convening from above at the early stage of constitution-making.

Chapter 5 will also employ this analytical strategy organized around empirical tests and alternate paths that both challenge and support our overall statistical findings. We review literature on social movements, interest groups, and deliberative democratic theory in order to explain the basis for democratizing constitutionalism "from below." Then for our second set of tests, seeking to explain the drivers of different modalities of constitution-making, we proxy for pre-constitutional bottom-up leverage with variables measuring mass mobilization and grassroots pressures. From there, that chapter analyses how seemingly participatory processes in Ecuador (2008) and Egypt (2011), failed to improve subsequent levels of democracy. We explain why these cases, where constitutionalism had participatory qualities at the convening stage and beyond, are inconsistent with the overall statistical pattern. The chapter considers Tunisia (2011) and Colombia (1991) as examples of successful constitution-making from below.

A goal of these two chapters is to disentangle the democratizing effects of participatory constitution-making from the prior political contexts that lead to this modality. Taken together, they respectively test whether "top-down" and "bottom-up" pressures have significant impacts on the design of constitutional processes, and through careful analysis of paired case studies, offer compelling accounts of the causal forces at work in the statistical results. We note that the distinction between imposed (top-down) and popular (bottom-up) owes more to the informal conditions and context of constitutional processes than the resulting texts themselves. Recall also from Chapter 1 that we seek to explain participation in terms of aggregation of popular views, "exchange of reason" or deliberation, and elite pacting or bargaining. We argued that in imposed constitutions – those featured in this chapter – the normatively inferior elite pacting or bargaining is the main mode of participation. Such cases offer minimal popular participation as social movements and opposition parties press from outside the process rather than getting a co-equal voice in the drafting process (deliberation), or any space inside the room at all (aggregation).

The principal finding of this chapter is that constitution-making processes with lasting democratizing effects can and do emerge across a broad of range of regimes and regions. These effects are independent of the preexisting democratic conditions or the precise legal language in the constitution itself, meaning the parchment is less important than the process that generates it. As per the bargaining and elite pacting literature on democratization, we start by discussing research on "pacted" transitions to democracy, on authoritarian constitutions and institutions, and some relevant constitutionalist thinking about the benefits of elites in constitution-making. Even though democracy is not our dependent variable in this chapter, these literatures provide a basis for understanding elite behavior, its institutional contexts and procedural modalities.

LITERATURE REVIEW: CONSTITUTIONS AS
PACTS – DEMOCRATIC OR OTHERWISE

The fall of the Berlin Wall in 1989 generated powerful images of social movements at work, as Germans literally chipped away at a boundary between dictatorship and democracy. By serving as such a powerful metaphor, the Wall's fall emphasized popular power in a booming literature that questioned (or marginalized) the role of elites in democratization. Within this literature, a constructive tension between these respective perspectives played out through discourses variously labeled as structure versus agency, historical context plus contingency, or macro- and micro-oriented perspectives. The literature review here re-introduces the democratization literature's early work on "pacts" in order to extend some of its insights to elite behavior during constitution-making. Pacting research was accused of being regionally specific, but it helps identify elite incentives and broader contexts shaping the bargaining environment as well as the causes of outcomes that were "normatively good" – despite the best efforts of autocrats. We also reference how analysis of authoritarian institutions has emerged as an extension of comparative institutional analysis previously focused on democratic regimes. Finally, we briefly characterize the constitutionalists' case for top-down constitution-making. This includes criticisms of direct participation and deliberative democratic theory. These skeptical views of participation resurrect Burkean notions of trusteeship, highlight potential benefits of secrecy, urge procedural insurance against popular whim, and privilege elite involvement. "Ordinary people did not understand what was going on," said a Constitutional Commissioner from Uganda's long drafting exercise, culminating in the 1995 constitution. "The opinion of elites really mattered."[2]

When O'Donnell and Schmitter (1986) characterized democratization as a chess game, they suggested that the interests of regime incumbents who favored democratic transitions and those who opposed them could be analyzed as a binary, strategic calculus. As mentioned in Chapter 1, this pioneering work divided regime incumbents into "hardliners," who sought to defend the authoritarian *status quo* and limit political uncertainty, and "softliners," who saw openings as opportunities for the opposition to let off steam and therefore stabilize the regime. "Pacts" were agreements between these elite factions about the terms of a transition, which could occur, for example, when hardliners became convinced that attempting to hang onto power put them at greater risk than the insurance they would receive through a compromise.

---

[2] Interview with a Constitutional Commissioner from West Nile, Uganda (name withheld). Kampala, Uganda. June 25, 2012.

Like chess, transitions were games in which each move was conditioned by the anticipated moves of the other player. Przeworski elaborated on this conceptual framework, casting a further distinction among the softliners, which divided them into "reformers" and "radicals" (Przeworski 1991, 68–9).

Using clever inductive logic, these pioneers in the field of transitions observed that democratizing pacts emerged in Southern European and Latin American cases when the moderate interests of softliners within the ruling coalition aligned with the reformer opponents of the authoritarian regime against the hardliner authoritarians and the radical regime opponents. The coalition of the political center could withstand pressures from the authoritarian hardliners (often bolstered by the military or one-party rule) and the radicals, whose street protests threatened to destabilize and undermine the entire political system (O'Donnell and Schmitter 1986c). Linz and Stepan (1996) further qualified transitions as a four-player game, since hardliners and softliners could have allies outside the regime; transitions would only occur, they argued, if the moderates outside the regime had sufficient autonomy to organize.

O'Donnell and Schmitter do not mention constitutions at all in *Transitions from Authoritarian Rule*, except in a footnote where they state that socioeconomic pacts may be linked to political pacts "especially given the extensive attention that issues of economic management, worker rights, and social welfare have received in the convening of modern constitutions, such as those in Italy, Portugal, and Spain" (O'Donnell and Schmitter 1986a, 9). However, Przeworski does anticipate a fundamental question raised in this chapter: why would incumbent authoritarians initiate constitution-making from above, and if they do, will societal actors have any reason to believe they are sincere in any efforts to liberalize the polity? To him:

> Constitutions adopted to fortify transitory political advantage, constitutions that are nothing but pacts of domination among the most recent victors, are only as durable as the conditions that generated the last political victory. In turn, constitutions that allow everyone to introduce substantive demands, constitutions that ratify compromises by enshrining substantive commitments [. . .] are often impossible to implement. (Przeworski 1991, 36)

In other words, constitutions that are too rigid and imposed may not be credible and may not quell popular discontent and thus not endure, whereas those that admit too many interest group compromises may be flimsy and thus not endure. This relates to important questions concerning regime stability after constitutional change (Maboudi 2016), but our tasks here and in Chapter 5 are limited to identifying the origins of constitution-making processes conducive to democracy. The role of constitutions and constitutionalism remained generally unclear in the early transitology literature.

Relevant to our study of elite pacts and bargaining, the pacting literature has not been without its critics, who claim that "freezing" the polity along lines that existed when the agreement was reached could create as many tensions as it solved (Encarnación 2005). Such critiques seem particularly problematic where pacts have been codified in constitutions, as in Spain's Moncloa Pact incorporated into the 1978 constitution. This formalization is precisely the problem according to some analyses, since pacts contain both the rules of procedure and policy prescriptions intended to protect elites rather than advance citizen participation. "In essence, they are antidemocratic mechanisms, bargained by elites, which seek to create a deliberate socioeconomic and political contract that demobilizes emerging mass actors" (Karl 1990, 12). Empirically, the early years of democratization's Third Wave were kind to these early analyses of democratization through pacting in Southern Europe and Latin America. But paths to democracy elsewhere in the developing world soon differed in visible ways, as neopatrimonial regimes held out against liberalization or ethnic politics hardened elite preferences (Bratton and Van de Walle 1997; Chabal and Daloz 1999).

Nevertheless, the work of O'Donnell, Schmitter and Przeworski initiated a wave of process-driven studies of democratization based on interest groups which forms the basis of our analysis over the chapters ahead. For example, Higley and Gunther (1992) and Linz and Stepan (1996) reinforced the explanatory power of "process-driven" democratization by associating different paths to democracy with different probabilities of democratic consolidation. By re-introducing conceptual frameworks for thinking about interest groups that institutionalist and behavioralist approaches had hastily discarded in the 1960s and 1970s, the pacting literature paved the way for veto-player theory, which explores how the expression of preferences through institutions, organizations, and individuals impacts policy change (Konig et al. 2010).

More to the point of our work, analyzing elites as interest groups also helped usher in new institutional approaches to authoritarian regimes. In other words, a generation of scholars in the 1990s demonstrated that interest group approaches were relevant across regime types, rather than just in the case of democracies. Roeder (1993) thus accounted for the collapse of the Soviet Union not because of the state's weak links with society, but because of the unsustainable equilibrium between policy-makers and the bureaucrats they became dependent on. Similar arguments attributed economic reforms in China to a dependence on technocratic expertise in the provinces, despite the durability of communism at the center (Shirk 1993). The literature does still consider transitions, both abrupt, such as the Arab Spring revolution that recently spread across the Middle East (Brownlee et al. 2015), and gradual, such as the protracted Mexican transition studied by Eisenstadt (2004) and others (Magaloni 2006; Greene 2007). But a thriving "analytic authoritarianism" research agenda now centers on explaining how autocracies and their institutions work, rather than asking when they will democratize (Gandhi and Lust-Okar 2009; LeVan 2014). How elites share power with each other within the regime is just as important for understanding governance as how they relate to societal pressures (Svolik 2012; Boix and Svolik 2013), including elections (Ekman 2009). And many authors in this new literature build explicitly on the O'Donnell and Schmitter "interest group transitology" tradition (see for example Stoner and McFaul 2013; Geddes et al. 2014).

The O'Donnell and Schmitter literature of 1986 fell out of use for around 10 years, but was resuscitated over the last decade or so, in time for our extensive usage of their approach. Within the democratization literature, theories of elite political behavior faced intellectual challenges from structuralists and a new camp of institutionalists in the 1990s. One famous debate centered on whether presidential or parliamentary systems were more conducive to democratic accountability, public policy performance, and "coup-proofing" (Shugart and Carey 1992; Linz and Valenzuela 1994; Cheibub 2007). These scholars posited that elite behavior was conditioned by the incentives they faced, meaning that the key to understanding a broad range of outcomes was the institutional environment. Another debate centered on the importance of elections, including charges that they fueled "excessive voluntarism" by attributing too much agency to elites (Karl 1990). International election observation and foreign aid to civil society organizations dramatically increased (Hyde 2011), since the "transition paradigm" (as O'Donnell and Schmitter's critics labeled their work) presumed that elections were the ultimate expressions of citizens' agency and aid to Civil Society Organizations could shape the political context, making it more amenable to democratization and reformers in suspect regimes (Carothers 2002). O'Donnell and Schmitter's model seemed to be inapplicable in important, symbolic cases such as Ukraine, where an autocratic president's attempt to ally with hardliners in the private sector failed (Way 2005). It also seemed less relevant as presidents such as Uganda's Yoweri Museveni mastered the art of electoral manipulation. "What is a constitution?" asked a leading opposition figure. "He doesn't believe in democracy. He uses these instruments to legitimize his dictatorship."[3]

---

[3] Interview with Mira Matembe. Kampala, Uganda. June 12, 2012.

Setting up our "bottom-up" or popular origin constitutions discussed in Chapter 5, structuralists pushed back against elite models of democratization for different reasons, arguing that they underestimated the stickiness of these political contexts and overlooked structural variables (such as the strength of labor movements) capturing socioeconomic conditions (Collier and Collier 1991; Rueschemeyer et al. 1992). Some structuralists, for example, started looking more at how economic conditions enabled and constrained individual authoritarian agents and coalitions (Haggard and Kaufman 1995). The success of popular protest in the former Soviet States and Africa prompted process-oriented scholars to increasingly emphasize the democratizing effects of social movements (Bratton and Van de Walle 1997; Kubik 2000; Bunce 2003; Eisenstadt 2004). These movements were more than merely allies of regime softliners though – they were interpreted as social forces larger than any single group of elites and as empirical indicators of critical historical junctures.

The debate stimulated a constructive tension about whether emerging democracies were the result of "top-down" enterprises dominated by exiting authoritarians and the institutions they designed to ease their exits from power (Barros 2002), and "bottom-up" advocates, who emphasized a strong civil society as a necessary condition for democratic transitions (Bratton and Van de Walle 1997; Wood 2000). The chess metaphor returned, but softliners and their radical allies outside the regime no longer tilted the game toward transitions. Instead, wily authoritarians who had formally given up power seemed to be winning by manipulating elections, limiting political competition, intimidating the media, and bluffing the international community regarding their democratic intentions. "Hybrid" regimes (Diamond 2002), semi-authoritarianism (Ottaway 2003), and "democracy's doubles" (Krastev 2006) swiftly populated the literature. A central puzzle seemed to be how elections, which had served as symbols of agency and presumed as mechanisms of popular control over elites, could coexist with such illiberal regimes. Were elections periodic rituals that lent a veneer of legitimacy to authoritarianism (Schedler 2006; Hyde 2011), or were they the essential procedural component to democratization itself (Lindberg 2009)? This was a relevant question for institutionalists, since electoral incentives and institutional design were supposedly sufficient to produce good governance. It was, however, a question we will largely set aside. This new literature considering interest groups in democratization is extensive, but it addresses types of regimes (authoritarian, hybrid, democratic), elections (as per Schedler and Hyde above), and now, transparency (Nadi 2017). Having argued for the legitimacy of this literature, we now turn to its application to the informal "low politics" processes surrounding the crafting of constitutions.

THE FREQUENT COINCIDENCE OF IMPOSED
CONSTITUTIONS AND ELITE BARGAINS

Constitutions were not so much a missing variable here as one that was often misunderstood for many of the reasons outlined in Chapter 2; new constitutions accompanied transitions during the 1990s but they hardly caused them. Research on Eastern Europe (Przeworski 1991; Sunstein 2001), Latin America (Loveman 1993; Gargarella 2010), and the United States (Dahl 2002) brought in a new set of ideas about the role of pacts in democratization, and finally specified how Third Wave constitutions were actually different from earlier ones. Constitutions may encourage a societal convergence of actors around norms embodied in a series of institutions to channel conflicts (Knight 1992), but they are not contracts as there is no third-party enforcement (Hardin 1989; Przeworski 2003). O'Donnell himself, as if disenchanted with the teleological implications of his pioneering text with Schmitter, noticed a glaring weakness in new democracies, which nullified many of their benefits to self-rule and autonomy.

As he famously argued in stating that the checks and balances of "horizontal accountability" were needed to balance the strong "vertical accountability" of executive dominance, constitutions played a central role (O'Donnell 2007). However, he drew a distinction between two "poles" of constitutionalism: a republican/democratic pole that grants collective rights, and a liberal pole that favors private rights (or "civil rights") above all else, each with different kinds of effects on democratization. One pole invokes linkages we explore between social contract theories and more deliberative forms of constitution-making, including the constitutionalists who undertook change from below assessed in the Chapter 5. The other pole lends itself to "window-dressing" constitutionalists from above analyzed in this chapter by binding rights to agency and to a large extent, elite autonomy.

"TRUSTEESHIP" ELITISM AND POLITICAL THEORISTS'
ARGUMENTS FOR CONSTITUTIONAL STEWARDSHIP

O'Donnell and Schmitter (1986) seemed interested in showing the agency of transitions, and were ultimately disappointed that so few authoritarian softliner-opposition reformer alliances could actually yield enduring and meaningful transitions where democracy actually improved citizens' day-to-day lives (Schmitter 2010). A more normatively pessimistic set of theories implies that citizens are too fickle and "passionate" (Elster's word) for constitutional politics to begin with. This classic conservative school of thought claims that pacted constitutionalism was more than merely window-dressing for autocrats in democrats' clothing. In fact, elites have an essential role to play in protecting the people from their lesser impulses and aptitudes. For example Burke's "true principles of government" asserted that government is not made from natural rights, meaning that liberty requires surrender to the state and only a power above the people can subdue their "passions" and wield experience for their benefit (Burke 1999). Indeed, this position was also the basis for James Madison's enduring constitutional principles. After declaring in "Federalist Number 49" that "the people are the only legitimate fountain of power," he warns that when the public's agreement on an issue grows, so does its confidence. Therefore "the passions ought to be controlled and regulated by the government" (Madison 2006b, 117–20). In much the same spirit, he describes factions in "Federalist Number 10" as any number of citizens in the minority or majority united "in common impulse or passion," and concedes that the causes of faction are "sown in the nature of man." But since abolishing the sources of faction cannot be accomplished without abolishing liberty, the only way to "break and control the violence of faction" is to control its effects (Madison 2006a, 84–5). Like pacted transitions, argument for checks and balances was only a short step away from a reasoned argument for pacted constitutions. Just as the public had to be protected from itself, elites needed to limit their abilities to threaten each other; pacts were an institutional means of controlling the pernicious potential effects of their differences.

These conservative arguments about the nature of individuals offer an additional elite-level justification for "imposed constitutions" beyond the O'Donnell and Schmitter (1986)-based elite bargaining arguments that address collective interests rather than individual ones. Burkean notions of governance through trusteeship rather than participation have gained appeal from several contemporary political developments. One stems from the rise of methods of direct democracy including referendums and different forms of citizen input into policy-making, often initiated from the top (i.e. by governments) (Morel 2001). Direct democracy devices are used almost twice as frequently today as they were 50 years ago, and almost four times more than 100 years ago (Altman 2011, 65). Conservative critics of "plebiscitory rule" resurrected the case for trusteeship, asking whether there was in fact too much democracy. In this view, representative democracy remained both relevant and the best insurance against the "populist myth" in the United States, where advocates of direct democracy on the left seek increased citizen engagement for more progressive policy while advocates on the right see it as a tool to limit the size of government (Haskell 2001).

In this sense, the US Tea Party movement constitutes a paradox: a grassroots wave that chose representation as the measure of its success, sweeping conservative candidates into state governments and the US House of Representatives in 2012, rather than hewing to traditional populist calls for more direct democracy. Right-wing populism in Germany, France, Austria, and Italy has been fueled by support for exclusion via narrow terms of participation and citizenship, manifest in the founding of small and xenophobic new political parties (von Beyme 2011). By contrast, Latin America's populism from the left, as discussed in Chapter 5, has been substantially driven by the politics of inclusion through social movements "from below," which have in some cases succeeded in overthrowing governments and forcing their issues onto policy agendas. The opposite of "trusteeship," populism claims that the needs of the populace must be addressed now, even at the expense of a nation's long-term interests (such as a balanced budget). Populists do not often formulate their reasoning in abstract philosophical terms, as the Burkeans do. They follow a political imperative to get immediate support now, usually to achieve electoral popularity or other immediate political ends (Ascher 1984; Roberts 2006). But they are the conceptual opposite of the elite trustees, seeking constitutions that favor citizens now, or favor other short-term imperatives (as opposed to longer-term benefits), such as executive re-election (Eisenstadt et al. 2016).

As further elaborated in Chapter 5, representation cuts both ways. For example, Brazil's leftist Workers' Party (PT in Portuguese) has fostered inclusion through mass movements in order to institutionalize itself as a "catch-all" party. The right in Europe and elsewhere has used representation to seek placement for a small cadre of like-minded politicians and to exclude others. With democracy facing such crises of representation from all sides, constitutional referendums presented an odd dilemma at the time they were seeing a dramatic increase in frequency: Tierney (2012) notes that they could either save republican government through direct participation, or as their critics contend, referendums could magnify the failings of modern democracy. Constitutions can be at the center of these political machinations when a credible proposal is introduced to break log jams.

A second development that helped legitimize notions of trusteeship as a justifying rationale for constitutionalism "from above" – in addition to the conduct of "top-down" plebiscites – was skeptical responses to deliberative models of democracy that had become popular in political science (Dryzek 2000). Pacted constitutionalism could offer a way out of what we might call "Tierney's dilemma" by acknowledging the benefits of elite engagement. By this argument, romanticizing popular participation could be dangerous, and implementing it could be impractical – especially if was implemented broadly, meaning beyond narrowly defined policy questions. As scholars of deliberative democracy themselves reasoned, "top-down" constitutions can constrain rulers and contribute to democratization. In his classic essay on the topic, Elster (1998) points to the Prussian Constitution of 1848, the Japanese Constitution of 1946 (imposed by occupying powers), and several French constitutions (including Charles de Gaulle's in 1958) among his examples of "top-down" constitutions that deliver democratic improvements.

The literature on pacts along with the research on democratization, institutionalism, and democratic trusteeship leaves us with several important lessons for contemporary constitutionalism. Elites may form pacts to advance democratization or to forestall it. Softliners and hardliners alike can fail, and the outcomes of the process may diverge from their intentions. This makes it hard to adhere to solely inductive theories of rational interest or structural theories dismissive of voluntarism. In addition, pacted constitutions may be less common than they were just a decade or two ago, and as highlighted in Chapter 2, international norms have certainly moved against them. But elite buy-in is still important, as Horowitz (2013) argues in the case of Indonesia, and even in compelling cases from the Arab Spring that began in 2011. Elites there have been central to many new "ruling bargains" in the new regimes, whether they are moving toward democracy or not (Kamrava 2014). For example, autocrats in Jordan, Turkey, Egypt, and Morocco have found hardliner-style allies in religious minorities who fear an erosion of religious freedom under democratic majoritarian rule (Belge and Karakoc 2015). Yet a critical difference between the Arab Spring bargains and those described by the earlier pacting literature is the late entry of elites into the process – typically under pressure from protest movements – rather than initiating the process (Brownlee et al. 2015). This intersection between bottom-up and top-down democratization generates two questions, which we address in the next section: why would elites opt to bind their hands with a constitution, and why would grassroots movements delegate deliberation or promulgation to them at all?

EMPIRICAL STUDIES OF WHY ELITES MIGHT BIND THEMSELVES TO CONSTITUTIONS

Why would elites bind their hands by negotiating and promulgating constitutions? Arguably, elites in democracies and dictatorships share some important similarities. Constitutions can limit their discretionary power but also distribute risk, making it harder to assign blame to the chief executive or any single actor. They can expose unpopular deals which would otherwise likely be left confined to smoke-filled rooms, and thus bolster regime legitimacy. They can pre-commit leaders to a shorter tenure than they want, but also reduce uncertainty about succession, thus deterring leadership challenges and reducing regime instability. Constitutions establish rules for resource distribution, representation, and rights.

In democracies, constitutions are "expected" so elites go through the motions for all of these reasons, even without significant pressure from below. For dictators, the calculus is more complicated because they hope to avoid any unintended democratizing effects of constitutions; they want the benefits outlined above without the risks. Thus, explaining why elites in dictatorship adopt constitutions is the harder question. Some of the literature mentioned above already hinted at answers. Here, we bring in this literature more explicitly and integrate the logic of O'Donnell and Schmitter (1986) and Przeworski (1991), who argue that authoritarians are compelled to negotiate pacted departures (or partial departures) from power when their unity collapses and softliner incumbents make common cause with reformer regime opponents. These groups generally fear the radical opponents, and also may fear that reprisals by hardliner authoritarians against them may further enflame regime opposition.

Ginsburg and Simpser (2013, 5) inventory the roles of constitutions in authoritarian regimes as "operating manuals, billboards, blueprints, and window dressing." Similar to the "hand-binding" role suggested by the existence of transparent electoral institutions in authoritarian regimes (Eisenstadt 2004, 32–8), Ginsburg and Simpser write that the "operating manual" offers a means of binding authoritarians so that their colleagues do not act outside of prescribed norms: "billboards" advertise the claims of constitutions "signaling the intentions of leaders within the regime to those outside of it; when serving as "blueprints," constitutions describe societal aspirations rather than political institutions as they exist; and under the "window-dressing" function, "the text is designed to obfuscate actual political practice" (Ginsburg and Simpser 2013, 6–8).

On the whole, authoritarians seek to control their challengers within the authoritarian coalition, signal intentions of reform (whether genuine or not) to regime opponents (domestic and international), and, perhaps, bargain over transitions of power and possible future regime conditions. In terms of content, "democrats innovate in the formal constitution, while dictators tend to imitate formal democratic institutions, saving their innovations for the informal realm" (Ginsburg and Simpser 2013, 143). Whatever the case, societal pressures for liberalization, as per the softliner-reformer alliance in the O'Donnell and Schmitter and Przeworski cases, constitutes part of the reason for authoritarian constitutionalism. Authoritarians need stability, they aim to distribute risk, and they seek also information to control actors inside and outside their coalition through sanctions.

In the following analysis, we pair democratizing and non-democratizing instances of imposed constitutions, following the logic outlined in the book's introduction: two cases conform to our statistical expectations and our theory (Venezuela and The Gambia), and two constitute confounding cases (Chile and Nigeria). Important to our empirical consideration of forms of participation, we assess the first two cases, the imposed constitutions, as clear instances of elite pacting/bargaining participation. The second two cases are more ambiguous, as they both started as elite pacts/bargains but then opened up somewhat to include other interests that were also aggregated. The analysis of both the modality of the process (imposed or popular) and the form of participation is important in order to understand how countries adopt elitist constitution-making processes as well as why democratization might occur anyway in outliers. Chapter 5 will mirror this case selection strategy through an examination of bottom-up constitution-making in two cases that led to democracy – Tunisia and Colombia – alongside a critical analysis of Ecuador and Egypt, where participatory processes failed to deepen democracy.

Venezuela (1999) is perhaps the quintessential recent Latin American "top-down" constitutional process consolidating authoritarianism. As per the "imposed" cases first identified in Chapter 3, that constitution yielded a tighter authoritarian regime, based on a few central institutional constraints that constitution imposed on challengers to the president. Why did Hugo Chávez "constitutionalize" his authoritarianism rather than just imposing it through informal institutions, as per the Elkins, Ginsburg, and Melton argument above? We explore a few of the main components of this constitution in order to then process-trace convening and promulgation to understand why Chávez might risk his executive discretion by calling for a constituent assembly, but also how he tightly and successfully managed a constitutional process that did not yield democratization. We then examine the lesser-known but important case of The Gambia, where a military dictator accommodated inclusiveness and allowed for public input – but only as a ruse for his own ruthlessness. In our dataset, constitution-making processes in both of these cases began with imposed convening and concluded with participatory referendums.

We then analyze Chile and Nigeria, which also adopted imposed constitutionalism. But unlike Venezuela and The Gambia, and contrary to the statistical pattern identified in Chapter 2, this pair of cases experienced post-promulgation democratization. This comparative methodology enables us to examine why similar processes (constitutionalism from above) led to different outcomes (Gerring 2011; Weller and Barnes 2014). Augusto Pinochet's regime in Chile transitioned to a euphemistically labeled "protected democracy," envisioned as a "presidential political system, with restricted participation and exclusive representation, tutelary power of the armed forces, and the untouchability of institutions in order to assure the regime's permanent authoritarian character" (Garreton, as cited in Ensalaco 1994, 410). Pinochet and his military authoritarians lost control of Chile's democratic transition, and the restrictive negotiation of the 1980 constitution backfired. Nigeria's hasty and closed constitutional reform process launched in 1998 similarly resulted in a successful transition in May 1999. The handover to an elected civilian president, (a former dictator himself) broke a 16-year-old pattern of transition plans announced and betrayed by military governments (Diamond et al. 1997; Bach et al. 2001).[4]

CASES IN POINT: TOP-DOWN CONSTITUTIONAL LEGACIES

Top-Down Constitutionalism Not *Improving Democracy: Venezuela and the Gambia*

Venezuela epitomizes the "top-down" imposed modality of convening. Hugo Chávez advocated for a popular convening process prior to Venezuela's promulgation, stating that "there is no reason to doubt that the constitutional process in itself will be absolutely democratic and this is the warranty that the result will be democratic" (Garcia-Guadilla and Hurtado 2000, 17). It seems this was wishful thinking, however, as Chávez launched a Constituent National Assembly (CNA) the day he took office in February 1999, which took a much more imposed approach. He had discussed the need for a national "re-founding" since his attempted *coup d'état* in 1992, which would have followed our "aggregated participation" type. Instead, the populist leader imposed a referendum to assess public support for the election of a CNA along the lines of the elite pacting/bargaining approach to participation, pervasive among the cases considered in this chapter. After the convocation of a constitutional process was approved by a wide margin, the CNA was elected in July 1999 using "a particular version of the mixed-member proportional system designed by Chávez himself" (Segura and Bejarano 2004, 225). While the CNA members were elected, President Chávez picked 94.5 percent of them himself, meaning that the assembly was selected as "window dressers," making

---

[4] Chile only modestly democratized following the 1980 constitution, improving its Polity score from −7 to −6.6 during the three-year time lead used in Chapter 2's regressions. It experienced higher levels of democracy following significant constitutional amendments in the late 1980s and a plebiscite on Pinochet's continued military rule.

"negotiations and alliances unnecessary" (Garcia-Guadilla and Hurtado 2000, 23). In fact, the "hand-raising participation" of the assembly members was not even needed, as "only a minority of the constituent members of the Polo Patriotico [the Chávez faction] actively participated in discussions during the final phase of integrating the work in the Commissions" (Garcia-Guadilla and Hurtado 2000, 23).

The imposed elite bargain Chávez pushed through the CNA mandated increased state involvement in the economy (including in Venezuela's all-important oil sector, where privatization was prohibited), and also did guarantee universal health care, education, employment, and pensions. However, it also extended the length of the president's term, empowered the president to call national referendums at will, granted presidential authority to name the vice president (with a heightened role), and permitted the president to dissolve the legislature. Perhaps most averse to democratization was the provision that the president could promulgate laws in any policy area (rather than just in the economic realm, as in the past) by passing an enabling law in the legislative branch, which Chávez simplified from bicameral to unicameral (Garcia-Serra 2001, 275–6). Furthermore, the constitution granted the unicameral National Assembly the authority to remove public officials.

These constitutional provisions were utilized, as President Chávez did use the Constitution of 1999 to diminish Venezuela's already low level of democracy. In 2001 the Chávez-controlled National Assembly dismissed the People's Defender (ombudsman) and the Prosecutor General; in 2002 it dismissed several judges of the Supreme Tribunal; and in 2004 it dismissed judges on the electoral court who were entertaining the possibility of a presidential recall referendum (Brewer-Carías 2010, 173–4). Having removed all possible venues for "deliberative participation," Chávez set about constructing his own "top-down" bodies, which he cynically claimed allowed for such participation. In 2006, the Chávez government passed the Law of Communal Councils, establishing presidential funds around the country to exercise public works, outside of the purview of elected local governments. By most accounts, these *rondas Bolivarianas* are clientelist entities designed to promote support for the president rather than execute public policy (McCarthy 2012, 123–48). After three years of "trial balloons," Chávez in 2009 had a constitutional amendment approved, allowing him indefinite re-election.

Chávez's authoritarian consolidation of power was interrupted only by his death in 2013, and his successor Nicolás Maduro has benefited also from the authoritarian institutions and practices established in the (1999) Constitution, and bolstered subsequently in practice. The case offers few surprises to our study of constitutions, as it conveys how authoritarian leaders using imposed constitutional convening processes can manipulate constitutions in their own interests and achieve legitimacy for institutionalizing their authoritarianism, even as they curtail citizens' rights. Similar to Venezuela (1999), The Gambia (1997) also offers a case of authoritarian consolidation via top-down decree imposition.

The road to The Gambia's (1997) Constitution, which we code as "imposed," began with a *coup d'état* in 1994 that overthrew Dawda Jawara, president since independence from Britain in 1965. Jawara's People's Progressive Party (PPP) had governed the small West African country under a philosophy of so-called *sembocracy*, a reference to the Mandika word for "power" or "force" that implied a strong ruler who acted on behalf of the people. After Jawara survived a failed coup attempt in 1981, the term was used by the regime's critics to point to the PPP's heavy-handed authoritarianism beneath a veneer of democracy. For example, parties had little political freedom despite the country's formal multiparty status. By 1992 the PPP was rife with internal factionalism and its popularity was in decline due to a wave of corruption scandals and President Jawara reneging on a promise to not seek another term (Saine and Ceesay 2012). The 1994 coup leader, Lieutenant Yahya Jammeh, quickly replaced the PPP with an Armed Forces Provisional Ruling Council (AFPRC). A two-year process of designing a new constitution culminated with 90 percent of the population approving the new text by national referendum, through a process that did feature aggregated participation, with Jammeh donning civilian clothes to announce his candidacy for the presidency. However, the participation quickly turned to the elite bargaining/pacting form, as Jammeh delayed the election and issued decrees to ban former ministers from participating and imposed restrictions on the press. He won the presidential election in 1996, and again in 2001, 2006, and 2011, and continues to this day to limit the media, civil society, and political organizing. How did the constitution-making process, with a semblance of participation and under the watchful eyes of the international community, help enable a familiar autocratic playbook?

In the aftermath of Jammeh's July coup, "political parties were banned, civil society organizations did not have rights, and there was tyranny from the top," according to the Halifa Sallah, the head of the only pre-coup opposition party – the Peoples' Democratic Organization for Independence and Socialism (PDOIS) – that remained legal. Like Chávez in Venezuela, Jammeh had eliminated any chance of deliberation by restricting the range of ideas that could be expressed. By November, the clampdown had split elites in the AFRPC: "the military itself, they were not united," which is why there was another (failed) coup attempt, he says.[5] The junta also faced tremendous

---

5   Interview with Halifa Sallah. Banjul, The Gambia. July 2, 2013.

international pressure to hand over power to a civilian regime.[6] To soothe its softliners and reformers, the regime announced a participatory component of the constitutional convention stage. In 1995, a National Consultative Council (NCC) toured communities throughout the country to solicit input on a new constitution. On one level, the process seemed sincere due to its perceived inclusiveness. Religious leaders, traditional rulers, and former politicians were all part of the consultations, according to a prominent government critic who conceded that the process had elements of inclusiveness – despite its secrecy.[7] But since these people who took part did not have a legal background, "they lacked the depth of understanding of what a constitution means," says one prominent legal scholar.[8] In the end, "the public participation was not really meaningful, and a decade later, people still lived in fear," according to another scholar.[9] The military's control over constitution-making, even at the early stages, is apparent at the level of the process as well as in terms of the outcomes of the constitutional text.

In terms of the process, mystery to some extent still shrouds how members of the Constitutional Review Commission (CRC), the body charged with actually drafting the constitution, were chosen. During this period of rule by military decrees, says a former Acting Chief Justice of the Supreme Court, "they were not at all transparent."[10] Some government sympathizers defended this kind of elite-driven convening process with Burkean logic, saying in interviews, "there is a limit as far as the contribution of the public is concerned" and "experts" are necessary.[11] According to one of the junta's close advisers, "they were chosen directly by the AFPRC. That is the only body that had the authority."[12] Thus the NCC was ultimately a kind of ruse, according an official involved: "Our purpose of going to consult with them was not for them to have input into the constitution. It was to explain the constitution to them." So the people participated in the process, but "that doesn't mean that the consultations produced substantial input from the community."[13] The NCC was also apparently directed at international critics; Jammeh had expelled the National Democratic Institute, which had carried out civic education under an invitation from the previous government, because he said the country director "organized workshops without permission" and declined to

[6] Interview with Emmanual Joof. Banjul, The Gambia. July 3, 2013.
[7] Interview with Suwaibou Touray. Banjul, The Gambia. July 4, 2013.
[8] Interview with Gambian Scholar #1 (name withheld). Banjul, The Gambia. July 1, 2013.
[9] Interview with Johannes Buaben-Baidoo, Banjul, The Gambia. July 1, 2013.
[10] Interview with Raymond Shock, Banjul, The Gambia. July 4, 2014.
[11] Interview with Gambian Scholar #1 (name withheld). Banjul, The Gambia. July 1, 2013.
[12] Interview with Saji Taal. Banjul, The Gambia. July 3, 2013.
[13] Interview with Gambian Scholar #6 (name withheld). Banjul, The Gambia. July 3, 2013.

discuss its mandate with the junta (el Walid Seye 1995). When the junta then launched a Civic Education Panel to explain the constitution's content to voters in preparation for a referendum on the constitution, Jammeh directed his ire toward donors: "I have been seeking every opportunity at every occasion to try and bring our development partners on board to sail with us," Jammeh said, but "they put obstacles on our way to impede our progress" ("Rawlings, Jammeh, Jawara, The International Community" 1995).

In terms of the text, the constitutional drafters ignored popular public demands voiced to the NCC and changed several constitutional provisions before and after the referendum. "When subsequent drafts came, things were completely doctored," recalls one former magistrate and practicing international lawyer.[14] According to him and other interviewees, the most prominent omission was the removal of presidential term limits – the very issue that had helped make Jammeh's 1994 coup popular. Ultimately, recalls the head of the opposition PDOIS, "one of the key demands was term limits" but that was removed from the constitution.[15] According to one legal analysis, it was "perhaps the most prominent, if not deliberate constitutional omission" (Jeng 2012, 132). By the time the constitution got to the voters, it was not only a *fait accompli* – they didn't have accurate information about what was in it.

The actual voting on the referendum was generally free and fair, and our dataset codes it as a popular process. But the military now wearing civilian clothes played a trick on voters by naming Jammeh's political party "Alliance for Patriotic Reorientation and Construction" (APRC). Only one letter off from the "AFPRC" acronym for the junta, the APRC label was designed to deliberately confuse voters into thinking that a vote against the party would be a vote against the military, according to an adviser who proposed the name.[16] In other words, they offered more elite bargaining/pacting participation, but it was masked as an aggregated form of participation. The Gambia's rulers cultivated confusion about the referendum by telling voters that a "no" vote would mean the military would stay, and that a "yes" vote was a vote for the transition.[17]

Like Venezuela's imposed constitution, The Gambia's produced legal lineages that have helped entrench autocracy. For example, when student protesters were shot by government forces in 2001, the government passed an Indemnity Act expanding the president's powers and placing certain constitutional provisions – that could make government officials subject to

---

[14] Interview with Emmanuel Joof. Banjul, The Gambia. July 3, 2013.
[15] Interview with Halifa Sallah. Banjul, The Gambia. July 2, 2013.
[16] Interview with Saji Taal. Banjul, The Gambia. July 3, 2013.
[17] Interview with civil society activist (name withheld). Banjul, The Gambia. July 4, 2013.

prosecution – no longer eligible for amendment (Jeng 2012). In one prominent case, the government changed the constitution to describe The Gambia as "a sovereign secular republic." Even though the Supreme Court ruled that the constitution had been improperly modified when the word "secular" was added, the term remains.[18] The "opacity" of the constitution, argues one analysis, was used by Jammeh's government to portray it as "incomplete" and not necessarily a "secret" document (Hultin 2013). Harassment of the media continued, and the press was banned from attending a public seminar organized by lawyers on prison conditions in June 2013. According to one journalist, the president regularly shut down radio stations, and when Jammeh was accused of killing a journalist, he said, "I don't kill journalists, I jail them."[19] Media harassment and censorship in Venezuela is also widespread. But if oil gave Chávez a powerful populist tool of patronage, it also increased the regime's vulnerability to international price fluctuations, stimulating factional tensions among party elites (Corrales and Penfold-Becerra 2011). Rather than exposing these deep elite divisions, the institutions created by the imposed constitution have helped manage them, and in the midst of modern populism, perpetuated the window-dressing constitutional myth crafted by Chávez and cultivated by his successor (Tinker Salas 2015).

Top-Down Constitutionalism Improving Democracy: Chile and Nigeria

In his uniquely comprehensive account of the politics behind Chile's 1980 constitution, Barros (2003, 168) narrates that, contrary to popular belief, "the charter does not embody any single position which emerged during the 1977 debate over the structure of the [military] Junta [. . .] least of all Pinochet, who as we shall see would have preferred to rule with no constitution at all or else one radically distinct from that promulgated." Indeed, the function of the authoritarian constitution here seemed to be to limit the discretion of challengers within the authoritarian coalition, and also to constrain opponents. The constitution was clearly launched through an elite pacting/bargaining form of participation, but the military did not shut down all deliberation; they merely delimited the range of debate. To wit, the constitution did revive the Constitutional Tribunal as a maximum judicial body and reinforced the bill of rights, but, at the same time, it also guaranteed a set of non-elected members to the Senate, the "insulation" of military appointments from politics and "elevation of the armed forces to the status of guarantors of the institutional order"

[18]   Interview with Gambian Scholar #1 (name withheld). Banjul, The Gambia. July 1, 2013.
[19]   Interview with Sam Sarr, Sarakuna, The Gambia. July 4, 2013.

(Barros 2002, 169). Term limits to military rule were established, as was a plebiscitary ratification of the constitution, but leftist parties (which had governed from 1970 to 1973, when Pinochet led a coup) were outlawed. The constitution was a mishmash of republican institutions, liberal rights, and military-led prerogatives. It restrained deliberation, but did not eliminate that form of participation, even as it instated a powerful elite bargain. Perhaps several decades of democracy and the fact that Pinochet was replacing a democratically elected social democrat may have circumscribed limits (or perceived limits) on the military's ability to shut down participation all at once.

Consistent with our broader argument and those made elsewhere (O'Donnell and Schmitter 1986; Holmes 1988; Eisenstadt 2004), it seems the constitution was an effort to bind the hands of the authoritarians, as softliners within that coalition did not want hardliners to fortify their internal positions. As stated by Barros (2002, 179), "Given the other junta members' aversion to granting Pinochet absolute control, liberalization was unacceptable insofar as it implied a weakening of the Junta, and as a result the organization of power during the transitory period remained largely identical to the period which the regime allegedly was stepping away from." So the elite pact was only a partial one; deliberative participation remained, but within a narrower space, which would eventually broaden as Chile democratized under the same constitution.

A Constituent Commission was named to draft the new constitution in 1975, but it was forced by the ruling junta, over objections, to do so. However, efforts in 1976 to allow this Commission to draft the document were frustrated, as the junta entirely reworked the constitution draft. In this process, efforts to fit their authoritarian prerogatives into more democratic norms generated controversy among junta members, as some sought to establish a constitution of transition (a "blueprint"), while others strove to offer "window-dressing" democratic appearances while at the same time retaining authoritarian prerogatives via informal negotiation of a "shadow constitution" (Barros 2002, 191). In 1978, amid international pressures generated by international publicity of the Pinochet regime's apparent assassination of Orlando Letelier in Washington, Pinochet announced that the junta would enact a new constitution for a democratic transition and then subject this "top-down" imposed constitution to public approval (precisely the kind of process we learned in Chapter 2 does not improve levels of democracy). Pinochet had handed down a memo late in 1977 on "Basic Orientations for the Study of the New Constitution" and allowed the Constituent Commission to negotiate the basic document, in consultation with the junta, which named the members, over the next couple of years. The text had to be unanimously approved by the

Council of State (the junta "cabinet"), however, ensuring that the 1980 constitution would "appear as little more than a cosmetic device for perpetuating the dictatorship" (Barros 2002, 216).

The final text of the constitution was prepared by four non-elected military commanders and gave Pinochet eight more years in office and expanded repressive capabilities. There was no record of the final drafting of the text, but it was promulgated as an "operating manual" in March 1981 with fanfare. While most renderings of Chilean democratization argue that the country's real liberalization occurred after the celebrated 1987 plebiscite on continued authoritarian rule, which General Pinochet seemingly allowed due to a dramatic miscalculation that it would legitimize his regime rather than destabilize it, Barros, consistent with our Chile data entry, dates the liberalization of Chilean authoritarianism back to 1983–4. The constitution re-established a Constitutional Tribunal, whose members did not seem to understand they were to be "window dressers" rather than norms enforcers, and circumscribed the junta's authority so that "the main body of the constitution grew apart from its authoritarian double" (Barros 2002, 256). Deliberative participation, which had been dormant during the years of negotiation between hardliners and softliners within the junta, became more public as other societal interests agitated for inclusion. The fortification of the junta vis-à-vis the president constrained Pinochet's ability to repress mass protests in 1983 and 1984, tempering "Pinochet's impetuous tendency to meet each protest or affront by ratcheting up emergency powers or by enacting impromptu, draconian repressive legislation" (Barros 2002, 257). The dictator failed to see that his own hands were being bound along with those of his authoritarian coalition challengers, and was soon forced to abide by checks and balances he never anticipated would take on the actual authority *de facto* that he allowed them to be granted *de jure*.

As in Chile, Nigeria's embrace of elite-centered constitutionalism in 1998 is paradoxical, and runs contrary to the statistical pattern documented above as well as our theory's expectations. For starters, when a transitional government decreed a constitution in 1999 with virtually no public input, Nigeria ran against the tide of participatory constitution-making that we identified in Chapter 2 as an emerging international norm. This was especially surprising since civil society had played a significant role in agitating for democracy by demanding political liberalization, organizing labor strikes, and forming powerful international allies sympathetic to democratization (Edozie 2002; LeVan 2011b). In 1993, popular protest brought the country to a virtual standstill for nearly two months after the dictator Ibrahim Babangida annulled the presidential election results (Suberu 1997). Western countries soon imposed an oil embargo to boost civil society morale and lend credibility to its demands (Lewis et al. 1998). Babangida's successor, Sani Abacha, was even more brutal, unleashing massive repression that drove many pro-democracy forces underground and crushed softliners within the regime. Starting around 1996, he specifically targeted those sympathetic to installing the winner of the annulled 1993 election, Moshood Abiola. By then the broad-based "rainbow cabinet" he assembled after taking over, which included prominent elites from Abiola's party, had been thoroughly dismembered and crushed (Amuwo 2001; LeVan 2015). Democrats and softliners exiled from the regime got a break when Abacha died suddenly in 1998.

With a history of at least five coups and only one successful transition from military to civilian rule (in 1979, which only lasted until 1983), there were good reasons to believe history was about to repeat itself as the 1998/9 transition got under way. The security services repeatedly injected themselves into the constitution-making process by screening political candidates.[20] More poignantly, the military vetoed constitutional provisions supported by Abdulsalaami Abubakar, chair of the transition, to limit the president to one term and rotate the office around six geopolitical "zones" of the country.[21] "In compacting its constitutions," wrote one scholar shortly after the 1999 transition in reference to its constitutional pact, "the country has never adopted a participatory or process-led approach involving the various nationality groups and the various communities" (Ihonvbere 2004, 257). Almost immediately, the constitution was dismissed by social movement activists and regime softliners as a doomed project to establish democracy by undemocratic means. "Constitutionalism has been subverted under the imposed 1999 Constitution," asserts one study (Falana 2010, 125). The elite-driven process seemed to ignore widespread demands for a Sovereign National Conference (SNC) styled after Benin's, which could put the most fundamental questions on the table – including the possibility of national disintegration to advance minority rights and cast off colonial institutions once and for all. Abubakar opposed the idea of an SNC because he saw it as usurping his power to oversee the transition (Onwudiwe 1999). More importantly, elites generally viewed an SNC as a risky proposition after so many previous transition plans over the previous 16 years had been usurped by the military.

How then did the country avoid the mistakes of the past and somewhat unexpectedly make the ensuing transition successful? This is an important question since we code the constitution as imposed. Not only did the head

---

[20] Interview with Governor Clement Ebri. Abuja, Nigeria. March 16, 2010.
[21] Interview with Governor Okwesilieze Nwodo. Abuja, Nigeria. March 8, 2010.

of the transition government adopt positions at odds with his social movement sympathizers, the earliest moments of Nigeria's pacted transition showed hallmarks of an "original sin" of elite imposed constitution-making that we have argued is difficult to remedy. One factor that accounts for the eventual democratizing effects of the 1999 constitution is that it is almost identical to the 1979 constitution, which though crafted under the watchful eye of an outgoing military regime, embraced deliberative important qualities. For example, its widespread consultation with the public generated enough political leverage for reformers to successfully reject some of the military's recommendations (Gboyega 1979). A second factor is that when Abubakar's interim government took over, the military was deeply divided over what to do with the 1993 election results; one of Abubakar's key rivals for head of the transition was inched out due to his sympathies for Abiola (Niboro 1998). But with the unexpected death of Abiola in 1998, the thorny question of whether he should be instated as the victor in the still-unresolved 1993 elections, or perhaps ordained as the frontrunner candidate in new elections, was avoided. With the most divisive issue in the junta now moot, activists and softliner elites who had fought for democracy had more space to maneuver. The military had been very concerned that Abiola, a wealthy businessperson from the southwest, would purge the northern-dominated military, perhaps as revenge for Abacha's neutralization of softliners from the southwest in 1997–8 (Olorunfewa 1998); such fears were now less relevant. A third factor that worked in favor of the emergence of deliberative qualities stemmed from Abubakar's wise decision to assign his transitional cabinet's top portfolios to northerners (Mumuni 1998). This further reassured Abacha's sympathizers, especially military elites, who historically hailed from the north. Finally, the election of Olusegun Obasanjo, a former war hero and the dictator who had overseen the 1979 transition, proved conducive to a democratizing political context despite the "imposed" constitution. He was from the south and had suffered gravely in prison under Abacha, giving him credibility among many pro-democracy activists; two weeks after he became president he established a truth commission with the goal of reconciliation. But in an important gesture to the military, the so-called Oputa Commission had no subpoena or prosecutorial powers (Constitutional Rights Project 2002). The military had a politician it could trust and whose southern ethnicity could close the door on the debacle of the annulled 1993 election. In fact, the most strident protests in 1993 had come from Obasanjo's southwest corner of the country. In the end, elite inclusion dictated by ethno-regional politics and powerful social movements alike, nudged Nigeria toward democracy and a more deliberative constitutionalism.

How did undemocratic constitution-making processes facilitate successful democratization in Chile and Nigeria? Nigeria's Polity score improved from −4.3 to +4.0 over the three years after the transition. Chile followed a longer path, with only slight improvement from −7.0 to −6.6 in the three years after the 1980 constitution (but with a much more robust transition later). Both outgoing military regimes were composed of soldiers and generals who feared the personal consequences of transitional justice, and in the end faced little accountability for their past transgressions. However, the elites in both countries also seemed to support limited deliberative participation; that is, debate and discussion on issues outside of their own historic roles and future prerogatives. In Nigeria, the People's Democratic Party (PDP), pushed to democratize by international donors as well as the massive domestic social movement for political reform that had formed in the 1990s, settled on an internal understanding that power would alternate between north and south, the central cleavage. No less important was the toothless truth commission, the Oputa Commission, which left elites with nothing to fear since it had no prosecutorial powers and its report on human rights investigations was never released. Interest in changing the constitution began shortly after the transition with failed efforts by the National Assembly. Most recently, in 2014 President Goodluck Jonathan hosted a costly "national confab" (a national dialogue) with hundreds of delegates. After taking nearly a whole month debating the rules of debate and then spending tens of millions of dollars on discussions, it made no amendments. The constitution has withstood such challenges, and democratization advanced significantly with Jonathan's defeat at the polls in 2015, which has effectively closed the chapter on the transition begun in 1998 under Abubakar. Nigeria seems to have opened to deliberation on the terms of its constitution, but over a decade after the document was imposed. In Chile the regime had to balance rivalries within the ruling authoritarian coalition as well as class tensions still visible as scars from the 1973 coup that overthrew the democratic socialist Salvador Allende. Though many details are difficult to discern even in retrospect, elite pact participation in both countries' constitutional processes reassured elites that their privileges would continue. The slow pace of constitutional change gave them less to fear: it was not until 2006 that Nigeria's president attempted to extend his tenure in office, failing because the legislature had separate interests and sovereign power that popular forces rose to defend, and it was not until 1990 that Chile took a meaningful stride toward democracy, with Pinochet losing a plebiscite he never thought he would ever lose. If pacts can reassure elites, they can also divert attention from the democratic institutions that legitimize civic power.

CONCLUSION: HOW TOP-DOWN CONSTITUTIONALISM
REPRODUCES THE FLAWS OF PACTS

At least since Madison declared "liberty is to faction what air is to fire" in "Federalist 10" (Madison 2006a), elites have been worried that the radicals would overwhelm the reformers and scare the hardliners and even the soft-liners into "cracking down" and stopping any regime transition in its tracks. Constitutions, it would seem, have, of late, been one way for authoritarians to control challengers within the authoritarian coalition, signal intentions of reform (whether genuine or not) to regime opponents (domestic and inter-national), and, perhaps, bargain over transitions of power and possible future regime conditions. This chapter has argued that authoritarians need institu-tional certainty as much as democrats do, and they need information about the behavior of their fellow elites to control actors in their own coalition as well as outside it. Hence even elites sympathetic to deliberative participation, such as Chile's softliners who did not want to be the ones to besmirch Chile's democratic tradition, part from positions in the tradition of elite bargaining/ pacting participation. Constitutions can force the hand of incumbent elites to display their democratic credentials, but, simultaneously, to reveal support for elite prerogatives in any transition. Unlike earlier eras of democratization, constitutions in the Third Wave have often not accompanied transitions from authoritarianism to democracy or the reverse; they have played many different roles and are fundamental to the new wave of hybrid regimes that slouch inde-terminately between those two more clearly determined categories of regimes rather than ever really moving from one to another.

Our case studies here reinforce three central findings from the statistical tests in Chapter 3. First, the most significant factor in shaping top-down con-stitutional decrees is the level of participation of opposition parties. In other words, when incumbent elites open the political process for other groups to participate (whether through mere aggregation, as in Nigeria, or with deliber-ation, as in Chile), they force their hands in pacts that yield more democratic openings. The more multi-partisan political processes are, the more likely they will succeed in launching constitutional participation that can transition regimes toward democracy. But if the political process is closed to the oppo-sition, such as in Venezuela (1999), where the constituent assembly was 95 percent hand-picked by the president, and The Gambia (1997), where no one even knows how the constituent assembly was picked, "window-dressing" con-stitutions imposed from above are more likely to be drafted. Incumbents may wish to appear to be seeking deliberative participation, but in fact in these cases (but not in Chile and Nigeria), they sought only to reinforce imposed constitutions via elite pacting/bargaining participation.

Second, and consistent with a broad range of new research on comparative authoritarianism (Brownlee 2007; Gandhi 2008; Frantz and Ezrow 2011; LeVan 2015), all four of these cases further reinforced the statistical finding that strong executives are not the only drivers of illiberal constitutions. That is, term limits on the executive and the existences of a system of checks and balances do not necessarily result in popular constitutions. On the contrary, our case studies show that incumbent executives can, and usually do, abolish the executive term limit and the existing systems of checks and balances against the executive either during the constitution-making process (as in The Gambia) or after the constitution promulgation, via constitutional referendums (like in Venezuela). As discussed above, in the few years following the constitution of 1999, Chávez (working through the National Assembly) dismissed the ombudsman, the prosecutor general, and several judges, and in 2009 he amended the constitution to guarantee himself indefinite re-election. The imposition of constitutional change to loosen term limits on incumbent executives is a *bona fide* pattern in Latin America (Hartlyn and Luna 2009; Eisenstadt et al. 2016), and not uncommon elsewhere as well.[22]

Our third (and principal) empirical finding is that constitution-making processes with lasting democratizing effects can and do emerge across a broad range of regimes and regions. These effects may be independent of the preexisting democratic conditions or the precise legal language in the constitution itself, meaning the parchment is less important than the process that generates it. While in most cases the precondition of democracy did not affect whether deliberative participation occurred, we did argue that Chile's democratic tradition may have self-censored Chilean softliners, preventing them from cutting off all policy debate, except in areas directly impacting their own prerogatives and futures. Our pairings of cases revealed two different modalities of imposed constitutionalism. In Chile and Nigeria, consistent with the logic of O'Donnell and Schmitter (1986), pacts over the new constitution provided elites enough insurance to mitigate the risks of democracy, while the softliner alliances, bridging the gap between the government and the people, took imposed constitutions and fashioned democracies. In Chile's case, the softliners found new allies in students and workers who launched three years of massive protests in 1983 (Schneider 1995). In Nigeria, the Abubakar transition government was haunted by the ghosts of the annulled 1993 election, which were finally buried with the sudden death of the presumed winner. Labor unions in the oil-producing south, human rights activists in Lagos, and civil

---

[22] Eisenstadt, dos Santos and Stevens (2016) identify Burundi 2015, Congo 2015, Rwanda 2015, and Tajikistan 2016 as other recent efforts at term limit liberalization through constitutional refounding.

society allies with transnational ties provided political capital for softliners, taking the struggle for democracy from the streets to the policy arena in the capital. These cases represent confounding results in our statistical analyses, yet the circumstances of their relative success stand out. The cases confirming our statistical results from Chapter 2 are less surprising: Chávez in Venezuela used popular support for state intervention in the economy to dominate politics, manipulating the CNA at each step of the process and constructing the autocracy his successor inherited. Jammeh in The Gambia adopted an inclusive process, which critics and allies alike say included religious leaders, traditional rulers, and various political activists. But that provided a thin veil of participation for the survival of a tight circle of military elites who, according to their own advisers, had little intention of listening. The ruse worked, and like Venezuela, the regime became invested in autocracy.

The elitist nature of top-down imposed convening processes generates additional problems. As Encarnación has argued, pacts (including constitutions) "freeze cleavages," that is, they make divisions permanent by codifying them, rather than creating flexibility for later compromise and negotiation. Such parchment may serve Burkean notions of trusteeship, but they do not allow societies to evolve in accordance with changes in the popular will. Rigid constitutions, which have a high threshold for amendments, are particularly open to this criticism. Furthermore, the elitist nature of constitution-making from above, where lawyers of a nation's affluent interest groups negotiate on their behalf, leaves out others. These elite stewards of incumbent interests may be technically proficient experts at writing constitutions, but the threshold of expertise needed to participate precludes the majority of citizens from having any involvement.

Ultimately, we argue through this chapter, combined with the next one, that deliberation and consensus are more durable than imposition. As our database has demonstrated, constitution-making "from below" does improve levels of democratization, even when popular participation in the subsequent stages of constitution promulgation – drafting and ratification – does not impact levels of democracy. This means that if incumbent elites incur the "original sin" of convening "from above," no amount of input from below can grant the final document democratic credibility. In other words, incumbent elites signal through the people they include at the convening table, what kind of regime they really want. And authoritarians do not want democracies unless they have to settle for them. Sometimes they do have to accede to the winds of change as in Chile, Nigeria, and more recently Tunisia (considered in Chapter 5). But an insincere commitment to constitutionalism in order to defuse social tensions can often unleash democratizing civic forces, even if these have not yet swept through Venezuela or The Gambia. As the chair of Uganda's constitutional drafting committee in the 1990s said, "You can never suppress the rights of people indefinitely. Sooner or later they will come up."[23]

Chapter 5 explains how this pressure from below works, and why it too sometimes fails. Using proxies for pre-constitutional bottom-up leverage, measuring the impact of strikes, popular mobilizations, and other grassroots pressures on the process variables, we test the drivers of different modalities of constitution-making and popular participation by illustrating the Chapter 3 statistical models with confirming and disconfirming cases, as we have done in this chapter. Ultimately, we show how social movements and new modalities of deliberative participation can push incumbent elites – autocrats and democrats alike – into more popular constitution-making procedures with lasting benefits for democracy.

[23] Interview with George Kanyeihamba. Kampala, Uganda. June 26, 2012.

5

The Logic of "Bottom-Up" Constitutionalism:
How Popular Processes Tilt the Odds
in Favor of Democracy

Despite the compelling evidence we presented in Chapters 2 and 3 supporting an expansive role for citizens in constitution-making, this chapter establishes how our view of participation differs from some of the expectations generated by the literatures on social movements, democratization, and plebiscitary processes. Cases involving the most intense grassroots "bottom-up" social movements, such as the genuine social revolution in Nicaragua in the 1970s (constitution in 1987) and the radical reordering of the post-apartheid regime in South Africa (social movement in the 1970s and 1980s, constitution entered into force in 1994), present several challenges. In terms of analysis with our Constitutionalism and Democracy Dataset (CDD), more than the three-year average after constitutional promulgation, as considered in Chapter 2, is needed to improve levels of democracy in these cases, or even to measure the lasting effects of a constitution. Constitutions that at first blush appear to be institutional breaks with previous regimes may in fact amount to far less radical re-orderings, with elites embracing the path of least resistance in the face of popular pressures.

This chapter demonstrates that the circumstances that enable successful bottom-up pressures, as in Benin, Tunisia, and a handful of other cases, are relatively unusual. More typically, social movements that succeed in destroying the old political order struggle to replace it (Grodsky 2012). They must articulate, mediate, and occasionally moderate demands, rather than spontaneously present them at anti-constitution-writing protests. This chapter argues that where interest groups performed such mediating or aggregating roles, social movements were more likely to successfully translate progressive politics into formal positions at constituent assemblies. We define interest groups as factions of interests that maintain credibility both with restless social movement leaders and worried elites. In other words, we extend the O'Donnell and Schmitter framework from Chapter 4 by specifying how social movements are more successful imposing their demands on elites when they are able to articulate their demands as broader interest groups. This differs from some of the more radical visions of participatory politics, but we maintain that it explains important differences between bottom-up movements that advanced democracy and those that derailed democratic transitions.

In the pages that follow, we present the paired comparison (Mill 1888; Lijphart 1971) cases introduced in Chapter 3, which illustrate the range of outcomes of "bottom-up" popular constitution drafting. The chapter seeks to give more concreteness to the ideal typical patterns of "bottom-up" constitutional participation arrived at through the statistical analysis in Chapter 3, and to complement, through opposition, the imposed or "top-down" cases elaborated in Chapter 4. The cases discussed in this chapter illustrate that participation itself is necessary but not always sufficient, and that while deliberation is the normatively ideal form that participation should take, popular participation can also take the form of mere aggregation, and even then that does not rule out a constructive role for elite pacts. Democracy-improving constitutions require structured participation directed into specific proposals at constituent assemblies. Social mobilization, online suggestions, and Facebook "likes" of provisions (see discussion of Egypt below and also Maboudi and Nadi 2016) are not sufficient. Iceland, and other cases where democratically negotiated constitutions are never implemented, like Eritrea 1996 (see Selassie 2010, 76), helped turn our focus away from the social movements literature, and toward the intersection of where such movements attain political opportunities to reconfigure themselves as interests promoting constitutional provisions or processes. In other words, cases like Eritrea and Iceland instruct us that all the social movement participation in the world cannot generate greater democracy. Deliberation requires that groups participate at the constituent assembly bargaining table, rather than just bang on the barricades outside.

Indeed, constitution-drafting from below is not simply about social movements; it is about prompting social movements to ally (and trust) intermediaries, in the name of citizens, more broadly, when they see political opportunities, and to focus on the construction of equitable, representative, and participatory institutions for channeling substantive disagreements. Przeworski presciently reminded us that while democracy cannot result from substantive compromise, it can emerge from institutional compromise (Przeworski 1988). Even more pointedly, he later warned that "the people" as political subjects must be differentiated from "the people" as a source of governing authority. "We are ruled by others," he writes, "and the only authority that justifies this fact is that the rulers act on bequest of 'the people' expressed in elections" (Przeworski 2010, 165). We would add constituent assemblies as a means through which political subjects need to have a role in expressing their preferences for the types of institutions constructed. The process is extremely political, but the result should be the routinization of conflict through institutional channels with less discretionary and subjective resolution. "The people" must think they are playing a role in the construction of government, just as they do in Przeworski's regular elections in democracies.

THE POWER OF "BOTTOM-UP" POPULAR CONSTITUTION DRAFTING WHEN REFORMERS TAKE THE LEAD

The twenty-first century opened with democratic backsliding, semi-authoritarianism, and hybrid regimes. These new realities make it all the more important – from empirical and normative perspectives – to consider the contexts and consequences of new constitutions. This new generation of constitutions also coincided with shifts in constitutionalism. Prevailing approaches to constitutions focus on content, the conditions influencing successful implementation, or their impact on subsequent institutional configurations, such as presidential or parliamentary government. But, as we showed in Chapter 2, democratic "content" measured as the existence of independent human rights commissions, the head of state selection method, and voter restrictions does not determine post-promulgation levels of democracy.

Rather than assuming that constitutions amount to foundational documents, this book has sought to show how constitutions often come to be viewed as precursor "contracts" to founding elections. As elaborated in Chapter 4, O'Donnell and Schmitter (1986) portrayed constitutions as core elements of pacts during the Third Wave that would lock in place elite "buy-in." This view of constitutions as contested expressions in ongoing historical and political processes seems more consistent with less teleological views of democracy as evidenced by the twenty-first-century reality of authoritarian reversion and hybrid regimes. As of 2015, democracy showed more declines than gains in civil and political rights worldwide for a full decade (Freedom House 2015). Indeed, considering constitutions as mere iterations in decades-long intra-elite bargaining processes becomes all the more important from empirical and normative perspectives. The Arab Spring, like Uganda's constitution-making process that appeared to have all the hallmarks of popular participation (at least in terms of number of citizens involved), has thus far yielded only limited symbolic societal gains. Institutional advances have proven ephemeral due to elite pacting/bargaining management of processes that aspired to deliberative democracy.

As we saw in Chapter 4, elite-imposed constitutions tend to produce authoritarian outcomes through elite pacting/bargaining forms of participation.

Are "bottom-up" popular processes any better at establishing or improving democracies? The answer is a qualified one. While elite-driven pacting through constitutions does not yield democratic openings, popular bottom-up processes only do so under particular circumstances. Indeed, we have empirically established that true deliberative and participatory constitution-making has lasting, positive impacts on democracy. Statistical tests in Chapter 2 demonstrated a strong correlation between our *process* variable and different measures of democracy at different points of time, establishing that popular convening of constitutional processes does improve levels of democracy later. The tests withstood robustness checks for endogeneity and across a broad range of controls. But what does such popular participatory constitution-making look like, and under what circumstances does it occur? And what is the line between genuine popular participation with deliberation on the one hand, and elite-induced populism with mere aggregation of popular demands, on the other hand? In other words, how can we tell that incumbent rulers are seeking to foster genuine societal participation in good faith, rather than just getting citizen "rubber stamps" to legitimize whatever they decide? In Chapter 3 we turned our independent variable, *process*, into a dependent variable in order to identify conditions conducive to popular participation in constitution-making since 1974. Our goal with that chapter was to test whether imposed "top-down" and popular "bottom-up" pressures respectively, have significant impacts on constitutional processes. We also provide strong theoretical justifications for each hypothesis, grounded in the comparative literature and illustrated through a discussion of cases. Just as Chapter 4 probed our empirical findings from Chapter 3 with regard to top-down cases, in the current chapter we explore bottom-up cases.

We do not claim the people's will should be automatically revered, but we do show theoretically and empirically that it need not be feared either. Thus, much as the social movement literature has made the case since the 1960s that ordinary citizens are capable of collective action, here we claim that those same citizens are capable of collective judgment through deliberation, and that constitution-making generates a popular rationale for doing so. Explorations of direct democracy, including the use of ballot initiatives, citizen initiatives, and participatory budgeting largely focus on governance rather than the constitution of government itself. Participation forms, including deliberation, explore how participation outside of voting (and in-between elections) is more than merely a democratic ideal.

Not all constitutions are popularly authorized, as the summary statistics for the CDD make clear. But a central empirical finding of this book is that when constitutions are sovereign expressions of peoples' participation, constitutions better promote and protect democratic rights. In other words, citizens are better off when they live in a political world of their own making. Moreover, "when citizens see a connection between participation and outcomes they are more likely to take part," says Pateman (2012, 12). We do not mean to romanticize protest, or to argue for some variety of direct democracy for all cases at all times, though we are hopeful about new modalities of participatory politics whittling away at the routinization of representation. Constitutions are departures from the routine regardless of whether they are a part of transitions to and from democracy, since they establish how representation operates (Altman 2011). Grassroots mobilization for democracy over the last few decades is a manifestation of ordinary people's willingness and ability to shape the boundaries of politics, and not just participate in them.

But sometimes, even grassroots participation is not enough. Adhering mostly to the structure introduced in Chapter 4, considering "top-down" constitutionalism, the focus of the current chapter is on "bottom-up" constitutionalism. After considering the fit of such popular constitutionalism into the deliberative models of the democratic theory and the democratization and social movement literatures, we consider two cases from our dataset of successful post-constitutional democratizers, 1991 Colombia and 2014 Tunisia, and compare these with two cases of failed post-constitution democratization, Ecuador 2008 and Egypt 2012. These four cases are used to highlight findings from Chapters 2 and 3, that popular convening can lead to more democratic outcomes, under some conditions. However, to better understand when "bottom-up" democratization does not yield democratic improvement, we present three conditions of failed popular convening processes, owing more to the politics surrounding constitution-making than to the convening itself.

These failures to democratize, even after popular constitution-making processes are: (1) popular drafting of a new constitution is more an exercise in populism by an incumbent hybrid leader than an effort to promote democracy (Ecuador [2008] offers an exemplary case discussed further below); (2) the formal rules of the new constitution are undermined by a set of informal institutions (Mexico [1917], and the successive 70 years, offers the classic example); and (3) popular constitution-making is undermined by a lack of elite consensus, meaning that "bottom-up" constitutionalism can be blocked by elites (Iceland [2012] exemplifies this problem). We conclude this chapter by noting that constitutions drafted and negotiated as part of the political elite pacts/bargaining considered in Chapter 4 cannot be studied in isolation. Chapter 6 acknowledges the limits of evaluating constitutions without their political context but also shows that, for policy-makers and scholars alike, there is much we can tell about constitutions and democracy from the level of inclusiveness of the drafting process.

Below we discuss the Tunisian case as an example of elite splits combined with mass mobilization, and Ecuador (2008) as an example of unified elites who recognize that their continued incumbency depends on cutting deals with parties and movements. We draw conclusions about the central role of interest groups and "from below" constitutionalism in Chapter 6. In the next section of the current chapter, we consider the democratic theory and its implications for interest groups' mediation and social movements (and their limits in constitutional processes) and also the molding of such movements by populist leaders. We then discuss the findings from the Large N study of constitutionalism from Chapter 3, and contrast this with specific and illustrative cases.

DEMOCRATIC THEORY, CONSTITUTIONALISM FROM BELOW AND INTEREST GROUP MEDIATION

The current deliberative moment in democratic theory has deep roots in the rejection of Plato and Burke, who saw those at the helm of government as ethical guides. In these more aristocratic notions of politics, process was hardly the point since a well-governed state was merely an extension of virtuous leaders who wielded the respect of the *demos*. How leaders were chosen thus mattered less than their character; the study of politics thus significantly entailed how to cultivate leadership values among the few alongside the followership of the many, whose bonds of loyalty were strengthened by the emergence of nationalism and then adapted to political science in the early twentieth-century embrace of civics. Schumpeter therefore argued that "the judgment of a qualified leader is generally better than the pooled judgment of lesser beings," as one of his critics puts it (Mackie 2012, 293). This view remains apparent in popular conservative interpretations of republicanism, in which democracy more resembles merely communicative expressions between rulers and subjects than a process that establishes a delegative relationship with the perpetual possibility of accountability for the exercise of public authority.

The alternatives that emerged presented new challenges though. Pluralism, modeling democracy as the competition of organized interests, was difficult to apply beyond American contexts, and excluded political demands lacking articulation through organized interests. It further introduced corporatism as a means of channeling the people's wants but casting doubt upon their authenticity or sincerity as they were filtered through official channels

(Schmitter 1977; Lijphart 2012). Tocqueville's civil society varied a great deal in Latin America – and indeed in inter-war Europe – in its voluntariness. So who really rules? Downs (1957) issued a completely different challenge to democratic theory: the problem wasn't how to translate the genuine will of the people into governance, since the universal franchise had arrived. The problem was that by aggregating citizen preferences, voting and appealing to voters paradoxically weakened democracy. For starters, the "costs" of voting were greater than the likelihood that a vote would have an impact, making abstention more rational than participation. In addition, as preferences clustered around a theoretical median voter, politicians would deliberately strive for ambiguity in order to increase the breadth of their appeal to the largest number of voters. Naturally, this further increased the information costs to voters struggling to determine which candidate statements were sincere and which were "strategic" – calculated to capture the most votes through ambiguities. The meaning of Downs' 1957 classic *Economic Theory of Democracy* was that as citizens act rationally upon their right to participate, the polity is inevitably left with an irrational, suboptimal outcome – a conclusion that spawned early variants of rational choice theory (Riker 1962).

Large voter turnout, especially in new democracies across the developing world, challenged Downs' speculations about "rational abstention." But the greater challenge came from social movements that erupted in the 1960s, leading democratic theorists to question the analogy of voters as consumers and to reject elitist notions of leadership. According to participatory democracy, popular participation facilitated a virtuous cycle because citizens became enlightened through acts of participation (Pateman 1970).

The turn to deliberative democracy has questioned whether it is enough to consider such enlightenment as a mere "by-product" of participation, and it has further doubted whether increased voting through referendums adequately enshrines democratic principles. "The essence of democracy itself," says Dryzek, "is now widely taken to be deliberation, as opposed to voting, interest aggregation, constitutional rights, or even self-government" (Dryzek 2000, 1). Perhaps even more boldly, deliberative democrats claim that the expansion of participation is not merely an exercise of rights – it is epistemically superior (Landemore 2013). Far from the suboptimal outcomes suggested by Downs, expansive and inclusive popular debate generates a "wisdom of crowds" (Surowiecki 2004). Until recently, empirical studies associated this with either a "miracle of aggregation," suggesting that a statistical law of averages simply canceled out inaccurate answers to a given question, or alternatively that voters can achieve a better average as long as they vote sincerely and independently. Deliberative democrats have countered that the key mechanism is actually "cognitive diversity" – the interaction of people's different models for interpreting and predicting the world (Landemore 2012; Hong and Page 2012). The interactive component is more co-constitutive and constructive, than simply aggregative.

Arguably, we shed little new light on theories of collective wisdom. But our theory is nevertheless important because it suggests that cognitive diversity improves constitution-making outcomes through a process that utilizes deliberation for making judgment and arriving at compromise, rather than estimating the truth through aggregation or averaging. In this sense, cognitive diversity is the social psychology behind what political science calls "inclusion" when it adopts proxies such as ethnolinguistic diversity. Moreover, our theory introduces interest groups as deliberative mechanisms. Cognitive diversity eventually reaches a point of diminishing returns, creating strong incentives for citizens to free-ride on the information-gathering of others, a phenomenon that Bentham observed in the British parliament (Elster 2012). In our view, interest groups thus constitute bundles of preferences; they perform functions such as providing expertise and reducing information costs. This means that citizens are not necessarily delegating away rights to participate or passively observing any miracles of aggregation. Rather, citizens are acting through interest groups as mid-level institutions that channel their preferences.

In practical terms, this participation takes different shapes. For example, a key finding of Lijphart's (2012) seminal study on models of democracy is that countries have either strong corporatist traditions that foster consensus, or lively multiparty systems that mediate citizens' demands – but countries do not need both. Our understanding of interest groups is similar in that they reduce the "noise" of individual voices without compromising them, and it is broader in the sense that we are not discussing interest groups in the pluralist tradition of politics. Interest groups constitute the moment when mediation occurs, and it is this moment in which citizens obtain sustainable leverage that can translate preferences into constitutional language for drafters.

Recall from Chapter 3 our argument that "top-down" and "bottom-up" pressures do affect constitution-making. In Chapter 4 we illustrated the form taken by "top-down" constitution-making, based on findings from Chapter 3 showing how some forms of executive constraint and limits on electoral competition impacted the form of participation taken by constitution-making. In the current chapter we show how "bottom-up" pressures from society – through interest group mediation – also affect constitutionalism. As shown statistically in Chapter 3, the greater the number of strikes, which we take as a proxy for targeted, organized, and peaceful civilian pressure, the more likely a society – and its elites – will undertake popular constitution-making processes.

Demonstrations (as measured by Banks and Wilson [2016], as were strikes) do not have a similarly significant effect, and violence (also measured by Banks and Wilson [2016]) has a negative but insignificant effect on prospects for a popular drafting process.

In Chapter 4 we addressed why elites would bind their hands – or perhaps believe they are not doing so – by drafting a new constitution via elite pacting/bargaining (i.e. as a deal between hardliners and softliners inside the incumbent's coalition). Using the cases of Venezuela (1999) and The Gambia (1997), we showed how closed systems do indeed gravitate toward elite control, and that democracies *do* sometimes adopt top-down elite-controlled constitution-making modalities. This reinforces our claim that the modality of constitution-making participation is not endogenous to regime type. We also described a second pair of cases where, despite elite pacting, events on the ground overwhelmed plans for authoritarian perpetuation, yielding more democratic regimes in Chile (1980) and Nigeria (1999) despite the absence of deliberative participation.

Here, we discuss interactions between social movements and interest groups and incumbent elites in power in order to explain the basis for successful democratizing constitutionalism "from below." Then we consider a pair of cases illustrating our theme here, that citizen participation can readily yield popular constitution-drafting, especially when the political vacuum created by elites' division is filled by strong civil society and interest groups that represent the general public. Tunisia (2014) and Colombia (1991) are examples of successful constitution-making from below that integrated actual deliberation into participation. In these nations the elites were at a crossroads, facing constraints due to either religious cleavages or drug violence and a strong left–right divide. They loosened up the forms of popular participation in the constitutional process as a way of breaking political stalemates. Then we consider how seemingly participatory processes in Ecuador (2008) and Egypt (2012) failed to improve subsequent levels of democracy. We explain why these cases, where constitutionalism had popular qualities at the convening stage and beyond, are inconsistent with the overall statistical pattern. In Ecuador, popular involvement, expressed in the massive participation in the constituent assembly, was ultimately sacrificed to populist efforts by the president to forge a governing coalition. In Egypt, popular aggregation (but not deliberation) fell by the wayside when elites lost control of the process, cracked down on participation, and even failed to reinstate a limited form of elite pacting/bargaining.

Recall that O'Donnell and Schmitter (1986) suggested the interests of authoritarian regime incumbents who favored democratic transitions and those who opposed them could be analyzed as a binary, strategic calculus, usually between "hardliners," who sought to defend the authoritarian *status quo* and limit political uncertainty, and "softliners," who saw openings as opportunities for the opposition to let off steam and therefore stabilize the regime. While such analysis was mostly suitable for the elite pacting constitutions from above (analyzed in Chapter 4), it was Przeworski who brought regime opponents within the model (according them agency beyond just how they impacted softliner positions) and divided them into "reformers" and "radicals" (Przeworski 1991, 68–9). That logic is critical to this chapter, as reinforced by Linz and Stepan (1996), who further qualified transitions as a four-player game, since hardliners and softliners could have allies outside the regime; and transitions would only occur, they argued, if the moderates outside the regime had sufficient autonomy to organize. Elite agreement within the ruling coalition remains essential for a democratizing constitution, just as it does for a democratic transition, by this logic, but events outside the coalition are also decisive. Indeed, Przeworski's vital distinction opens the way for considering social movements as interest groups pressuring from outside.

Social movement theorists McAdam et al. (1996, 132) famously defined political opportunities (as a cause of social movements) as arising for movements from several factors highly relevant to popular constitutions: "(a) increasing popular access to the political system, (b) divisions within the elite, (c) the availability of elite allies, and (d) diminishing state repression." The presence of any of these political opportunities provides citizens with a unique opportunity to influence their constitution. During moments of transition, citizens use their "collective judgment" and rally around "reformers." Empowered by "bottom-up" pressure, "reformers" are more likely to ally with softliners within the regime, as was the case in Colombia and Tunisia, where sympathetic softliners elevated their form of participation from mere aggregation to deliberation. Scholars like Goodwin and Jasper (1999, 28) have criticized the political opportunities structure approach to the study of social movements by McAdams and others such as democracy scholars Tarrow (1994) and Tilly (2007) as "tautological, trivial, inadequate, or just plain wrong." However, Goodwin and Jasper's preferred approach, based on structural explanations, undermines the agency of political actors and is of little or no use in trying to understand the importance of processes such as the drafting of constitutions. As noted extensively, the agency of factions within the incumbents and the opposition motivate change in the interest group approach we have adopted.

In this chapter we consider social movements and outline their interactions with (or "family resemblances" to) interest groups pressuring for new constitutions. Using Przeworski's extension of O'Donnell and Schmitter, we apply this interest-based framework to a range of cases, describing a few that succeed (Colombia [1991] and Tunisia [2014]), and others that fail. Failure to democratize as a result of constitution implementation can occur for many reasons, as demonstrated statistically in Chapter 2.

We show here that in the presence of political opportunities, such as when elites lose control (as in Colombia [1991]) or when there is elite division (as in Tunisia [2014]), if interest groups or Przeworski's "reformers" take control of the process, it will yield bottom-up or popular constitutional participation. The bottom-up process will fail, however, if no interest group can fill the gap between popular pressure and elites; mass action without interest aggregation into the constitutional process yields ineffectiveness. The case in point is Egypt (2012), where there was no strong interest group to utilize the political opportunity created by severe elite division (Stepan and Linz 2013). Similarly, when the incumbent elites are guardians and promoters of the bottom-up process, but only for populist reasons (as in Ecuador [2008]), the process will not yield democratization. Other problems, such as competing informal institutions, and lack of elite support to begin with (Iceland [2012] and also Egypt [2012]), can also obstruct the successful implementation of bottom-up constitutions.

Well-developed social movements are necessary but far from sufficient for "bottom-up" constitutionalism as they must be channeled off the streets and into the constituent assembly chamber. Hence, interest groups play an important role in mediating between popular participation and the incumbent elites, and, as evidenced in Chapter 2, some are much more democratic than others. So why would elites, especially in authoritarian and hybrid regimes, want new constitutions? And how are they sometimes cornered into constitutional change they didn't seek? One answer, as argued in particular for the wave of presidentialist cases in Latin America (Hartlyn and Luna 2009; Eisenstadt et al. 2016), is that presidents want to be re-elected beyond the term limits prescribed and hence rewrite the entire constitution to get new ones. But the broader answers we offer are two: (1) either there is no consensus among authoritarian and hybrid (or even transitional) rulers and hence interest groups constituted by social movements, parties, or other reformers or radicals are able to fill power vacuums (the Colombian and Tunisian cases discussed in the sections that follow); or (2) populist authoritarians/hybrid rulers think they can steer these outsider movements into the hallways of constituent assemblies without losing control (partial explanations for the Chilean and Nigerian cases discussed in Chapter 4). The Ecuadorian case is one where social movement interests were directed by a populist leader, whereas the Egyptian case is one where these interests could not be steered. Neither

Ecuador nor Egypt resulted in a higher level of democracy after promulgation of the new constitution. Most social movements still determine their power entirely on the strength of numbers (aggregation in its purest sense), whereas the power to affect the language of a constitution requires deliberation, or at least a role in any elite pacting/bargaining.

Before proceeding to the cases, definitions of populism are in order. To Roberts (Roberts 2006, 217), populism is "the political mobilization of mass constituencies by personalistic leaders who challenge established elites." The populists he studies bypass traditional power elites to gain support directly through the public by granting favors, programs, and material benefits. Other scholars in the economic tradition, such as Ascher (1984) and Sheahan (1987), define populism more specifically as, "extensive intervention usually intended to favor inclusion, with some cases of genuine achievements but with self-destructive regard of the constraints necessary for a functional economic system" (Sheahan, 1987, 29). In other words, populists put their own short-term interests (like re-election and popularity gained from granting favors and material goods) ahead of the long-term interests of the nation, like a balanced budget or national savings. As we will show below, Ecuador's president Rafael Correa epitomizes the use of a constitution-making process in 2008 for populist ends. His staff proposed the first-ever constitution granting "nature" human rights (even though, as Gudynas [2009] and Kauffman and Martin [2014] note, there was no evident way to implement this) while at the same time basing the country's extensive new program of welfare and redistribution on royalties obtained through extractive industries. We elaborate on this case of popular constitution-making that did not improve democracy, but first consider two cases of popular constitution-making that did improve levels of democracy.

CASES IN POINT: BOTTOM-UP CONSTITUTIONAL LEGACIES

Bottom-Up Constitutionalism Improving Democracy:
Colombia and Tunisia

Colombia's constituent assembly leading to the 1991 constitution achieved popular participation status based on several indications. First, elite efforts to negotiate the new constitution purely through elite pacting/bargaining had failed. Second, the populace (and especially students) had strongly advocated for such a "bottom-up" re-founding of the nation through a series of aggregation-based shows of strength. Finally, Colombia was trying to recover from catastrophic violence perpetrated by leftist insurgents, narcos, and paramilitaries, and by including some of these groups in the pacting/bargaining, the

Colombian elites demonstrated how much of an impasse they had reached through other means. The country was truly divided, and the hardliners and softliners had to involve the reformers and even the radicals, because not involving them sooner had yielded decades of political and narco violence.

The political context surrounding the constitutional process illustrated profoundly the level of division in Colombian society. In 1989, presidential candidate and frontrunner Luis Carlos Galán was assassinated, prompting some 20,000 students to march on the streets of Bogota. To Boesten, "it was the students and their movement that gave the project of reform an unmistakably democratic legitimacy and drove the process until a national plebiscite was held alongside the presidential elections in 1990" (Boesten 2016, 77). Colombia's governing elites had signed a pact in 1958 to govern that country among the two conservative political parties, to the exclusion of the left, which in part moved outside the system in protest. The elites' refusal to allow the far left to participate in Colombia's political process had prompted activists to splinter off and form Latin America's most ideological and lethal insurgent groups – such as the Revolutionary Armed Forces of Colombia (FARC, after the initials in Spanish) and the April 19 Movement (M-19) – outside of Cuba and Central America. Given the history of polarization and exclusion, what prompted the Colombian elites to allow the public – including demilitarized M-19 leftist insurgents – to have a popular vote regarding a constitutional "refounding" and then actually convoke a plural constituent assembly where dozens of former insurgents were given political platforms alongside the traditional elite families who had run Colombia for generations? The answer would seem to mostly lie in the elites' desperation to stop the violence.

Galán had apparently been slain by associates of Medellín Cartel boss Pablo Escobar. This assassination came after a 1985 M-19 guerrilla take-over of Colombia's Supreme Court building, which culminated in the slaying of a dozen justices and the burning of meticulously gathered evidence against Escobar and other drug kingpins. The homicide rate skyrocketed in the late 1980s and early 1990s as journalists, judges, and law enforcement officials were killed by the cartels, and political officials, outgunned and undermined by internal corruption, grew increasingly desperate. The students managed to publish a manifesto in Colombia's most important daily newspaper, ally with a broader student movement pushing directly for a constituent assembly, and in 1990 win the support of President Barco, who was desperate to stop the violence and reform the political system after his own constitutional reform efforts failed. Boesten (2016) argues that it was Barco's desperation to achieve constitutional reform, coupled with the national media's interest – after several journalist slayings – to restore order but through democratic means, allowing the student initiative to get on the 1990 ballot.[1]

After the public overwhelmingly supported the election of a constituent assembly in their 1990 plebiscite, the Supreme Court ruled that the constituent assembly could not be limited in scope, and the election was held in December 1990. Of the 70 delegates, only 45 came from the traditional parties, which did not seem to campaign hard for their candidates, while fully 19 of the demobilized leftist insurgent M-19 party were elected, two came from the communist party and related Patriotic Union, two came from national indigenous group representation, and two were from the rightist Christian Union (Segura and Bejarano 2013, 10). The M-19 rotated with Liberal and Conservative party leaders at the head of the assembly, and one of the five commissions, on justice reform, was headed by a student leader with a demilitarized insurgent from the Popular Liberation Army (EPL after the Spanish initials) as vice chair. The vast majority of the constituent assembly decisions were made unanimously, and the Liberal–Conservative alliance fell apart (Boesten 2016, 89–90). President Gaviria managed to leverage successful peace negotiations with the M-19 "and a window of optimism throughout the country to carry forward a bold constitutional reform project to open the political process" (Fox et al. 2010, 475). Negotiations benefited from "the absence of a strong ideological polarization in the assembly," according to Segura and Bejarano (Segura and Bejarano 2013, 11), and yielded one of the most inclusive constitutions of the era.

The exclusion from the Constituent Assembly of other major insurgents, the FARC and the National Liberation Army (ELN, after the Spanish initials), did restrict the ability of the document to deliver peace (Fox et al. 2010). But the fact that the document was much more inclusionary than any earlier national pacts did help political actors accept the existence of a new democratic space that had not existed there under the National Front. Under that Front, the two major parties (excluding emerging third-party forces which by the 1970s had evolved into full-blown insurgencies) undertook a constitutional reform via plebiscite, which "locked" Liberal and Conservative alternation in power – without participation of third parties – from 1957 until 1982. Had such intra-elite negotiations succeeded prior to 1991, which had provided authoritarian stability during the National Front

---

[1]   Starting in 1988 Barco, of the Liberal Party, had tried to meet with the Conservative Party's leader to hash out a referendum to call for a new constitution, but without success. Barco then tried to launch a bill in Congress calling for a constituent assembly, but that proposal failed, upon being linked to the controversial peace process and negotiations with the M-19 (Boesten 2016, 87).

decades, the Colombian constitutional promulgation might have played out differently. However, the lack of elite consensus, the external threats to stability from drug lords and, increasingly, by leftist insurgents and rightist paramilitaries, and the public's fatigue with violence, allowed the elite softliners to compromise with the reformers, and the cooptation of some – but not all – of the radicals. This lack of elite consensus, combined with a strong push by social movement interests, with softliner articulation, opened the constitutional process dramatically. Students and mainstream insurgents participated actively in the drafting of the constitution, elevating their level of participation to deliberative participation.

Tunisia is another example of successful "bottom-up" constitutionalism. Similar to Colombia, in Tunisia a division within the post-Ben Ali elites created a political opportunity for citizens to influence the constitutional reform process by rallying around strong and politically active civil society organizations and interest groups such as the labor union, the Bar Association, or the Human Rights League that allied – and had direct channels – with moderate forces in the Constituent Assembly. Following the Tunisian Revolution, which inspired the Arab Spring, the country's first free and fair election for a constituent assembly was held on October 23, 2011.[2] The National Constituent Assembly (NCA) was composed of diverse social and political groups from Islamists to seculars, leftists to rightists, and liberals to conservatives. The NCA was a dual-purpose assembly as it was composed of both "legislative" and "constitution-drafting" committees. Its constitution-drafting committees initiated an inclusive process, working with the larger body of NCA, even non-elected NCA election candidates, all political parties, civil society organizations, and the general public. Ironically, Tunisia was the first Arab country to adopt a written constitution in 1861 (Brown 2002) and it successfully adopted the Arab World's first democratic constitution in 2014. The NCA, however, faced severe elite divisions, challenges, and threats that could have derailed the country's democratic transition, as happened in Egypt. These elite divisions, combined with a power vacuum created by the departure of the country's authoritarian incumbent, helped social movements gain footholds in the constituent assembly via softliners.

Perhaps the most prominent threat to the country's stability was the severe political division between the Islamists and non-Islamists, which was exacerbated after the political assassination of two secular leaders. In February 2013, Chokri Belaid, a secular leader, was assassinated, allegedly by Salafi extremists

[2] The Tunisian revolution of 2010–11 is commonly referred to as the Jasmine Revolution, after Tunisia's national flower.

who wished to derail the country's transition to democracy by breaking the alliance of the moderate Ennahda and other non-Islamist parties. This assassination resulted in several protests organized by non-Islamist political groups that boycotted the NCA and demanded the resignation of the Ennahda-led government. The political turmoil reached its peak six months later, when Mohamed Brahimi, another secular political leader, was assassinated on July 25. Islamist militants also attacked several police stations and military bases and checkpoints around the country, leaving dozens of soldiers and police dead or wounded. After these deadly incidents, Ennahda and non-Islamist opposition groups engaged in a national dialogue that led to the resignation of Ennahda's prime minister, Ali Laarayedh, and his cabinet, and the formation of a "national unity government." Ennahda eventually lost both presidential and parliamentary elections in 2014, but its political compromises paved the way for the country's transition to democracy. A more divided elite could hardly have been imaginable.

Protests after the second major assassination sent shockwaves throughout the country. Those protests, combined with NCA representatives' threats to withdraw from the Assembly, forced Ennahda-majority constitutional committees to change several constitutional provisions, in accordance with the national dialogue agreements. In other words, the political turmoil and resultant political opportunities allowed the national dialogue to assume a true deliberative form of participation, rather than merely strive to gain some indirect input through efforts to forge a new elite pact. This could not have been possible without citizens rallying around politically active interest groups like the labor union and their alliance with the moderate forces in the NCA. The divisions in the Constituent Assembly allowed the labor union and other interest groups to lead the transition by hosting the National Dialogue. The alliance of "the people" via civil society organizations and interest groups and the moderates forced the Ennahda-led ruling coalition (known as the *Troika*) to change its position on several constitutional provisions. Unlike its counterpart in Tunisia, the Muslim Brotherhood (MB)-led Constituent Assembly in Egypt was not pressured by civil society organizations, rather only by its political opponents, and it was not yet ready to compromise despite the withdrawal of 40 percent of the Constituent Assembly members.

A key difference between Tunisia and Egypt was the role that the civil society played in the transition process. While the civil society in Egypt was influential in the fall of Mubarak and mobilizing participants for the constitution-making process, it was not successful in building national reconciliation and crafting new rules of the game to pave the way for democratic transition (Stepan and Linz 2013). Egypt's civil society could not break through the elite pacting/bargaining barriers and impose terms of deliberation on the process. In Tunisia, on the other hand, without the involvement of the General Union of Tunisian Workers (UGTT, after the initials in French) – a major group of the Nobel Peace Prize-winning umbrella – reaching national reconciliation may have been impossible (Chayes 2014). The UGTT, founded in 1946, with more than half a million members (5 percent of the Tunisian population) and branches in every Tunisian province, is a grassroots organization that has played a significant political role since its foundation. After the breakdown of negotiations in 2013 on the fourth constitutional draft (known as the June constitution), the UGTT joined forces with other civil society organizations, including the Employers' Union (UTICA, after the initials in French), the Tunisian Bar Association (founded in 1887), and the Human Rights League (the first independent human rights association in the Arab world), and hosted the national dialogues with leaders of different political groups in Tunisia (Chayes 2014). These four groups, which later came to be known as the National Dialogue Quartet, made political compromise possible. The democratic constitution that resulted from this compromise was approved by the NCA with 94 percent approval. The power of this union and its civil society allies illustrates, perhaps better than any other case, our statistical finding that *Strikes* (our proxy for organized and peaceful bottom-up pressure) has a positive and significant impact on constitutional processes. When strong civil society organizations exist to mobilize peaceful protests, elites are more likely to open up the constitution-making process. The UGTT played such a role in Tunisia, not only by mobilizing protests against Ben Ali, but also by organizing demonstrations throughout the constitution-making process, and holding national dialogues between the major actors after the fall of Ben Ali.

The successful "bottom-up" cases of Colombia and Tunisia shared three important traits. First, constituent assemblies were selected through popular elections that were advocated by both citizens and social movements exploiting divisive political environments. Second, political opportunities such as elite division (as in Tunisia) or diminishing elite control (as in Colombia) created a power vacuum and opportunity for interest groups to influence the constitution-making process. In Colombia these hardliners were particularly heinous; they were the emerging paramilitary vigilantes, who increasingly took matters into their own hands by committing violent acts against the leftist insurgents and the drug barons (and may have contributed to the merging of interests of the leftist insurgents who later financed their operations through alliances with drug traffickers). The violent and draconian measures taken by these hardliners gave the social movements an agenda, and their constant pressures wedged the constitutional process into a more participatory position.

In Tunisia the assassination of secular political leaders and Ennahda's controversial draft constitution (the June Constitution) increased the political division and created a political opportunity both for citizens and social movements to influence the process. Third, these political opportunities resulted in a popular bottom-up constitution only because strong social movements and interest groups were able to exploit them. Colombia provided an illustrative case in point. Constituent assemblies were less threatening to the elite *status quo* than the vigilante paramilitary "purges" undertaken by the hardliners in the military and civilian ranks, and the leftist threats of social revolution, which were proposed by the insurgents who did not follow the M-19's lead and demilitarize to form a new political party (the Patriotic Union). In Tunisia, the National Dialogue Quartet utilized the division between Ennahda and the non-Islamists as a political opportunity and advocated a democratic constitution that reflected everyone's view. In both of these cases, elite divisions created opportunities for social movements and regime opponents to participate as full deliberators in the convening stage of new constitutions. Weak and threatened elites could not control pacting/bargaining, and did not even try. Social movements had more than merely aggregated numbers on their side; they had mechanisms for more deliberative forms of participation that could translate popular cries into practical political demands at the constitutional table.

Bottom-Up Constitutionalism Not Improving Democracy: Ecuador and Egypt

In our database, Ecuador 2008 was coded as popular. However, the nation yielded negative overall impacts on levels of democracy during the average of three years after its constitutional promulgation (and has strayed further from democracy since, as per de la Torre and Ortiz Lemos 2015). Given President Correa's central position in the "new left" populism (Levitsky and Roberts 2011; Cameron et al. 2012) and his effort to win support through constitution-making, how do we explain the decline in his country's level of democracy after the constitution's promulgation? While inconsistent with our argument that authoritarians seek to bind the hands of others in their coalitions, create an "operating manual," and "window dress," it would seem, in this case, that the president of Ecuador really wanted to paint a utopian but impractical (and not readily implemented) vision of "the good society" (a very strong blueprint, in the words of Ginsburg and Simpser 2013), rather than implement a constitution that would diminish his own authority. Like the other remaining stalwart of Latin America's twenty-first-century left turn, Evo Morales of Bolivia,

Correa led an Andean nation with a large indigenous population[3], ran for president on a strong platform of promoting indigenous rights, and, like his role model Chávez in Venezuela, campaigned to "refound" democracy, pledging to anchor this process in the promulgation of a new constitution.

Taking a nod from some of Chávez's post-constitution referendums in Venezuela[4], Correa bypassed the Congress, which was empowered by the 1998 constitution to constitute a constituent assembly, and instead called for a national plebiscite early in 2008. After congressional opponents filed complaints about this plebiscite and Correa's subsequent one to "elect" his candidates to that assembly rather than going to Congress for that, Correa publicly threatened Congress and the Electoral Court, both of which buckled to his will (Conaghan 2008). While a direct plebiscite is considered more popular than a congressional vote – in general (and in our variable coding) – this one seems to have been an end run around the organized political opposition, which was in the Congress. While appearing to allow aggregate participation by staging a plebiscite, Correa was really stage managing elite pacting/bargaining.

According to the Constituent Assembly chair Alberto Acosta (interview 2015), Correa managed to "impose" 80 out of 130 members through this process of "apparent election." Acosta said he agreed to lead the effort if the president and drafters did not rush the process. Hundreds of citizens journeyed to the historic town of Montecristi, where the assembly was held, and after the initial six months of testimony and drafting, Acosta sought a three-month extension to adequately conclude. The president denied the request, and the government started rushing texts through the approval process. "The assembly lost clarity in its public participation and in the quality of the text. This partly explains the diminishment at this time of what had been a 'constitutional fervor.'" Acosta said in an interview that he quit President Correa's *Alianza Pais* party, convinced that "the constituent [assembly] process was just one more point in the president's effort to concentrate evermore his power. Correa is a *caudillo* ["chieftain"] for the twenty-first century."

Despite any diminishment in constitutional fervor, Correa's constitution was highly popular at the time and soon ratified, although not all of its language was implemented. As noted by Becker (2011, 47), "the political outcome

---

[3] Bolivia is 60 percent indigenous, whereas 30 percent of Ecuador's population is considered indigenous (see Eisenstadt and Torres 2016).

[4] Chávez's most notorious referendum was the one in 2007 where the populist president ensured high turnout in the referendum by putting a proposed scale-back of the Venezuelan work week on the ballot at the same time he asked voters for additional terms in office, beyond those specified in the constitution.

of the new constitution depended not on the actions of the constituent assembly but on whether organized civil society could force the government to implement the ideals that the assembly had drafted," and the answer is that civil society could not. Despite mentions of multicultural rights and indigenous autonomy in the text, the constitution proved difficult to implement (see discussion below) precisely in these areas where populist language was put into the document, but seemingly without prospects for implementation. In particular, Martínez Novo (2013, 120) references "indigenous territories and control of nonrenewable natural resources" as "problematic and ambiguous."

A centerpiece in each of the constitutional platforms of President Correa was a nationalist and ethnic deference to indigenous rights groups, and by extension, to environmental protection. Elements of the indigenous and environmental rights cosmovision were included in Bolivia and Ecuador, but both leaders quickly found them in conflict with their economic imperatives of funding social programs through oil, natural gas, and mineral extraction royalties. Given the choice between indigenous rights/environmental protection and, in direct opposition, the need to finance ambitious improvements in education, health care, and infrastructure in both countries in order to propel themselves to multiple re-elections, both have chosen extractivism, with all the environmental degradation and repudiation by their former indigenous allies. They established glorious constitutional blueprints of "harmonic life" (each repeatedly using the term in Spanish, *buen vivir* and Kichwa/Quechua *sumak kawsay*), and then utterly failed to live up to them in both countries.

"Harmonic life,"[5] a phrase taken from the Kichwa/Quechua cosmovision, was enshrined prominently in Ecuador's 2008 constitution (and in Bolivia's a year later) by an elected constituent assembly led by a highly credible academic lawyer, who codified the term (Acosta and Martinez 2009). Indeed, Ecuador 2008 was the first constitution in the world giving Mother Nature (in Kichwa/Quechua, the "Pachamama") "human" rights (Gudynas 2009, 2011). That lawyer, Alberto Acosta, said that the codification of indigenous rights and the rights of nature were due to the participation of hundreds of people who journeyed to Montecristi, the town selected for the Constituent Assembly based on its historic significance (Ecuadorian Eloy Alfaro had been born there). And Kauffman and Martin also strongly affirmed the participatory nature of the constituent assembly of 2007 (2014).

---

5   "Harmonic life," as interpreted by (Seiwald 2011, 22), is a fluid and relational concept, establishing a constantly adapting bond between humanity, nature, spirituality, and a responsibility for maintaining this bond for future generations. It prioritizes non-material benefits, a pervasive sense of place and fit with nature and among other people, and a sense of well-being derived relationally from one's historic place (Recasens 2014, 55–72).

However, in order to understand the populism of President Rafael Correa, we must understand what happened subsequent to implementation of the constitution. Correa claims to have adopted a developmental model based on the indigenous philosophy of *sumak kawsay*, aptly summarized by Kauffman and Martin (Kauffman and Martin 2014, 43) as a concept that bypasses the Western duality where humans dominate or conserve nature, because humans are believed to be an active part of nature rather than separate from it. Under *sumak kawsay*, "[r]ather than a linear progression of accumulation, development is understood as the attainment and reproduction of the equilibrium state of *buen vivir*, which refers to living in harmony with nature" (Kauffman and Martin 2014, 43). Codifying all of this in the constitution was an elite pacting/ bargaining gambit, as the left, where the populist Correa needed to stake his political claim, was dominated by Ecuador's powerful indigenous movement. That movement had, through aggregative participation, felled presidents before their terms ended in 1998 and 2000. In giving this group "window-dressing" in 2008, even though he would increasingly subject their lands to strip-mining and oil-drilling with low – and diminishing – environmental standards after about 2010, Correa won their allegiance for a time.

Scholars question the democratic nature of contemporary Ecuador (see for example Martínez Novo 2013; Conaghan 2015; de la Torre and Ortiz Lemos 2015; Eisenstadt and West 2017) as soon after Correa's extensive homage to indigenous constituents and their role in preserving nature, he undertook "populist polarization" (de la Torre and Ortiz Lemos 2015) and "extractive populism" (Eisenstadt and West 2017), where he simultaneously praised the sanctity of Ecuador's rainforests, mountains, and other environments, while opening these up to oil-drilling and mining by Chinese companies, which had the lowest environmental standards, to pay for his extensive agenda of social programs without raising taxes. Funding redistribution through resource extraction royalties, Correa by 2013 was directly contradicting his earlier *sumak kawsay* pledges by opening up national parks, like the Yasuní Reserve, one of the most biodiverse rainforest sanctuaries in the world, to oil concessions.

The danger of populism is a real one. As evidenced in Ecuador (and in Venezuela in Chapter 4), leaders on the left often sought to use the negotiation of a new constitution as a means of propelling themselves into office. While Correa was more democratic in allowing the election of a constituent assembly than Chávez (hence the "popular" coding of the convening process), and Ecuador remains more democratic than Venezuela, Correa's constitution does remain at least partly unimplemented, à la Mexico 1917–2000, particularly with regard to the rights of nature and of indigenous people to be

its stewards. Correa did not emerge as part of an authentic radical social movement subsequently moderated in negotiations with softliners and reformers.
Rather, he was a self-styled radical who shrewdly appropriated the most powerful symbol of the Ecuadorian left, the Pachakutik indigenous flag (which
had helped topple two presidents in 1998 and 2000, at the height of its power).
As a populist trying to maximize his immediate support rather than concern
himself with long-term political advancement of the nation, Correa's lack of
genuine grassroots backing grew increasingly evident after he negotiated –
but failed to implement – the 2008 constitution. The coda to the story is that
Correa did lead a move, spearheaded by his partisan majority in the legislative
National Assembly, to amend the Ecuadorian constitution in 2015, in part to
cut all term limits and allow all office holders indefinite re-election.

In Egypt, too, the bottom-up constitutional process failed to yield democratization, but not because of populist policies of the executive. Rather, it
failed because there was no strong interest group to exploit the severe political
divisions in this most populated Arab country. Egypt had the social movement
strength to win the battle of aggregation, but no way to convert the gains to
deliberation. The Arab Spring, starting in Tunisia, spread to the rest of the
region only after the Egyptian protesters took to Tahrir Square in Cairo. The
extremely publicized Egyptian Revolution, however, did not lead to democracy. On the contrary, it eventually resulted in authoritarian resurgence as military elites recuperated their positions and quickly converted some wayward
social movements into elite pacting/bargaining participants and ruthlessly
crushed the rest. The transitional period, marked with two "free and fair"
elections and a democratic constitution-making process, failed after a military coup backed by popular protests revoked the six-months-old constitution
and removed the first and only democratically elected president in Egyptian
history. The failure of the Egyptian bottom-up constitution can be well understood when we compare it to the constitutional process of Tunisia.

The constituent assemblies in both countries opened the constitutional
process to the public, but for different reasons. In Egypt it was to gain popular legitimacy, but in Tunisia the constituent assembly was already legitimate
(because it was directly elected by the people), and public inclusion was a
decisive tool to assist the troubled constitutional process. All three major players after the fall of Mubarak in Egypt (the military junta, the MB, and the secular liberals) strived to legitimize their actions, mainly because they were not
playing according to the democratic rules of the game and were increasingly
losing popular support. Both the MB and secular liberals were suspicious of
each other, accusing the other group of not adhering to the democratic rules,
and as such preferred to pact with the military. Soon after the fall of Mubarak,

liberal protesters began arguing than the MB was not trustworthy to lead the country's transition to democracy. After all, they were right to some extent. The Brotherhood's official website displayed its 2007 party platform, which manifested many non-democratic features. The MB did not even hold any meeting with the liberals in the first six months after the revolution and did not attempt to show a moderate view on women or non-Muslims (Stepan and Linz 2013, 23).

The MB did not make any efforts to improve its image as an illiberal political group. Nor did it reconcile with the non-Islamists and secular liberals. Rather than pacting with the non-Islamist revolutionary groups, the Brotherhood decided to side with the Supreme Council of the Armed Forces (SCAF). The harsh attacks of the non-Islamists on the Brotherhood over MB's illiberal policies and practices convinced the Brotherhood that the military is a better partner than the non-Islamist revolutionary groups. In other words, the MB preferred to share power with the military elites than with the non-Islamists, whether softliner or hardliner. After decades of political isolation, bans, and imprisonment, the Brotherhood wanted to rule, even if with limited powers. The text of the 2012 constitution written mostly by the MB depicts such arrangements. The constitution gave, more power to the military, elites than, arguably, all previous constitutions in the country. Article 195, for instance, stated that only serving military officials can be appointed as defense minister; Article 198 allowed the prosecution of civilians in a military court. The non-Islamists, on the other hand, tried any necessary and even undemocratic means to stall the constitutional process. When they failed, they decided to cut a deal with the military and overthrow the democratically elected MB president. The military used this environment of mistrust and the division between the non-Islamists and the Islamists to prevent the transition and eliminate both rivals. This was the moment when aggregation participation failed, as the military authoritarian elites managed to regain power, and did not feel the need to placate the public further.

A similar situation, more or less, existed in Tunisia. But in Tunisia citizens seized on this political opportunity and aligned with the civil society organizations and interest groups to influence the course of constitution-making. This is not to say that the Egyptians were not capable of "collective judgment." The reason that the Egyptian citizens could not use the political opportunity to their benefit was two-fold. First, contrary to the situation in Tunisia, in Egypt the whole society was divided into two rival camps: Islamist vs. non-Islamist (with a third group of bystanders). And second, in Egypt, civil society and interest groups were not strong enough to influence the constitution-making process (Stepan and Linz 2013). The lack of strong interest groups, with the ability to insist that their power from aggregation be respected, prevented Egyptian citizens from aggregating their voice and allying with the moderates in the Constituent Assembly, who were also weak when compared to the radicals. Effective deliberative participation requires the ability to leverage constituent claims as political demands, which the moderates in all political groups did not have. The whole process instead was steered by the radicals (both Islamist and non-Islamist) and the reinvigorated hardliners (acting through military elites), who were able to suppress all moderate voices through their own fortitude and ruthless willingness to repress.

The constitution of 2012 was forged under these volatile circumstances. In January 2012 the first democratically elected House of Representatives in Egypt began its duties including electing a 100-member Constituent Assembly. The first Constituent Assembly enjoyed democratic legitimacy (Brown 2012); however, it was dissolved on April 10, 2012, by Egypt's Supreme Administrative Court only one month into its activities, due to lawsuits by radical non-Islamist groups stating that the Constituent Assembly did not represent the full diversity of Egyptian society.[6] The second Constituent Assembly was elected only after SCAF threatened to impose its own Assembly if the different political parties involved did not reach an agreement on the allocation of seats to different groups. Finally, on June 7, 2012, an agreement was reached among representatives of 22 parties and the military.[7] In the new Constituent Assembly 39 members were elected from the sitting House of Representatives dominated by the MB's Freedom and Justice Party and the Salafist Nur Party. Six seats were allocated to judges and nine to law experts, and one seat each was allocated to the armed forces, police, and Justice Ministry. Thirteen seats were given to unions, five to al-Azhar University, four to the Coptic Orthodox Church of Egypt, and the remaining 21 went to public figures.[8]

The MB-dominated Constituent Assembly opened the process to the general public in order to demonstrate its legitimacy as a democratic institution working under democratic norms of transparency and public inclusion. The response from the public, which was already demonstrating for inclusive and democratic constitution-making in Tahrir Square, was profound. In fewer than four months, almost 100,000 people participated through official means (both online and in meetings), providing the Constituent Assembly with more than 113,000 suggestions for the constitution. But the large number of public contributions turned out to be meaningless because of the MB and secular liberals' struggles over the future of Egypt. The result was a call for the boycott

---

6   *BBC News*, Middle East. April 10, 2012.
7   *BBC News*, Middle East. June 8, 2012.
8   Ibid.

of the constitutional referendum by the non-Islamists and a very low turnout on the public side.[9] The constitution was eventually ratified with a 64 percent approval rate, but was voted down in Cairo and two other major cities. Frustrated citizens who saw their participation as a sham, used merely to legitimize the Brotherhood's constitution, sided with the non-Islamist opposition and started demonstrating against the constitution the very first day after it was promulgated. The result of this alliance was the *Tamarod* (Rebel) Campaign, which mobilized millions of anti-Brotherhood protesters throughout the country. General Abdel Fattah El-Sisi, seized the moment and orchestrated a coup against the MB government, and ordered a new top-down constitutional process. Shortly after, the military, in the name of stabilizing the country, arrested both the Brotherhood leaders and the non-Islamists who opposed its rule and secured the transition back to the authoritarian rule. Unlike in Tunisia, where the departure of Ben Ali created a power vacuum unfilled by any political group, in Egypt the military could immediately fill the power vacuum effectively in becoming the hardliner incumbents after Mubarak's resignation. The military incumbents did not miss any opportunity to ruthlessly crush any person or group that opposed their rule. Furthermore, powerful radicals in both the Islamist and non-Islamist opposition, who overwhelmed the ineffective moderate opposition, and a lack of strong interest groups that could act as mediators of public voices in the Constituent Assembly, made deliberative participation almost impossible. Participation was initiated at the aggregation level when all groups agreed on the formation of the second Constituent Assembly, but despite several attempts such as crowdsourcing, it failed to reach the bargaining/pacting and deliberation level.

CONCLUSION: PASSIONS, INTERESTS AND THEIR MEDIATION IN CONSTITUTIONALISM FROM BELOW

Przeworski, in discussing democratization in the Eastern European processes that formed the early basis for his later studies of democratization, wrote of the centrality of agreeing on institutions even when political actors could not agree on what they wanted these institutions to do: "The leaders of conflicting political forces can agree to the actions of institutions while they cannot agree to substantive outcomes in the absence of institutional guarantees" (Przeworski 1988, 79). The procedures of convening a constitution (i.e. the selection of rules for the constituent assembly and the types of groups who

---

[9] Fewer than one-third (31.62 percent) of eligible Egyptian voters participated in the constitutional referendum.

participate in the initial convening process) may be among the most important of these institutions, in democratizing and non-democratizing regimes. Social movements were important to these processes, to be sure, in that they generated a demand from below for constitutions, forcing the softliners within incumbent regimes and societal reformers to reckon with them and close ranks against threats from the social movement radicals and, equally or more threatening, from incumbent hardliners.

The Colombian and Tunisian cases offer models of incremental change involving social movement participation with successful aggregation but also radical and reformer negotiations with elites that achieved the quality of deliberation. Beyond those cases, more radical movements have also yielded new constitutions without elite pacting/bargaining "buy-in," but typically this elite acceptance occurred a few years after the radicals came to power. In cases such as Nicaragua (1987) and South Africa (1997), for example, constitutions were designed a few years after the radical movements consolidated authority, but designers realized these movements needed more popular support to sustain themselves. Elites accept constitutional arrangements that are suboptimal to their interests when they perceive that they have no choice. Let us briefly consider these two cases of extensive social movement "power in numbers" aggregation and show how the radicals were able to push constitutional processes beyond mere elite pacting/bargaining, but also how the elite maneuvering was mostly able to keep regimes stable even in the face of strong popular threats.

Concretely, the leftist Nicaraguan rebel Sandinista National Liberation Front (FSLN, after the initials in Spanish), which displaced the corrupt Somoza dictatorship through armed struggle in the late 1970s, grappled extensively with the construction of a constitution, as mass movements sought to consolidate a social democratic constitution, while the armed insurgents had their own interests, and Miskito indigenous communities, who openly rebelled against the new government, had to be placated through the granting of governance autonomy before the constitutional assembly could design and ratify a constitution in 1987 (Walker and Williams 2010). In South Africa, the complexities of dismantling apartheid and transitioning to democratic rule required several years of negotiations involving extensive public consultations, an interim constitution, and a constitutional court established prior to ratification. According to observers Ebrahim and Miller (2010, 112): "More time and energy were spent on negotiating the process of arriving at the final constitution than on negotiating the substance of it." Acceptance of the new constitution in South Africa was part of a larger political negotiation whereby, according to Wood, the apartheid-era non-black elites retained control of the economy but submitted to international and domestic demands to turn over political control to Nelson Mandela's African National Congress (Wood 2000). These cases of dramatic political and social reconfiguring, involving the convening of a new constitution but not centered on that act, did not fully register changes in levels of democracy within three years before or after the constitution's promulgation. Our data do better reflect more incremental "bottom-up" changes where the constitution was more of a centerpiece of change; a focal point of elite pacting/bargaining, but one where powerful social movements were able to aggregate their force into leverage for deliberation.

As we argued throughout this chapter (and showed also in Chapter 3), social movement pressures do matter for popular constitution-making, but incumbent elites enjoy large strategic advantages when it comes to forming a constituent assembly and selectively excluding groups. If reformers cannot successfully push their way into the constitutional reform processes and remain as alienated outsiders, then the country faces a broader state crisis with social movements and upheaval. This is the stuff of social revolutions, rather than parchment reforms. Cases like Nicaragua and South Africa threatened to take this course, but were steered back to moderation by incumbent elites who were realistic and understood that incremental opening through constitutions and other reforms was preferable to their fates and fortunes than being overturned. Wily social movement, opposition party, and interest-group leaders exploited power vacuums – where elites were split as in Colombia and Tunisia. In Ecuador, elites tried to "fake" popular interests as populists seeking to coopt opponents and bypass traditional elites, which enabled them to successfully fortify mass power bases. In Egypt, radical aggregation did not translate into bargaining power, because the social movement opponents had no interest groups to translate their protest slogans into constitutional provisions. If in Mexico, peasant leaders Villa and Zapata abandoned the constitutional process to go back to farming after winning the revolution, thus losing the elite pact, in Egypt the radicals were forced out by resurgent hardliners and also by their own inability to institutionalize their momentary social movement gains.

The successful "bottom-up" cases of Colombia and Tunisia, highlighted in this chapter, shared three important traits. First, constituent assemblies were selected through popular elections sought and won by social movement radicals exploiting divisive political environments. Participation through aggregation yielded participation in elite pacting/bargaining and even deliberation in both cases. Second, the softliners had failed to achieve "top-down" reforms and were thus open to allying with reformers (O'Donnell and Schmitter 1986b; Przeworski 1991) against the hard-liners, all but ensuring that all interests would play a role in convening the constitutional process. In Colombia these hardliners were particularly heinous; they were the emerging paramilitary vigilantes who increasingly took matters into their own hands by committing violent acts against the leftist insurgents and the drug barons (and may have contributed to the merging of interests of the leftist insurgents who later financed their operations through alliances with drug traffickers). In Tunisia the Islamist hardliners also antagonized the moderates, softliners, and other societal groups by assassinating two left/secular leaders. These political assassinations were aimed at creating a division between the incumbent moderate Islamist Ennahda and the non-Islamist opposition groups. Third, and also true to O'Donnell and Schmitter and Przeworski, the hybrid regime/authoritarian/semi-authoritarian incumbents seemed to prefer the reformers to the hardliners, and the reformers to the radicals. This preference ordering may have diminished the radicals' roles in constitution-making, but the radicals still did find their way in as allies of the reformers, or at least as threats that needed to be placated through inclusion rather than through repression.

The failed cases of incremental "bottom-up" constitution implementation had to do with failures to aggregate individual citizen preferences via political agency, as illustrated so vividly by Iceland's failed but highly participatory effort, but also, to some extent by the ultimate failure to integrate Egypt's social media discussion into any meaningful constitutional reform. Mainly, the failed "paired cases" of Ecuador and Egypt did not succeed because neither government executives (Correa and Morsi), nor social movement leaders (the indigenous Pachakutik social movement and the April 6 and other youth movements) had no incentives to cooperate with other actors. That is, in Ecuador, Correa campaigned as a radical, through populist gestures and actions, but took office as a softliner and really had no need to appeal more broadly for support once the international prices of export commodities like oil reached levels that allowed him a sufficient surplus to deliver improved services. So instead of being the environmental president, as promised, Rafael Correa became the extractivist president (Eisenstadt and West 2017). Even in 2011, Becker reports a strong ambivalence toward Correa on the part of the indigenous movement. This ambivalence only grew, making ever more true Becker's statement (Becker 2011, 60) that "it is not sufficient to draft new legislation [including constitutions]; social movements need to remain ever vigilant to ensure that the government follows through [. . .]" In both cases, the radicals had no advocates to bring them into constitutional processes, and the threats to all, unlike in Colombia and Tunisia, were insufficient to prompt elites to bring the radicals to the table for fear of the consequences of not bringing them in.

Social movements, as expressions of popular sentiment, benefit from mediation. In the case of constituent assemblies to draft new constitutions, these movements especially need interest groups to insure against populism and to translate mass opinion into concrete positions on draft language. If the movements come to power abruptly and cannot transform themselves from insurgents to editors with expediency because they need years or decades to consolidate national control or transit from opposition to party in power, constitutions will either be written but not enforced (the notorious Mexican case), or written only after years of struggle (Nicaragua and South Africa). Sometimes, as in South Africa, radical change is needed and constitutionalists just have to wait until the smoke settles. In other cases, such as our paired comparisons, success requires weakened hardliner and softliner incumbents, a strong will to change, and fortified reformers bolstered by threats from radicals. Populism can cut short anticipated democratic gains from constitution-drafting, as leaders such as Correa and Morsi were not truly motivated to govern for the people; only for themselves. But Gaviria did treat their people as citizens rather than clients, and democracy gains resulted. In Chapter 6, we generalize from these experiences about the roles of participation and deliberation in constitution-drafting to promote democracy, and consider policy implications.

6

Interest Groups Versus Individual Participation, and the Gap Between Ideal Constitutional Process and Real-World Practices

Constitutions advance democracy when the people are the authors of their own rights. This book's study of constitution-making processes around the world demonstrated that transparent, meaningful input from citizens generates vital path-dependent benefits for democracy. Such participation accounts for an important empirical puzzle overlooked during the Third Wave: in our Constitutionalism and Democracy Dataset (CDD), only about half of 144 new constitutions between 1974 and 2014 in 119 countries improved democracy. We further demonstrated that citizen participation during the earliest moments of constitution-making is the most important answer to this puzzle. This finding casts new doubts on the lasting benefits of referendums – an increasingly common device for ratifying constitutions. By showing that the modality of constitution-making matters much more than the mere promulgation of a new constitution, our research extends and corrects the democratization literature. Moreover, by showing that the process that generates legal language is typically more important than the text itself, the findings challenge prevailing legalistic approaches and add empirical heft to innovative ideas from democratic theory. As we parsimoniously put it in our previous work, "talk trumps text" (Eisenstadt et al. 2015). New international norms of participation are therefore clearly justified. But the means by which popular views are aggregated and articulated impact citizens' ability to design lasting democracy and deter dictatorship, placing interest groups as mediators – and sometimes moderators – near the center of the story.

We developed our argument and demonstrated our results in several broad steps. In Chapter 2 we described our primary independent variable, *participation*. We then summarized the participatory model of democracy, which highlights the benefits of referendums and other modalities for direct citizen input. We then developed our core argument around insights from deliberative democracy, which goes a step further by insisting that participation must mean more than merely voting or delegating authority. Deliberative democrats emphasize persuasion without coercion, and the public justification of preferences. Throughout the book, we associate these ideas with a bottom-up approach to constitution-making, implying large roles for social movements and various forms of popular pressure. Chapter 2 also notes that both the participatory and deliberative models emerged as challenges to classical notions of democracy as "trusteeship," articulated by Burke, as well as economic models of democracy from Downs suggesting that participation was "irrational." Those ideas inform our characterization of top-down constitution-making as processes controlled by elites, who sometimes "stage manage" participation.

We then refute such elitist notions of democracy through two sets of statistical tests: a "participation" hypothesis finds that popular participation throughout the constitution-making process positively impacts subsequent levels of democracy. These results hold at different time intervals and even use different measures of democracy. Next, we disaggregate the participation variable into convening, debating, and ratifying stages in order to test an "origination" hypothesis predicting that the first stage, convening, has the largest impact on democracy. We confirm that participation at this earliest stage is most critical: democracy improved in only 45 percent of cases that incorporated broad consultation at debate and ratification stages, but not at the convening stage. Contrarily, 82 percent of the cases in our data that used popular convening, regardless of popular participation in later stages, show such improvement. We admit that neither test presents an explicit test of the participatory and deliberative models of democracy, and we eagerly await future studies that could shed light on what deliberation sounds like, rather than focusing on its benefits. But by offering robust results with our rigorously constructed *participation* variable, our tests support the core principles of these democratic models that argue for deep citizen involvement, broad inclusion, and transparency. The results also hold across a broad range of controls for level of development, natural resource income, foreign assistance, ethnic heterogeneity, population size, and age of the existing constitution.

At that point, we undertook three important tasks in Chapter 3. First, since our independent variable, *participation*, has three different possible levels of participation (popular, imposed by elites, or a mixture) in each of three stages of constitution-making, we provide descriptive statistics for the 21 combinations out of the 27 possible processes. The most common pathway is imposed constitution-making at all three stages, covering 26 constitutional processes or 19 percent of cases in our dataset. The second most recurring pathway is mixed in all three stages, which includes 16 constitutions or 12 percent of our cases. The third most recurring pathway is mixed at the first two stages of convening and debating, and then popular at the ratification stage. These three pathways vary across different regime types and none of them correlate with any specific regime type. This is important because it means that more participatory constitution-making processes are not associated with democracy as a regime that permits participation by definition. In fact, only 28 percent of the constitutions in our sample were drafted under democratic regimes, while 35 percent were drafted under personalist or single-party authoritarian regimes.

Second, to further explore the drivers of different types of processes, we turned our independent variable into a dependent variable. By demonstrating that the transparent, participatory processes are not driven by a country's recent experience with democracy, we confront a potential endogeneity problem in our theory. Using executive constraints and term limits as proxies for elite control, tests of a "top-down" hypothesis were indeterminate. However, we did find that more closed political systems, in which no opposition party is allowed to participate and when they do participate they are not allowed to get a high percentage of vote share, tend to have imposed constitutional processes.

Finally, operationalizing popular participation in terms of strikes, demonstrations, or riots, tests in Chapter 3 of a "bottom-up" hypothesis offer robust evidence that nonviolent, organized protest is far more likely to lead to participatory constitution-making. The results suggest that the nature of bottom-up pressures has an impact on decisions for constitutional processes. Strikes, in fact, represent all types of targeted, organized, and peaceful civilian pressure, while violent pressures usually do not successfully open up the process for public participation. Instead, violent bottom-up pressure produces negative results and leads to more imposed constitutional processes. This is consistent with Chenoweth and Stephan's (2011) findings attesting to the efficacy of nonviolent "civil resistance," as well as Mansbridge et al.'s expectations that deliberative processes promote reasoned exchanges and a mutual respect among citizens. Finally, through a variety of proxies for the content of constitutions, including language creating a human rights commission, we empirically debunk the prevailing wisdom that the content of constitutions matters more for democracy. Once again, talk trumps text.

As Chapter 3 provided context for where participatory constitution-making comes from, Chapters 4 and 5 provide information about how it works – and sometimes does not work. Using case studies that do and do not conform to our results, these chapters mirror each other in offering representative cases of our bottom- up and top-down typologies of constitution-making. Through two pairs of case studies in each chapter, we demonstrate how deliberation as a form of participation is superior to either bargaining, which privileges elites, or aggregation that reduces citizenship to the ballot. In Chapter 4 we focused on elites, exploring why ruling elites would bother to enter the uncertain terrain of constitution-making, which runs the risk of opening up politics. In top-down processes, elites are *the* actors responsible for making the constitution, with no or minimal input from the public. We illustrated this through case studies, chosen from two cases that conform to our statistical findings and our theory: constitutions promulgated in Venezuela (1999) and The Gambia (1996) demonstrated why the gamble to change the constitution paid off for the respective rulers, as they maintained control of the process and democratization did not follow. By contrast, constitutions imposed in Chile (1980) and Nigeria (1999) represent outliers in our statistical tests since they did have subsequent democratizing effects, despite top-down constitution-making controlled by elites.

Chapter 5 elaborated on the circumstances of successful and unsuccessful constitution-making from below. We introduced interest groups, organized social movements, and opposition parties, which mediate demands through softliners and reformers, and different organizational actors who can serve as intermediaries between citizens and elites. Interest-group intermediaries help induce effective participatory processes where they can accomplish aggregation without agency loss; that is, where citizens' control is rendered efficient but not compromised. Case studies again show how deliberative participation is superior to bargaining or mere aggregation. The key feature of successful bottom-up processes is the inability of elites to dominate the process, and the best check against elite control is the participatory ingredients in the earliest stages. This does not necessarily entail exclusion of elites, as some critics of deliberative democracy contend. Instead, our findings from our case studies emphasize the hazards (for democracy) of excluding the public.

The successful "bottom-up" cases of Colombia and Tunisia, highlighted in Chapter 5, shared three important traits. First, constituent assemblies were selected through popular elections agitated for by social movement radicals exploiting divisive political environments. Second, the softliners had failed to achieve "top-down" reforms and were thus open to allying with reformers against the hardliners. Third, hybrid regime/authoritarian/semi-authoritarian incumbents seemed to prefer the reformers to the hardliners and the reformers to the radicals. This preference ordering may have diminished the radicals' roles in constitution-making, but the radicals still contribute to the process as allies of the reformers, or at least as threats who needed to be placated through inclusion rather than through repression. We attributed the failed cases of bottom-up constitutions in Egypt and Ecuador to failures to aggregate individual citizen preferences via political agency. Neither government executives nor social movement leaders had incentives to cooperate with other actors. In both cases, the radicals had no advocates to bring them into constitutional processes, and the threats to all, unlike in Colombia and Tunisia, were insufficient to prompt elites to bring the radicals to the table for fear of the consequences of not bringing them in.

Egypt's failure to integrate social media discussion into any substantive textual reform points to a "FacebookFallacy" and the complications of crowdsourcing content. Without interest groups or institutions such as parties to aggregate citizens' demands and generate political capital to act on them, it's difficult to translate the talk to text. The lesser-known but no less important case of Iceland provides a cautionary tale of participation without deliberative forms. This chapter proceeds first by elaborating on the caveat posed by Iceland that even technology and social media are no substitutes for a process that can air and aggregate individual wills, translating them into democratic constitutions by making these wills part of a collective movement. In this sense, Iceland appears to have learned what many deliberative democrats already knew: the only way to assess individual identification with constitutions would be through the use of public opinion, as Maboudi shows in Tunisia (2016). Even more importantly, absent an interest group to aggregate these individual wills into a group platform (regardless of how true they are to the "mean citizen" position), the ideas and constitutional language suggested by such individuals will not find their way into any constitution. Interest-group advocates must actively participate in negotiations as representatives of individuals. Elites always have interest groups at their disposal, and they often speak directly as special interests without even having to formally consult others. But the populace often does not possess a voice, and when they do, they experience agency loss and lose part of their message as they water it down in negotiations and struggle to aggregate one message from thousands or millions of individual positions. The constitutional playing field is tilted to be sure. When popular interests do get to fully participate, it takes interest groups to serve as both mechanisms of aggregation and as citizen leverage in order for dispassionate rationality to translate into seats with power and influence throughout the constitution-making process.

Next, this chapter lays out the argument and some of the recent evidence supporting ideals of deliberation and individual-level participation, for example through "mini-publics." Such modern mechanisms of popular participation strive to offer innovative solutions to problems of scale (can you have direct participation in larger countries?), scope (do complex tasks benefit from deliberative participation?), and competence (do ordinary people know enough?).

We also discuss the strengths and weaknesses here of the interest-group frame-work we borrowed from the democratization literature in Chapters 4 and 5, and summarize how interests may be different in different parts of the world, but that their drafting-stage input is still necessary if resultant constitutions are to improve levels of democracy. We underscore the discussion of inter-est-group centrality with illustrative cases from Egypt and Tunisia and then, more broadly, by considering the forms interest groups might take in different parts of the developing world (Africa and Latin America).

Finally, we extend this argument about the importance of interest groups to the second (drafting) and third (ratification) stages, connecting the implications of individual-level participation to earlier empirical findings on plebiscites. We review implications of our findings about the limits of participation through plebiscites, which have been favored by the international democracy-promoting community over the last few decades. Instead, we conclude that such resources might be much better spent recruiting "front-end" participation of interest groups and independent civil society organizations. From a practical stand-point, one of our principal conclusions is that technical and legal training could give even – and especially – the least prepared groups opportunities to mean-ingfully drat and deliberate new constitutions. Furthermore, incumbent exec-utives should know that they may be better off allowing space for alternative voices at the constitutional roundtables; if elites instead try to shout them down, then the most enduring effect of the resulting constitutions may be strides toward democratization without them. We also elaborate on our key findings with regard to the relative unimportance of constitutional content compared to process, thus linking the book's early empirical findings to our later elaborations of interest groups, elites, and popular participation.

ICELAND'S DECENTRALIZED DRAFTING:
AGGREGATION WITHOUT DELIBERATION

Probably the most decentralized constitution-drafting process ever, Iceland offers a cautionary tale about the need to aggregate participation of individ-uals into salient interest groups, regardless of how well informed and enthu-siastic those individuals may be when acting alone. Exploiting the Internet access by the great majority of that nation's population, Iceland channeled public frustration with the country's 2008 economic collapse through a constitutional process in 2012. That process resulted from a "Pots and Pans Revolution" in 2008–9, where citizens contested the catastrophic mismanage-ment of their nation's economy and pressured Parliament to draft the first constitution since 1944, but drafted by the people rather than by lawyers and politicians, according to Gylfason (2014, 3–6). In 2009 Parliament appointed a Constitutional Committee of academics from a range of fields to conceive of a constitutional process, and then in 2010, Parliament took the unprecedented step of convening a National Assembly of 950 citizens, who were drawn randomly from the National Register, to discuss terms of the document under the supervision of the academic experts.

The resulting text was drafted by this Constitutional Council and made public week by week for comment through an interactive website where special interests received no special treatment. The final text was approved in a 2012 national referendum, where the constitution received 67 percent support (Gylfason 2014, 16).[1] However, as the drafting process had bypassed political parties, those parties had no vested interest in the outcome, did not encourage referendum turnout (which was only 49 percent), criticized the results of the referendum *post hoc*, and filibustered the bill until 2013, when opponents of the bill were returned to power, stranding the constitution without passage (Gylfason 2014). Nothing notable has happened since then.

What lessons might be drawn from this process? One political theorist (Landemore 2017, 31–2) argued that rather than establishing the Constitutional Council to actually draft and post text, "it might be worth experimenting instead with a larger and randomly selected group of individuals" or "forgoing a specific assembly at all and instead trying a fully crowdsourced constitution which used the technique of commons-based peer production." However, she acknowledged the process might be risky as participants could self-select in a way that represents special interests rather than the general interest. Another lesson, suggested by Elster (2012), is that constitution-writing processes be hourglass-shaped, involving: a broad debate before delegates are elected, followed by more narrow, discrete – and even secretive – debate by delegates, and then another broad debate between the final drafting and its submission for public approval in whatever form that may take (2012, 169–70). However, as Landemore (2017, 8) points out, "the Icelandic process, by contrast, strived to be as inclusive as possible at every important stage, and particularly at the crucial stage of drafting the actual constitutional text."

However, it may also be, as implied by Gylfason, that the decentralization of the Icelandic process left it without any institutional champions in Parliament or the political parties. As also evidenced by a widely crowdsourced commentary on the Egypt 2012 process (Maboudi and Nadi 2016), broad public commentary on constitutional text does not guarantee political support.

---

[1] The actual question (Gylfason 2014, 16) was: "Do you want the proposals of the Constitutional Council to form the basis of a legislative bill for a new Constitution?"

In fact, the exemplary popular process in Colombia (1991), described in Chapter 5, may have succeeded in part by including regime opponents in the Constituent Assembly, but still involving other interests, the de-constituting government and a range of societal interests, in the process. Prominently featuring Colombian student leaders as heads of text-negotiating tables ensured both that the resulting language would stand above criticisms of exclusion and elitism, and also that full consideration of the issues would be given. Indeed, these societies were so polarized that their leaders supported a constituent assembly, knowing this could not bode well for their hold on authority.

Most important for this book, the Iceland case demonstrates the futility of citizen participation through mere aggregation, without interest groups to bring issues from the streets to the constituent assembly. As we mentioned with regard to Ecuador and Egypt in Chapter 5, the most important factor in "bottom-up" drafting processes may be the inclusion of interest groups and political parties to represent concrete positions, as opposed to individual-level participation. We showed in Chapter 2 that participation in the drafting moment matters for whether the eventual constitution is democratic or not. What we did not specify is whether that participation could be at the individual level (as specified by deliberation theorists and discussed below), or at the level of societal interests (labeled by Horowitz [2013] as inclusion). Such participation (whatever its form) improves levels of democracy in the convening stage but does not consistently improve constitutions' levels of democracy in Stage 2 (drafting) or Stage 3 (ratification). We have, furthermore, extended the logic to give a normative value to forms of group participation, arguing that deliberation is the highest order of participation, as it offers direct appraisals and precise recommendations for constitutional language. While deliberation may appear to be a process between individuals, we have argued that in fact it requires groups to ensure a place in the constituent assembly to their designated representative. Aggregation is the lowest form of group participation, as "power in numbers" may be useful in disrupting the repression of ruthless authoritarians, but it does little, in itself, to offer precise and proactive policy positions in the way collective wisdom arrived at through deliberation can. Elite pacting/bargaining can occur at the individual level when it involves governing elites, who may act on their own or explicitly as representatives of groups. But softliners, reformers, and radicals, privileged with positions in these debates, get into the room on the strength of aggregation and thus negotiate as representatives of interest groups rather than as individuals. Hence, while imposed convening may be by individuals, popular convening necessarily involves interest groups.

WHITHER INDIVIDUALS AND "MINI-PUBLICS"
IN A WORLD OF INTEREST AGGREGATION

Tunisia and the "Sovereign National Conferences" (SNCs) south of the Sahara raise a critical question about the moments when citizens successfully seize control of constitutional assemblies, claiming sovereign control: What then? Egypt reminds us that participatory publics generally learn very quickly that constructing a new regime is even harder than bringing down the old one, and there are important reasons to be skeptical that participation alone will generate participatory constitution-making. Participants need to surrender their passions and bring position platforms to the table as interest groups. In this section we focus on several recent innovations in theory and practice that we believe reduce such doubts about popular participation, and indeed identify some new evidence regarding its benefits applicable during constitution-making.

There are still those who would argue that individuals need to get their say in vital issues like constitution-making without merely aggregating their views into a more abstract position, to be represented for them by an interest group designee. For example, in response to James Madison's case for republican government (rather than direct democracy) as a necessary adaptation to eighteenth-century modernity, Manin (1997) posits that when presented this way, the choice between direct and indirect democracy is a false one: the important characteristic of ancient democracy was the practice of lot. Random selection encouraged and required citizens of Athens to participate in decision-making. Equal opportunity for selection created accountability, since you don't know who among you will rule tomorrow, as well as mechanisms for knowledge (as distinct from preference) aggregation. Athens had an effective combination of "sophistication and diversity" to make this work (Ober 2012). Lot also solves the problem of procedural fairness in selection, as well as inclusion since minority viewpoints at some point get a voice through leadership. But then they also generate a new problem related to consent: random selection of the people's delegates is a weaker expression of consent than the affirmative act of voting, protesting, or arguing for that matter.

"Mini-publics" offer a modernized adaptation of lot by randomly selecting a subset of the population. We outline this here as potentially suitable in some cases of constitution-making. They have emerged as one contemporary institutional innovation that gives procedural primacy to fairness and inclusion while enabling a stronger expression of consent through deliberation. They are "reasonably representative" deliberative forums of anywhere from 20 to 500 people empowered to develop public judgments on a specific issue

(Mackenzie and Warren 2012). Dahl's hope in developing such ideas, starting in the 1970s, was that focused and amplified public participation on an advisory basis could reanimate the energy of early (smaller scale) democracies. To this end British Columbia established a Citizens' Assembly to review electoral laws, as did Ontario, the results of which were linked to a referendum. The Civic Forum established by the Dutch government in 2006 took deliberation over electoral reform to a national scale but played only an advisory role without an automatic referendum. Such participatory experiments have been used elsewhere on a range of other issues such as city planning and controversial scientific discoveries. Therefore "deliberative democrats are quick to point out that the environment in which citizens interact in mini-publics can promote free and fair exchange between participants," even though their ultimate impact on policy itself may be less certain (Smith 2009, 109–10). Steiner (2012) argues that this equal opportunity to participate remedies what he calls an unrealistic expectation that ordinary citizens *should* be involved in the deliberative politics.

Mini-publics are clearly an interesting institutional innovation advancing participatory principles. But we do not know of cases where they have played a significant role in crafting constitutions. The reason has as much to do with scope as scale: constitutions are such fundamental texts, dealing with such a broad range of issues, that they generate different expectations for participation than reforming an electoral system. The typical remedy has been referendums because by lowering the costs of participation they expand the scope of issues citizens have a say on. In addition to approving (or amending) constitutions, referendums have also been widely used with the founding of new states, the establishment of complex new models of sub-state autonomy, and the transfer of sovereign powers from European states to the European Union (Tierney 2012). In Chapter 2 we identified their significant rise since the 1970s, as well as some of their weaknesses. They arguably bolster legitimacy for reforms, but since they tend to get approved, some scholars doubt whether they actually gauge public opinion (LeVine 1997). In Nepal, Kenya, and Sri Lanka, one study calls them "blunt and clumsy instruments for endorsing complex proposals on the structures of the state and the formulations of fundamental rights" because, in the end, they are "post facto devices for testing support" (Haysom 2007). One of our key empirical findings is that early participation generates important benefits compared to such *post facto* proceduralism and the explicit – but weak – consent that it generates.

Beyond the issues of fairness, scope of issues, and feasibility, another major concern is whether ordinary citizens are really up to the task of taking part in constitution-making. Until recently, much of what we know about the ability of citizens' participation comes from referendums, which unlike SNCs, greatly simplify the costs of participating and the complexity of the decision itself. A study by Lupia and Johnston on citizen involvement on complex policy issues offers an important clue, since they argue that "voters are not as incompetent as commonly portrayed." While voters may lack information, they do not lack competence. Information is data, and voters often get it wrong. But information costs in referendums are inherently low because the vote typically involves a binary choice, and additional shortcuts are available. Competence is different because it "is the ability to make accurate predictions" (Lupia and Johnston 2001, 195). However, they also claim that the idea that voters can control elites through referendums is also flawed. Elites determine the wording, time, and often the subsequent interpretation of the referendum; in this sense, they might even be responsible for voters' bad information. Lupia and Johnson conclude that voters and elites *both* need to be held accountable.

The notion of citizen competence is useful because it reframes citizens' ability to participate in terms of relational thinking about consequences, rather than intelligence or education. It enables their views to matter through reason rather than social privilege or power. As a guideline, Fishkin (2009) suggests that citizens should be able to debate ideas and information in a public space based on their merits rather than the social standing of the person making the argument, meaning that preferences should be weighed independently of who offers them. This limits the opportunities for expertise to become a back door for exclusion or de-legitimation of certain views. Deliberative frameworks strive to maximize opportunities for non-coercive participation, and minimize socially embedded or psychological barriers to participation.

Also, even if elites are not trying to dominate the discussion, citizens may still desire their expertise. Or better yet, citizens may desire their own experts, but as our case studies show, effective deliberation still seems to require citizen control over those experts. Where citizens are willing to delegate such tasks, how can the process still satisfy Lupia and Johnston's standards of accountability? Chambers argues that through deliberative democracy, processes can contain "a publicity principle" establishing strong presumptions of openness that compel those making the argument to back up a policy, proposal, or claim with reason. Exposure can undermine the process itself unless it is built into the process, whereas publicity holds deliberators to standards of reason and truth (Chambers 2004). Where transparency can guard against agency loss, in our view, the use of expertise improves the division of labor for the complex task of constitution-making while minimizing the risks of elites coopting the process into an imposed one.

Thus from the perspectives of deliberative democracy, not only is large-scale participation on complex issues feasible, there is reason to believe that it has inherent benefits, but, in the case of the radicals in popular convening, they must be backed by the power of numbers. Tocqueville, who is not typically associated with deliberative theory, associates scale with virtue in *Democracy in America*. Democracies essentially face a problem of adverse selection: it is doubtful, he argues, that the smartest and most qualified leaders can actually be identified procedurally, through voting. Those who should run, do not because they are too busy being successful in other endeavors; meanwhile those who do run pander to voters, whose opinions are inherently susceptible to flattery. A representative component of democracy may be necessary, but it is also inherently flawed in the leaders it produces. The "moral empire of the majority" offers a remedy. It is "the idea that there is more enlightenment and wisdom in many men united than in one alone" (Tocqueville et al. 2000, 236).

Various ideas from democratic theory today extend the virtues of scale to other terms and modalities of participation. Landemore, for example, makes an instrumental case for participatory democracy. Rather than arguing that democracy should be valued for procedural qualities of fairness, etc., she argues that the epistemic quality of deliberation is a function of the number of people deliberating. Deliberation among the many, she says, is more likely to produce "democratic reason," meaning collective intelligence or occasionally collective wisdom, which carries qualities of experience or virtue. The competence for deliberation is not merely about making predictions, as Lupia and Johnston proposed, because it also values the *moral* judgment of citizens. Deliberation is meant to enlarge the pool of information, distinguish between good and bad arguments, and generate agreement on the most reasonable solution. Deliberation, whether among representatives or by the people directly, "is superior to the deliberation among the few," concludes Landemore, "because to the extent that cognitive diversity is correlated with numbers and provided that citizens are at least moderately smart on average, the more numerous the deliberating group, the smarter it is" (2012, 264).

This is known as the "cognitive diversity trumps knowledge theorem." Whether the crowd is solving a problem or exercising judgment on an important issue, scholars such as Hong and Page (2012) argue that the group will always be more accurate and "wiser" than its average member. Numerous scholars, including several with essays in *Collective Wisdom* (2012), argue for conditions such as diversity and sophistication, the establishment of a "judgment aggregation" procedure, or possibly a minimal level of logical coherence among the people's choices. It is important to emphasize that cognitive diversity here does not refer to a range of exogenously determined preferences, but rather the varied psychological orientations through which people actually "see" issues differently, and arrive at their preferences through different kinds of paths.

These issues of individual-level participation and representation are important but subtle, perhaps too subtle, for the power politics of most constitutional processes. As demonstrated by cases like Colombia and Tunisia, where bottom-up popular participation yields democracy improvements, the ability to participate in deliberation is due to the empowerment of radical interests. These radical interests may gain clout because elites are weak and divided (as in both cases), because international norms conspire against elites' pillars of legitimacy (the South African case, where apartheid was universally challenged), or because elites are weak after war, economic crisis, or other strife (the cases of Nicaragua and Egypt, to name a few). And the radicals (and their reformer and softliner interlocutors with the hardliners) must have effective advocates who understand how to reasonably aggregate thousands and millions of individual positions into one powerful, coherent one, and who can effectively represent it (rather than opting to return to their farms, for example). Even given the caveats above regarding individual representation (and that of "mini-publics") in central, albeit "low" politics processes like crafting constitutions, the key is still interest-group representation, or inclusion, at the bargaining table. Even the radicals at the table must have the power to bargain credibly with over-privileged elites, and they must have the ability to achieve the normatively best form of participation, deliberation.

INTEREST GROUPS, INDIVIDUALS, AND CONSTITUTIONAL PROCESS

Successful SNCs are rare. These imply that there are no entrenched powers; that constitutional processes are starting from scratch. The Tunisian "democratization through constitutionalism," which was the way regimes transitioned at the start of the Third Wave in Eastern Europe and Latin America, may turn out to be exceptional worldwide in the Arab Spring-era of hybrid regimes and authoritarian backsliding. In Tunisia, unlike other post-Arab Spring countries, the labor union and other civil society organizations made a crucial difference. Tunisia was the first country in the Middle East and North Africa to have a written constitution in 1861 (Brown 2002). Although that constitution was suspended three years later, constitutionalism continued to exist (at least to some extent) through several NGOs and professional organizations that maintained their independence despite several attempts by the state to subordinate, isolate, or manipulate them. Among these organizations, the Tunisian

Bar Association, the Tunisian League for Human Rights, the Employers' Union (UTICA), and the General Union of Tunisian Workers (UGTT) played a significant role in Tunisia's current transition toward democracy. All these organizations are old, resourceful, politically active, and with strong ties to the general public. For example, the Tunisian Bar Association (among the first in the region) was founded in 1887, or the Tunisian League for Human Rights was the first independent human rights association in the Arab world (Chayes 2014). Among the most resourceful organizations is the UGTT, with more than half a million members (5 percent of the Tunisian population) and branches in every province in Tunisia.

In no other Arab country has civil society played a significant role in transition toward democracy, and thus, had interest groups been ready for full participation in constitutional deliberations. The Egyptian state has been successful in subordinating the civil society, even if it did so after getting a sense of the consequences of aggregation participation. Although Egypt has a larger civil society than Tunisia, its political society was underdeveloped and it had no way of translating that aggregation power into interest-group participation. As Stepan and Linz (2013) argue, a civil society can play a role in the destruction of the authoritarian regime, but for the construction of democracy a political society is also needed. Although several Egyptian NGOs and independent organizations participated in protests against Mubarak, they were less effective in shaping the country's transition. Several independent organizations participated in the 2012 constitutional reform process during the Muslim Brotherhood short-lived rule, but they were once again marginalized by the military after July 2013. In many other post-Arab Spring countries, like Libya, Yemen, Syria, or Bahrain, independent interest groups either did not exist or, where they existed, their political ideology was divided along ethnic, religious, or even tribal lines (Meisburger 2012).

How generalizable is the Tunisian example? Chapter 5 aside (where we likened it to Colombia's "democratization through constitutionalism"), we do believe that the very existence of interest groups or at least a broad civil society coalition, as in Benin, is a critical precondition for promulgating constitutions that improve levels of democracy. Chapter 3 showed that social movements (in the form of strikes) conduce to democracy-improving constitutions, and here we address the argument from a slightly more structural position, that basic freedoms (like assembly and expression), combined with a modicum of economic development allowing citizens to move beyond the "politics of the belly" (Bayart 1993) are central. Where subsistence is still the economic norm, interest groups may form over geographical, clan, and ethnic divides. Where economies are more specialized, these divisions may be over representation of particular economic sectors or workers, and there may be more differentiated and more professionalized interest groups participating in constituent assemblies. Either way, everyone needs to be at the table.

THE CENTRALITY OF CONTENT

In Chapter 2 we argued that the content of constitutions did not affect whether and how these shaped democracy, using the existence or not of strongly democratic institutions (independent electoral institutions and human rights commissions) as proxies for "democratic content." Our negative findings, which by definition are difficult to feature extensively and thus were not discussed at length, do bear mention here because we need to distinguish between democracy as a regime type and democratic institutions. Our finding in Chapter 2 was that the existence of democratic institutions in the constitution does not increase the chance that the resulting regime will be more democratic. And we believe this to be due to the fact that authoritarians and hybrid regimes have grown increasingly adept at "playing to the [international lender] crowd" with provisions for utopian democratic institutions guaranteeing clean elections and human rights (and in the case of Nadi's 2017 dissertation, transparency), but really only offering such beacons of democratic light as olive branches (or favorable loan-term guarantors) for international rather than domestic constituents. However, just because text promises of clean elections and human rights (often unimplemented) do not correlate with improvements in democracy, we are in no way arguing that democratic constitutions can exist without such important safeguards. Constitutional guarantees of an ombudsman human rights commission may or may not deliver real improvements in human rights. But without such constitutional guarantees, we do know that human rights will NOT likely improve.

In general, the content of constitutions may have two democratizing effects: designing democratic institutions and regulating state behavior. First, the content of a constitution can contribute to democratization by creating democratic institutions. There is a wide and empirically important literature on the democratizing effects of various constitutional designs such as presidentialism versus parliamentarism (see Linz 1990; Cheibub 2007; Cheibub et al. 2014), federalism versus unitary governments (see Ghai 2002; Weingast 2008), and proportional versus majoritarian electoral systems (see Reynolds 2011; Meisburger 2012). The second area where the content of constitutions might be important for democracy is by changing a state's behavior through restrictions on its actions. Almost every constitution gives those living under its rule certain rights and freedoms and puts some constraints on the state's behavior to protect those rights and freedoms. A huge literature exists on whether constitutional provisions of citizen rights and freedoms have any impact on reducing human rights violations. One group of studies suggests that the best way to protect citizen rights and liberties is through the enumeration of rights in a constitution that provides protection from the state abuse of power (Rosenthal 1990; Elster 1993; Beatty 1994). Another group of scholars, however, argue that constitutions and their so-called democratic provisions are "worthless scraps of paper," conveniently used by dictators to window dress and regularly violated whenever necessary (see Sartori 1962; Andrews 1968; Howard 1991; Murphy 1993).

The empirical findings in the literature are mixed, providing support for both arguments, at least to some extent. For example, in a study of 39 countries from 1948 to 1982, Davenport (1996) shows that out of 14 constitutional provisions promising individual rights and liberties or restricting them, only three impact the state behavior. Specifically, he finds that (1) constitutional provisions of freedom of press reduce the probability of state use of political repression, (2) constitutional restrictions on freedom of press increase the state use of repression, and (3) the provision of the state of emergency clause in the constitution increases the probability of state repression. In a similar study, Keith (2002) shows that while constitutional provisions for individual freedoms do not affect the state behavior, provisions for fair and public trials significantly decrease the likelihood of states' abuse of human rights.

Overall, the empirical findings show mixed results regarding the democratizing effects of the content of constitutions. One of the reasons for these mixed results is the large variation in states' compliance with the rules that bind their hands. Let's go back to the human rights example. The Paris Principles, established in 1993 by the United Nations, serve as guiding principles for establishing human rights commissions and assessing their institutional capacity. The Principles expect National Human Rights Institutions (NHRI) to protect human rights – for example, by receiving, investigating, and resolving complaints, mediating conflicts, and monitoring activities. In addition, they must promote human rights through education, outreach, the media, publications, training and capacity-building, as well as by advising and assisting governments. A UN accreditation body then assesses the functionality of NHRIs (United Nations Office of the High Commission on Human Rights 2010). The Paris Principles gauge the autonomy of NHRIs based on the independence of the appointees, adequate funding and resources, and commissioners' protection from arbitrary removal (Hatchard 1999). Out of the 105 NHRIs evaluated by the United Nations, 70 countries were accredited as being in full compliance with the Principles' criteria as of 2014, while another 25 were "not fully" compliant. However, Freedom House that same year judged 10 of fully compliant countries as "not free" and another 26 countries as only "partially free." These figures suggest a tremendous variation in constitutionally established commissions' ability to impact human rights.

A mere constitutional provision on human rights commissions does not guarantee the state's compliance with the international rules and norms. Many authoritarian constitutions look very similar to their democratic counterparts. Elkins et al. (2013, 162) do find that "authoritarian constitutions tend to be less specific, protect fewer rights (especially those rights that are less common), and provide for less judicial independence." But they also find that authoritarian constitutions are very similar to the democratic ones in the levels of executive power and provisions of more common rights (such as freedom of expression). The constitutional provisions for rights and freedoms, however, have different functions in authoritarian regimes. As Ginsburg and Simpser (2013) argue, one of the main functions of authoritarian constitutions is window-dressing. Many authoritarian countries, such as most Middle Eastern states, have constitutions without constitutionalism (Brown 2002). These constitutions make promises for protection of their citizens' rights and freedoms, but the executive regularly violates those constitutional provisions.

Populist leaders insert "good-looking" provisions in their constitutions, mostly regarding rights and freedoms. In practice, however, many of these provisions are not implemented. As we discussed in Chapter 5, for example, Ecuador's populist president Correa included a provision in the constitution that guarantees "nature" its rights. Many of these window-dressing and populist provisions are either impossible to implement or not intended for implementation.

This takes us back to our finding in Chapter 2 that the process of constitution-making matters more than the content of constitutions in bringing democratic improvements. A democratic process is more likely to yield democratic constitutional provisions (Maboudi 2016) that will be respected by the state. If the process is imposed, however, even if the constitution promises various rights and freedoms, those provisions are more likely to be for window-dressing purposes. Our statistical analysis in Chapter 3 shows that certain authoritarian regimes are more likely to have imposed convening processes. The results show that there is a positive but insignificant relationship between being a democracy and having a democratic convening process. For non-democracies, only monarchies and mixed non-democracies have a negative and statistically significant relationship with the form taken by the constitution-making process. In other words, authoritarian monarchies such as the Persian Gulf states and countries with a mixture of different authoritarian typologies (such as Egypt during Mubarak), which according to Geddes's typology was a personalistic-single-party-military regime) are more likely to use imposed processes to draft their constitutions. There is, however, no correlation between personalistic, military, or single-party authoritarian regimes with the nature of constitution-making process.

Another important finding from this study concerns constitutional referendums. As noted in the book's introduction, referendums have been used as mechanisms of direct democracy for over two centuries, but their use overall and their use specifically as a preferred tool for changing constitutions is relatively recent and has especially increased over the last three decades. "Demographic and technological developments are fueling an unprecedented expansion of direct democracy," meaning that "legislatures are gradually being eclipsed as the primary creators of public policy," in some views (Matsusaka 2005, 157). Referring to a "new wave of direct constitutional democracy," Tierney notes that out of 58 "functioning electoral democracies" between 1975 and 2000, 39 of them conducted at least one national referendum (Tierney 2012, 1). There are arguably some regional patterns in this growth. For example, in Europe, the Americas, and the South Pacific, constitutional referendums remain popular, while close to two-thirds of Asian countries and a vast majority of Middle Eastern countries avoid them (Anckar 2014). Several advanced democracies, including the United States, Japan, and India, have never held a nation-wide referendum, even where they are common at the subnational level. In the United States they have been used to push for bilingual schools, gay rights, and the right to die, among other issues in the states (Braunstein 2004). Our study only included referendums on entirely new constitutions, and thus set aside important issues addressed in other research concerning their use for amending the constitution or for other major national questions. Countries such as Ireland and Australia are among the countries that have regularly used "mandatory referendums" to formalize decisions concerning territorial integrity or other issues (Schiller 2009). Other constitutional issues more commonly decided by referendum concern electoral reform (as in New Zealand and Canada), devolution of power, as in Puerto Rico, or treaties as in Denmark's consideration of European Union membership (LeDuc 2003), and of course the "Brexit" vote in 2016 yielding the decision by Great Britain to leave the European Union.

In his seminal study on the topic, Qvortrup says, "fundamentally, referendums challenge the basic assumption of the tried and tested specific representation of democracy. A referendum takes power of decision over a specific question back from elected representatives and returns it to the people" (Qvortrup 2006, 2–3). The direct nature of this participation is precisely the inspiration for referendums' critics, who have come from both the political left and the right (Qvortrup 2014). In contrast to the trust placed in ordinary citizens by deliberative democrats, opponents of referendums argue that they unnecessarily empower interest groups – especially those with substantial money – and they undermine representative government that is otherwise necessary for daily governance (Secrest and Norquist 1995). One analysis goes so far as to argue that European citizens should not be directly engaged in considering the creation of a confederation, concluding "the assent of the people is not necessary" (Podolnjak 2007). Others highlight the "strategic" uses of referendums by elites, who can manipulate the results by timing and wording (Walker 2003); this appears to have been the case in the rejection of Kenya's 2002 draft constitution, for example (Lynch 2006). Such strategies aim to legitimize the initiator of the referendum and amplify its preferences. But elites may also initiate referendums to avoid responsibility for a difficult decision, or because they seek to promote a policy otherwise opposed by a majority of legislators (Rahat 2009).

Our study is also notable for how its critique of referendums differs from such claims, since our findings embrace neither the Burkean defense of democracy as representative rule by elites nor the more radical notions of participation that can even be dismissive of voting as inadequate. A recent summary of the debate claims that both sides have missed the more important question of how referendums interact with "traditional" institutions of democracy (Hug 2009). Our concern is not too different: we fear that referendums have been routinized as devices for constitutional ratification without considering their broader effects on democratic participation.

CONCLUSIONS: FRONT-LOAD THE PARTICIPATION OF INTEREST GROUPS IN ORDER TO BACK-LOAD DEMOCRACY

Peasant hero Emiliano Zapata famously abandoned the presidential chair in Mexico City after sitting uncomfortably there for only a brief time (a famous photo shoot showed his discomfort) before acting on the realization that he felt more useful harvesting his crops in nearby Morelos State than governing and writing constitutions. His land reform pleas, which were the substantive agenda of the Mexican Revolution, were thus nowhere to be found in the otherwise progressive Mexican Constitution of 1917.[2] And Iceland's "frozen"

---

[2] The savvy populist and retired revolutionary general Lázaro Cárdenas in the 1930s took up this "unfinished business" from the Revolution and executed one of the most widespread land reforms in the twentieth century.

constitution remains thus, after perhaps achieving the distinction of being the draft constitution with the most public scrutiny (at least in terms of constitution draft commenters as a percentage of the adult population). When, as in the Mexican case, leading interests refuse to participate in drafting, or, as in the Iceland case, there are no obvious political parties or interest groups to champion constitutional provisions – or entire drafts – it is easy to envision these processes being dominated by those already in power. Successful constitutionalism "from below" is good news for democracy, but it is both a relatively recent phenomenon distinctly associated with the last few decades and it occurs under a relatively rare set of circumstances. Moreover, the Iceland and Mexico scenarios are likely to remain more common than the revolutionary conditions associated with Tunisia or the sovereign moments seized by citizens in Benin or Mali. Citizens have new rights to participate under international conventions, they increasingly have the competence and judgment necessary for substantive participation, and the innovations from the Iceland and Egypt experiments remind us how new technologies may afford them more time to participate as the costs of doing so decline. Even so, the effort and resources devoted to having citizens approve constitutions may be much more readily put forth as policy and legal training, and technical support, for interest-group leaders, and on efforts to twist the arms of incumbent executives to make sure they bring all parties to the constituent assembly table.

This book has clearly demonstrated that deliberation matters. And while more research needs to be done showing precisely how it matters and how it should be aggregated, we have, in this conclusion, argued based on logic and case-based evidence, more than on any statistical patterns, that interest groups are the key to drafting democratic constitutions. What we do know, based on case studies presented in Chapters 4 and 5, is that deliberation results when wily radicals manage to parlay "strength in numbers" into constituent assembly seats. And social movements can only really do this when there are interest groups readily able to absorb them and aggregate their positions into legal platforms tenable at the elite pacting/bargaining sessions that constituent assemblies inevitably become. We made the statistical case for the difference between the elite interests driving "top-down" imposed constitutions unlikely to improve democracy, and the "bottom-up" popular convening and drafting processes, which have the best chance of improving levels of democracy when the demands of social movements can be aggregated and mediated via interest groups, lending deliberative power to the people's voices. Borrowing from the democratization literature, we presented cases through an interest-group framework to further elaborate how democracy might be improved in popular processes when the incumbent elites initiate constitutional processes because they are divided or weak, and when there are social movements, opposition parties, and interest groups in the wings seeking engagement in the political system through full participation in constitution-drafting.

The lesson is to place constituents before assembly. But constituent demands still need to make their way to the constitutional bargaining table through interest groups that can both leverage popular pressures and mediate them. As the Third Wave's "foundation of democracy" constitutions in the 1970s and 1980s gave way to less democratic ones, over the last two decades, the puzzle emerged of why bother convening, drafting, and ratifying constitutions if they do not improve a regime's overall level of democracy? As with many explanations in politics, the precise motivations for non-democracy-enhancing constitutions, remain an area for future research, although it is increasingly clear that authoritarians, hybrid leaders, and even democrats might seek new constitutions to increase their own discretion as well as to improve the access of citizens to voice. This book has shown that whatever their motivations, incumbent executives "show their hands" at the all-important initial moment of drafting. It is that convening moment that matters, and hence should be the focal point of international and domestic efforts to ensure greater national participation in the resulting content of the constitution. It is time to restore some of the democratic agency to constitutional assemblies, which they used to have. The way to do this is to support underdog groups at the beginning, rather than whatever parchment emerges after this all-important process of citizen participation.

Additional Statistical Analyses as Checks on Robustness of Models

TABLE A.1. *Heckman selection model*

Variables	AVG Polity $t+1$ to $t+3$	Selection	Mills
Democracy_($t-3$ to $t-1$)	−0.11	0.04	
	(0.11)	(0.04)	
Process	0.97**	0.09	
	(0.39)	(0.14)	
Ethnic	−2.50	−1.28	
	(2.85)	(1.32)	
ODA	−0.09	−0.03	
	(0.06)	(0.02)	
Natural resources	−0.06	0.00	
	(0.05)	(0.01)	
GDP per capita	−0.00	−0.00	
	(0.00)	(0.00)	
Population (log)	−0.34	0.03	
	(0.48)	(0.18)	
Promulgation year	0.12	−0.10***	
	(0.10)	(0.03)	
New state[†]		−0.63	
		(0.72)	
lambda			−5.23
			(4.81)

(continued)

TABLE A.1. (*continued*)

Variables	AVG Polity t+1 to t+3	Selection	Mills
Constant	−230.70	203.47***	
	(206.70)	(62.31)	
Observations	92	92	92

Standard errors in parentheses.
***$p < 0.01$, **$p < 0.05$, *$p < 0.1$.
†Binary variable for whether the country is a new state born since 1974.

TABLE A.2. *Participation hypothesis and level of democracy stratified by regime type*

Variables	AVG Polity t+1 to t+3		AVG UDS t+1 to t+3	
	Democracy	Dictatorship	Democracy	Dictatorship
Democracy_(t−3 to t−1)	0.16	0.02	0.01	−0.04
	(0.22)	(0.10)	(0.07)	(0.07)
Process	0.14	0.90	0.02	0.09**
	(0.50)	(0.54)	(0.03)	(0.04)
Ethnic	−2.28	−2.55	0.14	0.37
	(4.41)	(3.09)	(0.22)	(0.27)
ODA	0.17	−0.09**	0.01	−0.01
	(0.11)	(0.04)	(0.00)	(0.00)
Natural resources	−0.03	−0.10	−0.00	−0.01*
	(0.11)	(0.06)	(0.00)	(0.00)
GDP per capita	0.00*	−0.00	0.00	−0.00
	(0.00)	(0.00)	(0.00)	(0.00)
Population (log)	0.96	−0.25	0.04	−0.01
	(0.69)	(0.54)	(0.04)	(0.05)
Promulgation year	−0.32**	0.05	−0.02***	0.01
	(0.12)	(0.07)	(0.00)	(0.01)
Constant	616.22**	−98.12	33.85***	−14.91
	(234.22)	(146.45)	(9.18)	(16.80)
Observations	22	64	20	59
R-squared	0.45	0.23	0.51	0.30

Robust standard errors in parentheses.
***$p < 0.01$, **$p < 0.05$, *$p < 0.1$.

TABLE A.3. *Stage one of the 2SLS models*

Variables	Process (AVG Polity $t+1$ to $t+3$)	Process (AVG UDS $t+1$ to $t+3$)
Strike	0.48***	0.46***
	(0.14)	(0.15)
Ethnic	1.37	1.21
	(0.83)	(0.87)
ODA	−0.02	−0.02
	(0.02)	(0.02)
Natural resources	−0.05***	−0.02
	(0.02)	0.02
GDP per capita	−0.00	−0.00
	(0.00)	(0.00)
Population (log)	−0.11	−0.10
	(0.13)	(0.12)
Promulgation year	0.04**	0.06**
	(0.02)	(0.03)
Constant	−75.26**	−113.63**
	(41.61)	(51.29)
Observations	81	80
R-squared	0.18	0.13

Robust standard errors in parentheses.
***$p < 0.01$, **$p < 0.05$, *$p < 0.1$.

TABLE A.4. *Stage two of the 2SLS models*

Variables	AVG Polity $t+1$ to $t+3$	AVG UDS $t+1$ to $t+3$
Fitted value of process	3.04***	0.26***
	(0.89)	(0.10)
Ethnic	−2.49	−0.02
	(2.99)	(0.27)
ODA	−0.06	−0.00
	(0.06)	(0.01)
Natural resources	−0.00	−0.00
	(0.08)	0.00

(continued)

TABLE A.4. (*continued*)

Variables	AVG Polity *t+1* to *t+3*	AVG UDS *t+1* to *t+3*
GDP per capita	−0.00	0.00
	(0.00)	(0.00)
Population (log)	0.38	0.02
	(0.42)	(0.04)
Promulgation year	−0.03	−0.01
	(0.07)	(0.01)
Constant	40.26	11.09
	(133.22)	(16.11)
Observations	81	80
R-squared	0.14	0.21

Robust standard errors in parentheses.
***p < 0.01, **p < 0.05, *p < 0.1.

TABLE A.5. *Correlation among the three-stage variables*

	Convening	Debating	Ratifying
Convening	1.00		
Debating	0.63	1.00	
Ratifying	0.26	0.43	1.00

TABLE A.6. *Test of collinearity*

Variable	VIF	Tolerance = 1/VIF
Lag of Polity	1.15	0.87
Convening	2.66	0.38
Debating	2.04	0.5
Ratifying	1.68	0.6
Ethnic	1.23	0.82
ODA	1.40	0.71
Natural resources	1.31	0.77
GDP per capita	1.55	0.64
Population (log)	1.23	0.81
Promulgation year	1.27	0.79
Mean VIF	1.55	

TABLE A.7. *Large sample model*

Variables	Average Polity score			Average Unified Democracy score		
	t+1 to *t+3*	*t+4* to *t+6*	*t+8* to *t+10*	*t+1* to *t+3*	*t+4* to *t+6*	*t+8* to *t+10*
Convening	3.71***	3.85***	4.15***	0.42***	0.45***	0.48***
	(0.86)	(0.86)	(0.91)	(0.09)	(0.10)	(0.10)
Debating	0.61	0.35	0.33	0.05	0.03	0.01
	(1.04)	(1.00)	(1.03)	(0.11)	(0.11)	(0.12)
Ratifying	0.95	1.87***	1.97***	0.16**	0.19**	0.21***
	(0.70)	(0.71)	(0.73)	(0.07)	(0.08)	(0.07)
Constant	−3.38***	−3.81***	−3.37***	−0.61***	−0.64***	−0.58***
	(0.91)	(0.88)	(0.93)	(0.10)	(0.10)	(0.10)
Observations	123	115	106	117	116	109
R-squared	0.26	0.33	0.35	0.29	0.31	0.33

Robust standard errors in parentheses.
***p < 0.01, **p < 0.05, *p < 0.1.

TABLE A.8. *Model using bootstrapped standard errors:*
bootstrap replications (1,000) seed (123)

Variables	Average Polity score			Average Unified Democracy score		
	t+1 to *t+3*	*t+4* to *t+6*	*t+8* to *t+10*	*t+1* to *t+3*	*t+4* to *t+6*	*t+8* to *t+10*
Democracy	−0.05	−0.05	−0.00	−0.12*	−0.10	−0.05
(*t−3* to *t−1*)	(0.10)	(0.11)	(0.12)	(0.07)	(0.07)	(0.07)
Convening	2.19*	3.24***	2.69*	0.30***	0.36***	0.35**
	(1.12)	(1.16)	(1.53)	(0.11)	(0.11)	(0.15)
Debating	1.26	0.37	1.21	0.03	−0.02	0.01
	(1.54)	(1.40)	(1.79)	(0.13)	(0.14)	(0.18)
Ratifying	−0.39	1.13	1.22	0.07	0.11	0.19**
	(1.02)	(1.02)	(1.10)	(0.09)	(0.09)	(0.09)
Ethnic	−2.44	−0.57	−1.39	0.31	0.18	−0.08
	(2.70)	(3.26)	(3.35)	(0.29)	(0.28)	(0.28)
ODA	−0.10*	−0.09*	−0.09	−0.01	−0.01**	−0.01
	(0.06)	(0.05)	(0.06)	(0.01)	(0.01)	(0.01)

(continued)

TABLE A.8. (*continued*)

Variables	Average Polity score			Average Unified Democracy score		
	$t+1$ to $t+3$	$t+4$ to $t+6$	$t+8$ to $t+10$	$t+1$ to $t+3$	$t+4$ to $t+6$	$t+8$ to $t+10$
Natural resources	−0.08	−0.02	−0.06	−0.00	−0.00	−0.01
	(0.06)	(0.05)	(0.09)	(0.00)	(0.00)	(0.01)
GDP per capita	−0.00	−0.00	−0.00	−0.00	−0.00	−0.00
	(0.00)	(0.00)	(0.00)	(0.00)	(0.00)	(0.00)
Population (log)	−0.18	0.03	−0.47	−0.01	−0.03	−0.04
	(0.50)	(0.54)	(0.60)	(0.05)	(0.05)	(0.05)
Promulgation year	0.07	0.04	−0.01	0.00	−0.00	−0.01
	(0.08)	(0.08)	(0.12)	(0.01)	(0.01)	(0.01)
Constant	−141.17	−86.59	31.12	−2.33	5.83	27.90
	(153.37)	(166.08)	(234.47)	(16.24)	(15.38)	(22.45)
Observations	82	74	63	78	76	67
R-squared	0.25	0.32	0.36	0.32	0.35	0.40

Standard errors in parentheses.

[***]$p < 0.01$, [**]$p < 0.05$, [*]$p < 0.1$.

Coding of Pathways According to
27 Possible Combinations

Pathway no.	Combination	No. of constitutions	Positive change	Negative change	No change	Missing
1	III	28	13 (46%)	10 (36%)	5 (18%)	
2	IIM	9	7 (77.77%)	1 (11.11%)	1 (11.11%)	
3	IIP	12	7 (58.33%)	4 (33.33%)	0	1 (8.33%)
4	IMI	5	2 (40%)	3 (60%)	0	
5	IMM	4	3 (75%)	1 (25%)	0	
6	IMP	6	3 (50%)	2 (33.33%)	1 (16.66%)	
7	IPI	0	0	0	0	
8	IPM	1	0	1 (100%)	0	
9	IPP	3	2 (66.66%)	1 (33.33%)	0	
10	MII	2	2 (100%)	0	0	
11	MIM	1	1 (100%)	0	0	
12	MIP	1	0	1 (100%)	0	
13	MMI	4	2 (50%)	1 (25%)	0	1 (25%)
14	MMM	16	11 (68.75%)	2 (12.5%)	2 (12.5%)	1 (6.25%)
15	MMP	16	10 (62.5%)	5 (31.25%)	0	1 (6.25%)
16	MPI	0	0	0	0	
17	MPM	3	3 (100%)	0	0	
18	MPP	8	6 (75%)	0	0	2 (25%)
19	PII	0	0	0	0	
20	PIM	0	0	0	0	
21	PIP	0	0	0	0	
22	PMI	1	1 (100%)	0	0	
23	PMM	8	6 (75%)	0	2 (25%)	

(continued)

Pathway no.	Combination	No. of constitutions	Positive change	Negative change	No change	Missing
24	PMP	1	1 (100%)	0	0	
25	PPI	0	0	0	0	
26	PPM	4	3 (75%)	0	1 (25%)	
27	PPP	4	2 (50%)	1 (25%)	1 (25 %)	
###	No data	7	–	–	–	
Total	–	144				

List of the Constitutions with the Most Recurring Pathways

Pathway	Cases
Imposed–Imposed–Imposed (28 constitutions)	Afghanistan (1990), Azerbaijan (1995), Belarus (1990), Bhutan (2008), Bosnia-Herzegovina (1995), Burkina Faso (1991), Burma (2008), Cambodia (1981, 1993), Central African Republic (1994), Chile (1980), China (1978, 1982), Congo Brazzaville (2002), Dominican Republic (2010), Equatorial Guinea (1982), Guinea (2010), Lesotho (1993), Nepal (1990), Nicaragua (1974), Oman (1996), Saudi Arabia (1992), Somalia (1979, 2012), Syria (2012), Thailand (1991), Uzbekistan (1992), Vietnam (1992), Zimbabwe (1979)
Mixed–Mixed–Mixed (16 constitutions)	Belgium (1994), Croatia (1990), Czech Republic (1993), Eritrea (1997), Finland (2000), Gabon (1990), Georgia (1995), Hungary (2011), Macedonia (1991), Malawi (1994), Moldova (1994), Mongolia (1992), Mozambique (1990), Trinidad & Tobago (1976), Ukraine (1996)
Mixed–Mixed–Popular (16 constitutions)	Armenia (1995), Brazil (1988), Burundi (2005), Chad (1996), Comoros (2001), Ghana (1992), Haiti (1987), Iraq (2005), Kyrgyzstan (1993), Madagascar (1992), Mali (1992), Peru (1993), Rwanda (2003), Senegal(2001), Serbia (2006), Zimbabwe (2013)

References

Acosta, Alberto. 2015. First Chair of the Ecuador Constituent Assembly of 2007. Interview on August 15 in Quito.

Acosta, Alberto and Esperanza Martinez. 2009. *El buen vivir: una via para el Desarollo*. Quito, Ecuador: Abya Yala.

Akiba, Okon. 2004. *Constitutionalism and Society in Africa*. Burlington, VT and England: Ashgate.

Al-Hibri, Azizah. 1992. "Islamic Constitutionalism and the Concept of Democracy." *Case Western Journal of International Law* 24 (1):1–20.

Alesina, Alberto, Arnaud Devleeschauwer, William Easterly, Sergio Kurlat, and Romain Wacziarg. 2003. "Fractionalization." *Journal of Economic Growth* 8:155–194.

Altman, David. 2011. *Direct Democracy Worldwide*. New York: Cambridge University Press.

2013. "Bringing Direct democracy Back In: Toward a Three-Dimensional Measure of Democracy." *Democratization* 20 (4):615–41.

Amuwo, Kunle. 2001. "Transition as Democratic Regression." In *Nigeria during the Abacha Years, 1993–1998*, edited by Kunle Amuwo, Daniel C. Bach, and Yann Lebeau, 1–56. Ibadan, Nigeria: Institut Francais de Recherche en Afrique.

Anckar, Dag. 2014. "Constitutional Referendums in the Countries of the World." *Journal of Politics and Law* 7 (1):12–22.

Andrews, William George. 1968. *Constitutions and Constitutionalism*. Vol. 1: New York, NY: van Nostrand.

Ascher, William. 1984. *Scheming for the Poor: The Politics of Redistribution in Latin America*. Cambridge, MA: Harvard University Press.

Bach, Daniel C., Yann Lebeau, and Kunle Amuwo. 2001. *Nigeria during the Abacha Years, 1993–1998*. Ibadan, Nigeria: Institut Francais de Recherche en Afrique.

Banks, Arthur S. and Kenneth A. Wilson. 2016. Cross-National Time-Series Data Archive, edited by Databanks International. Jerusalem, Israel.

Bannon, Alicia L. 2007. Designing a Constitution-Drafting Process: Lessons from Kenya. *Yale Law Journal* 116 (8):1824–72.

Barros, Robert. 2002. *Constitutionalism and Dictatorship: Pinochet, the Junta, and the 1980 Constitution, Cambridge Studies in the Theory of Democracy*. Cambridge, UK; New York: Cambridge University Press.

2003. "Dictatorship and the Rule of Law: Rules and Military Power in Pinochet's Chile." In *Democracy and the Rule of Law*, edited by Jose Maria Maravall and Adam Przeworski, 188–222. Cambridge: Cambridge University Press.

Bayart, Jean-François. 1993. *The State in Africa: The Politics of the Belly*. London: Longman.

Beatty, David M. 1994. "Human Rights and the Rule of Law." In *Human Rights and Judicial Review*, edited by David M. Beatty. Dordrecht: Martinus Nijhoff.

Becker, Marc. 2011. "Correa, Indigenous Movements, and the Writing of a New Constitution in Ecuador." *Latin American Perspectives* 38 (1):47–62.

Belge, Ceren and Ekrem Karakoc. 2015. "Minorities in the Middle East: Ethnicity, Religion, and Support for Authoritarianism." *Political Research Quarterly* 68 (2):280–92.

Benomar, Jamal. 2004. "Constitution-Making after Conflict: Lessons for Iraq." *Journal of Democracy* 15 (2):81–95.

Bessinger, Mark. 2008. "A New Look at Ethnicity and Democratization." *Journal of Democracy* 19 (3):85–97.

Boesten, Jan. 2016. Between democratic security and democratic legality: discursive institutionalism and Colombia's Constitutional Court. Doctoral dissertation. Vancouver: University of British Columbia.

Boix, Carles and Milan W. Svolik. 2013. "The Foundations of Limited Authoritarian Government: Institutions, Commitment, and Power-sharing in Dictatorships." *The Journal of Politics* 75 (2):300–16.

Bratton, Michael and Nicolas van de Walle. 1994. "Neopatrimonial Regimes and Political Transitions in Africa." *World Politics* 46:453–89.

1997. *Democratic Experiments in Africa: Regime Transitions in Comparative Perspective*. Cambridge and New York: Cambridge University Press.

Braunstein, Richard. 2004. *Initiative and Referendum Voting: Governing through Direct Democracy in the United States*. El Paso, TX: LFB Scholarly Publishing LLC.

Brett, Roddy and Antonio Delgado. 2005. "Guatemala's Constitution-Building Processes." Paper submitted to International IDEA's Democracy-Building and Conflict Management Programme.

Brewer-Carías, Allan R. 2010. *Dismantling Democracy in Venezuela: The Chávez Authoritarian Experiment*. New York, NY: Cambridge University Press.

Brown, Nathan J. 2002. *Constitutions in a Nonconstitutional World: Arab Basic Laws and the Prospects for Accountable Government, SUNY Series in Middle Eastern Studies*. Albany, NY: State University of New York Press.

2008. "Reason, Interest, Rationality, and Passion in Constitution Drafting." *Perspectives on Politics* 6 (4):675–89.

2012. "Egypt's Constitution: Islamists Prepare for a Long Political Battle." Carnegie Endowment for International Peace.

Brownlee, Jason. 2007. *Authoritarianism in an Age of Democratization*. Cambridge and New York: Cambridge University Press.

2011. "Executive Elections in the Arab World: When and How Do They Matter?" *Comparative Political Studies* 44:807–28.

Brownlee, Jason, Tarek Masoud, and Andrew Reynolds. 2015. *The Arab Spring: Pathways of Repression and Reform*. New York: Oxford University Press.

Bunce, Valerie. 2003. "Rethinking Recent Democratization: Lessons from the Postcommunist Experience." *World Politics* 55:167–92.

Burke, Edmund. 1999. *Reflections on the Revolution in France, Oxford World's Classics.* Oxford: Oxford University Press.

Cameron, Maxwell A., Eric Hershberg, and Kenneth Evan Sharpe. 2012. *New Institutions for Participatory Democracy in Latin America: Voice and Consequence.* New York: Palgrave Macmillan.

Carey, John M. 2009. "Does It Matter How a Constitution Is Created?" In *Is Democracy Exportable?*, edited by Zoltan Barany and Robert Moser, 155–77. Cambridge and New York: Cambridge University Press.

Carothers, Thomas. 2002. "The End of the Transition Paradigm." *Journal of Democracy* 13 (1):5–21.

Carpizo, Jorge. 1978. *El Presidencialismo Mexicano.* Mexico City: Siglo XXI Editores.

Carter Center. 2012. *Statement on Tunisia's Constitution Drafting Process.* Atlanta, GA: The Carter Center.

Chabal, Patrick and Jean-Pascal Daloz. 1999. *Africa Works: Disorder as Political Instrument, African Issues.* London, Bloomington: International African Institute in association with James Currey, Oxford. Indiana University Press.

Chambers, Simone. 2004. "Behind Closed Doors: Publicity, Secrecy, and the Quality of Deliberation." *Journal of Political Philosophy* 12 (4):389–410.

Chayes, Sarah. 2014. "How a Leftist Labor Union Helped Force Tunisia's Political Settlement." *Carnegie Endowment for Int'l Peace.*

Cheeseman, Nicholas. 2015. *Democracy in Africa: Successes, Failures, and the Struggle for Political Reform, New Approaches to African History.* New York: Cambridge University Press.

Cheibub, José Antonio. 2007. *Presidentialism, Parliamentarism, and Democracy.* Cambridge and New York: Cambridge University Press.

Cheibub, José Antonio, Zachary Elkins, and Tom Ginsburg. 2011. "Latin American Presidentialism in Comparative and Historical Perspective." *Texas Law Review* 89:1707–43.

Cheibub, José Antonio, Zachary Elkins, and Tom Ginsburg. 2014. "Beyond Presidentialism and Parliamentarism." *British Journal of Political Science* 44 (3):515–44.

Chenoweth, Erica and Maria J. Stephan. 2011. *Why Civil Resistance Works: The Strategic Logic of Nonviolent Conflict.* New York, NY: Columbia University Press.

2014. "Drop Your Weapons: When and Why Civil Resistance Works." *Foreign Affairs* (July/August).

Chernow, Ron. 2004. *Alexander Hamilton.* New York: Penguin Press.

Chesterman, Simon. 2004. "Imposed Constitutions, Imposed Constitutionalism, and Ownership." *Connecticut Law Review* 37 (4):947.

Collier, Ruth Berins and David Collier. 1991. *Shaping the Political Arena: Critical Junctures, the Labor Movement, and Regime Dynamics in Latin America.* Princeton, NJ: Princeton University Press.

Collier, Ruth Berins and James Mahoney. 1997. "Adding Collective Actors to Collective Outcomes: Labor and Recent Democratization in South America and Southern Europe." *Comparative Politics* 29 (3):285–303.

Colomer, Josep M. 1994. "Transitions by Agreement: Modeling the Spanish Way." *American Political Science Review* 85 (4):1283–1302.

Conaghan, Catherine. 2015. "Surveil and Sanction: The Return of the State and Societal Regulation in Ecuador." *ERLACS* 98:7–27.

Conaghan, Catherine M. 2008. "Ecuador: Correa's Plebiscitary Presidency." *Journal of Democracy* 19 (2):46–60.

Constitutional Rights Project. 2002. *Confronting Abuses of the Past: Issues at the Oputa Commission.* Lagos and Abuja. Reprint, In File.

Coppedge, Michael. 2012. *Democratization and Research Methods, Strategies for Social Inquiry.* Cambridge: Cambridge University Press.

Corrales, Javier and Michael Penfold-Becerra. 2011. *Dragon in the Tropics: Hugo Chávez and the Political Economy of Revolution in Venezuela.* Washington, DC: Brookings Institution Press.

Dahl, Robert. 1971. *Polyarchy: Participation and Opposition.* New Haven and London: Yale University Press.

Dahl, Robert A. 2002. *How Democratic Is the American Constitution?* New Haven: Yale University Press.

Davenport, Christian A. 1996. "'Constitutional Promises' and Repressive Reality: A Cross-National Time-Series Investigation of Why Political and Civil Liberties are Suppressed." *The Journal of Politics* 58 (3):627–54.

de la Torre, Carlos and Andrés Ortiz Lemos. 2015. "Populist Polarization and the Slow Death of Democracy in Ecuador." *Democratization* 23 (2):1–21.

Diamond, Larry Jay. 1994. "Toward Democratic Consolidation." *Journal of Democracy* 5 (3):4–17.

2002. "Thinking About Hybrid Regimes." *Journal of Democracy* 13 (2):21–35.

2016. *In Search of Democracy.* Milton Park, Abingdon, Oxon; New York, NY: Routledge.

Diamond, Larry, Francis Fukuyama, Donald Horowitz, and Marc Plattner. 2014. "Discussion: Reconsidering the Transition Paradigm." *Journal of Democracy* 25 (1):86–100.

Diamond, Larry Jay, Oyeleye Oyediran, and A. H. M. Kirk-Greene. 1997. *Transition without End: Nigerian Politics and Civil Society under Babangida.* Boulder, CO: Lynne Rienner Publishers.

Downs, Anthony. 1957. *An Economic Theory of Democracy.* New York: Harper.

Dryzek, John S. 2000. *Deliberative Democracy and Beyond: Liberals, Critics, Contestations.* Oxford and New York: Oxford University Press. Reprint, In File.

Ebrahim, Hassen and Laurel E. Miller. 2010. "Creating the Birth Certificate of a New South Africa: Constitution-Making after Apartheid." In *Framing the State in Times of Transition: Case Studies in Constitution Making*, edited by Laurel E. Miller and Louis Aucoin, 111–57. Washington, DC: United States Institute of Peace Press.

Eckstein, Susan. 2001. *Power and Popular Protest: Latin American Social Movements.* Berkeley: University of California Press.

Edozie, Rita Kiki. 2002. *People Power and Democracy: The Popular Movement against Military Despotism in Nigeria, 1989–1999.* Trenton, NJ and Eritrea: Africa World Press. Reprint, In File.

Eisenstadt, Todd A. 2003. "Thinking Outside the (Ballot) Box: Informal Electoral Institutions and Mexico's Political Opening." *Latin American Politics and Society* 45 (1):25–54.

2004. *Courting Democracy in Mexico: Party Strategies and Electoral Institutions.* Cambridge and New York: Cambridge University Press.

2006. "Mexico's Postelectoral Concertacesiones." In *Informal Institutions and Democracy: Lessons from Latin America*, edited by Gretchen Helmke and Steven Levitsky, 227–48. Baltimore, MD: The Johns Hopkins University Press.

2011. *Politics, Identity, and Mexico's Indigenous Rights Movements, Cambridge Studies in Contentious Politics*. New York: Cambridge University Press.

Eisenstadt, Todd A., A. Carl LeVan, and Tofigh Maboudi. 2015. "When Talk Trumps Text: The Democratizing Effects of Deliberation on Constitution-Writing, 1974–2011." *American Political Science Review* 109 (3):592–612.

Eisenstadt, Todd A., Daniela Stevens, and Barbara dos Santos. 2016. Presidential Re-election as a Driver of Constitutional Reform in Latin America, 1973–2014, typescript. Paper presented at the 2016 meeting of the Latin American Studies Association, New York, NY.

Eisenstadt, Todd A. and Marcela Torres. 2016. Interest Articulation in Indigenous Rural Latin America: From Corporatism to Bounded Pluralist "Interculturalismo." typescript.

Eisenstadt, Todd A. and Karleen Jones West. 2017. "Environmentalism in a Climate-Vulnerable State: Rainforests, Oil, and Political Attitudes along Ecuador's Extractive Frontier." *Journal of Comparative Politics* 49 (1):231–51.

Ekiert, Grzegorz and Jan Kubik. 1999. *Rebellious Civil Society: Popular Protest and Democratic Consolidation in Poland, 1989–1993*. Ann Arbor: University of Michigan Press.

Ekman, Joakim. 2009. "Political Participation and Regime Stability: A Framework for Analyzing Hybrid Regimes." *International Political Science Review* 30 (1):7–31.

el Walid Seye, Cheriff. 1995. "Chairman Jammeh's Thoughts, Concerns and Position on Burning Issues of the Day." *Foroyaa*, November 7, 1–6.

Elkins, Zachary, Tom Ginsburg, and James Melton. 2009. *The Endurance of National Constitutions*. Cambridge and New York: Cambridge University Press.

2013. "The Content of Authoritarian Constitutions." In *Constitutions in Authoritarian Regimes*, edited by Tom Ginsburg and Alberto Simpser, 141–64. Cambridge and New York: Cambridge University Press.

Ellickson, Robert C. 1991. *Order without Law: How Neighbors Settle Disputes*. Cambridge, MA: Harvard University Press.

Ellicott, K. 2011. *Countries of the World and Their Leaders Yearbook: 2012*. Farmington Hills, MI: Gale, Cengage Learning.

Elster, Jon. 1993. "Introduction." In *Constitutionalism and Democracy*, edited by Jon Elster and Rune Slagstad, 1–18. Cambridge and New York: Cambridge University Press.

1998. "Deliberation and Constitution Making." In *Deliberative Democracy*, edited by Jon Elster, 97–122. Cambridge: Cambridge University Press.

2012. "The Optimal Design of a Constituent Assembly." In *Collective Wisdom: Principles and Mechanisms*, edited by Helene Landemore and Jon Elster, 148–72. Cambridge: Cambridge University Press.

Encarnación, Omar. 2005. "Do Political Pacts Freeze Democracy? Spanish and South American Lessons." *West European Politics* 28 (1):182–203.

Ensalaco, Mark. 1994. "In with the New, Out with the Old? The Democratising Impact of Constitutional Reform in Chile." *Journal of Latin American Studies* 26 (2):409–29.

Falana, Femi. 2010. "Constitutionalism, Rule of Law, and Human Rights." In *Governance and Politics in Post-Military Nigeria: Changes and Challenges*, edited by Said Adejumobi, 125–43. New York: Palgrave Macmillan.

Feldman, Noah. 2004. "Imposed Constitutionalism." *Connecticut Law Review* 37:857.
    2009. "Islamic Constitutionalism in Context: A Typology and a Warning." *St. Thomas Law Journal* 7:436–51.

Fishkin, James S. 2009. *When the People Speak: Deliberative Democracy and Public Consultation*. Oxford; New York: Oxford University Press.

Fombad, Charles Manga. 2010. "The Constitution as a Source of Accountability: The Role of Constitutionalism." *Speculum Juris* 2:41–65.

Fox, Donald T., Gustavo Gallon-Giraldo, and Anne Stetson. 2010. "Lessons of the Colombian Constitutional Reform of 1991: Toward the Securing of Peace and Reconciliation?" In *Framing the State in Times of Transition: Case Studies in Constitution Making*, edited by Laurel E. Miller and Louis Aucoin, 467–82. Washington, DC: United States Institute of Peace Press.

Fox, Gregory H. 2000. "The Right to Political Participation in International Law." In *Democratic Governance and International Law*, edited by Gregory H. Fox and Brad R. Roth, 48–90. Cambridge: Cambridge University Press.

Fox, Jonathan. 2014. *Social Accountability: What Does the Evidence Really Say?*, *Global Partnership for Social Accountability*. Washington, DC: World Bank Group.

Franck, Thomas M. and Arun K. Thiruvengadam. 2010. "Norms of International Law Relating to the Constitution-Making Process." In *Framing the State in Times of Transition: Case Studies in Constitution Making*, edited by Laurel Miller, 20–56. Washington, DC: United States Institute of Peace Press.

Franklin, James C. 2013. "Repertoires of Contention and Tactical Choice in Latin America, 1981–1995." *Research in Social Movements, Conflict and Change* 35:175–208.

Frantz, Erica and Natasha Ezrow. 2011. *The Politics of Dictatorship: Institutions and Outcomes in Authoritarian Regimes*. Boulder: Lynne Rienner.

Freedom House. 2015. *Freedom in the World 2015 – Discarding Democracy: Return to the Iron Fist*. New York: Freedom House.

Galston, William A. 2011. "Pluralist Constitutionalism." *Social Philosophy & Policy* 28 (1):228–41.

Gandhi, Jennifer. 2008. *Political Institutions under Dictatorship*. Cambridge and New York: Cambridge University Press.

Gandhi, Jennifer and Ellen Lust-Okar. 2009. "Elections under Authoritarianism." *Annual Review of Political Science* 12:403–22.

Garcia-Guadilla, Maria Pilar and Mónica Hurtado. 2000. "Participation and Constitution Making in Colombia and Venezuela: Enlarging the Scope of Democracy?" Paper presented at Latin American Studies Association, March 16–18, 2000. Miami, Florida.

Garcia-Serra, Mario J. 2001. 'The "Enabling Law': The Demise of the Separation of Powers in Hugo Chávez's Venezuela." *The University of Miami Inter-American Law Review* 32 (2):265–93.

Gargarella, Roberto. 2010. *The Legal Foundations of Inequality: Constitutionalism in the Americas, 1776–1860, Cambridge Studies in the Theory of Democracy*. Cambridge; New York: Cambridge University Press.

Garrido, Luis Javier. 1989. *The Crisis of Presidencialismo*. Vol. 30: San Diego, CA: Center for US-Mexican Studies, Monograph Series.

Gboyega, Alex. 1979. "The Making of the Nigerian Constitution." In *Nigerian Government and Politics under Military Rule, 1966–1979*, edited by Oyeleye Oyediran, 235–58. New York: St. Martin's Press.

Geddes, Barbara. 2003. *Paradigms and Sandcastles: Theory Building and Research Design in Comparative Politics*. Ann Arbor, MI: University of Michigan Press.

Geddes, Barbara, Joseph Wright, and Erica Frantz. 2014. "Autocratic Breakdown and Regime Transitions: A New Data Set." *Perspectives on Politics* 12 (2):313–31.

Gerring, John. 2011. *Social Science Methodology: A Unified Framework*: Cambridge University Press.

Ghai, Yash. 2005. "Journey around Constitutions: Reflections on Contemporary Constitutions, A." *South African Law Journal* 122:804.

Ghai, Yash Pal. 2002. "Constitutional Asymmetries, Communal Representation, Federalism, and Cultural Autonomy." In *The Architecture of Democracy: Constitutional Design, Conflict Management, and Democracy*, edited by Andrew Reynolds, 141–70. Oxford: Oxford University Press.

Ginsburg, Tom. 2012. *Comparative Constitutional Design, Comparative Constitutional Law and Policy*. New York: Cambridge University Press.

Ginsburg, Tom, Zachary Elkins, and Justin Blount. 2008. "The Citizen as Founder: Public Participation in Constitutional Approval." *Temple Law Review* 81:361–82.

2009. "Does the Process of Constitution-Making Matter?" *Annual Review of Law and Social Sciences* 5 (5):201–23.

Ginsburg, Tom and Alberto Simpser. 2013. *Constitutions in Authoritarian Regimes*: Cambridge University Press.

Goodwin, Jeff and James M. Jasper. 1999. Caught in a winding, snarling vine: The structural bias of political process theory. Paper read at Sociological forum.

Greene, Kenneth F. 2007. *Why Dominant Parties Lose: Mexico's Democratization in Comparative Perspective*. Cambridge New York: Cambridge University Press.

Grodsky, Brian K. 2012. *Social Movements and the New State: The Fate of Pro-Democracy Organizations When Democracy Is Won*. Stanford: Stanford University Press.

Grote, Rainer and Tilmann J. Röder. 2012. *Constitutionalism in Islamic Countries: between Upheaval and Continuity*. Oxford; New York: Oxford University Press.

Gudynas, Eduardo. 2009. *El Mandato Ecologico: Derechos de la Naturalez 7 Politicas Abientales en la Nueva Constitucion*. Quito, Ecuador: Abya Yala.

2011. "Buen Vivir: Today's Tomorrow." *Development* 54 (4):441–7.

Guliyev, Farid. 2011. "Personal Rule, Neopatrimonialism, and Regime Typologies: Integrating Dahlian and Weberian Approaches to Regime Studies." *Democratization* 18 (3):575–601.

Gylfason, Thorvaldur. 2014. "Constitution on Ice," typescript. Centre for Economic Policy Research of the University of Iceland.

Haggard, Stephan and Robert R. Kaufman. 1995. *The Political Economy of Democratic Transitions*. Princeton, NJ: Princeton University Press.

2016. *Dictators and Democrats: Masses, Elites and Regime Change*. Princeton: Princeton University Press.

Hansen, Roger D. 1971. *The Politics of Mexican Development*. Baltimore: Johns Hopkins Press.

Hardin, Russell. 1989. "Why a Constitution?" In *The Federalist Papers and the New Institutionalism*, edited by Bernard Gofrman and Donald Wittman, 100–20. New York: Agathon Press.

Hart, Vivien. 2003. *Democratic Constitution Making*. Washington, DC: US Institute of Peace.

Hartyln, Jonathan and Juan Pablo Luna. 2009. "Constitutional Reform in Contemporary Latin America: A Framework for Analysis." Typescript.

Haskell, John. 2001. *Direct Democracy or Representative Government? Dispelling the Populist Myth, Transforming American Politics*. Boulder, CO: Westview Press.

Hatchard, John. 1999. "A New Breed of Institution: The Development of Human Rights Commissions in Commonwealth Africa with Particular Reference to the Uganda Human Rights Commission." *Comparative and International Law Journal of Southern Africa* 32:28–53.

Haysom, Nicholas. 2007. "Negotiating a Sustainable Political Settlement: Lessons from the South African Transition." In *Democratic Constitution Making: Experiences from Nepal, Kenya, South Africa, and Sri Lanka*, edited by Hari P. Bhatthari and Jhulak Subedi. Kathmandu: Nepal South Asia Center.

Higley, John and Richard Gunther. 1992. *Elites and Democratic Consolidation in Latin America and Southern Europe*. Cambridge and New York: Cambridge University Press.

Hirschman, Albert O. 1970. *Exit, Voice, and Loyalty Responses to Decline in Firms, Organizations, and States*. Cambridge, MA: Harvard University Press.

Holmes, Stephen. 1988. "Precommitment and the Paradox of Democracy." In *Constitutionalism and Democracy*, edited by Rune Slagstad and Jon Elster, 195–240. New York: Cambridge University Press.

Hong, Lu and Scott E. Page. 2012. "Some Microfoundations of Collective Wisdom." In *Collective Wisdom: Principles and Mechanisms*, edited by Hélène Landemore and Jon Elster, 56–71. Cambridge; New York: Cambridge University Press.

Horowitz, Donald. 1985. *Ethnic Groups in Conflict*. Berkeley: University of California Press. Reprint, Not in File.

Horowitz, Donald L. 2013. *Constitutional Change and Democracy in Indonesia, Problems of International Politics*. Cambridge, England; New York: Cambridge University Press.

Howard, Dick A.E. 1991. "The Essence of Constitutionalism." In *Constitutionalism and Human Rights: America, Poland, and France*, edited by Kenneth W. Thompson and Rett T. Ludwikowski. New York: Lanham.

Hug, Simon. 2009. "Some Thoughts about Referendums, Representative Democracy, and Separation of Powers." *Constitutional Political Economy* 20:251–66.

Hultin, Niklas. 2013. "Law, Opacity, and Information in Urban Gambia." *Social Analysis* 57 (3):42–57.

Huntington, Samuel P. 1968. *Political Order in Changing Societies*. New Haven and London: Yale University Press.

Hyde, Susan D. 2011. *The Pseudo-democrat's Dilemma: Why Election Observation Became an International Norm*. Ithaca: Cornell University Press.

Hyden, Goran. 2001. "Constitution-Making and Democratisation in Africa." In *Constitution-Making and Democratisation in Africa*, edited by Goran Hyden and Denis Venter, 202–20. Pretoria, South Africa: Africa Institute of South Africa.

Ihonvbere, Julius. 2004. "Constitutionalism and the National Question." In *Nigeria's Struggle for Democracy and Good Governance*, edited by Adigun Agbaje, Larry Diamond and Ebere Onwudiwe, 243–66. Ibadan: University of Ibadan Press.

Jeng, Abou. 2012. "From Hope to Despair: Travails of Constitution Law-Making in Gambia Second Republic." In *State and Society in the Gambia since Independence*, edited by Abdoulaye S. Saine, Ebrima Jogomai Ceesay, and Ebrima Sall, 113–50. Trenton, NJ: Africa World Press.

Kailitz, Steffen. 2013. "Classifying Political Regimes Revisited: Legitimation and Durability." *Democratization* 20 (1):39–60.

Kamrava, Mehran. 2014. *Beyond the Arab Spring: The Evolving Ruling Bargain in the Middle East*. London: Hurst & Company.

Karl, Terry Lynn. 1990. "Dilemmas of Democratization in Latin America." *Comparative Politics* 23 (1):1–21.

Kauffman, Craig M. and Pamela L. Martin. 2014. "Scaling Up Buen Vivir: Globalizing Local Environmental Governance from Ecuador." *Global Environmental Politics* 14 (1):40–58.

Keefer, Philip. 2005. "Database of Political Institutions: Changes and Variable Definitions." Development Research Group of the World Bank. www.iadb.org/en/research-and-data/publication-details,3169.html?pub_id=IDB-DB-112

Keith, Linda Camp. 2002. "Constitutional Provisions for Individual Human Rights (1977–1996): Are They More than Mere 'Window Dressing?'" *Political Research Quarterly* 55 (1):111–43.

Knight, Jack. 1992. *Institutions and Social Conflict*. Cambridge: Cambridge University Press.

Konig, Thomas, George Tsebelis, and Marc Debus. 2010. *Reform Processes and Policy Change: Veto Players and Decision-Making in Modern Democracies*. New York: Springer.

Kramon, Eric and Daniel Posner. 2011. "Kenya's New Constitution." *Journal of Democracy* 22 (2):89–103.

Krastev, Ivan. 2006. "Democracy's 'Doubles.'" *Journal of Democracy* 17 (2):52–62.

Kubik, Jan. 2000. Between the State and Networks of "Cousins": The Role of Civil Society and Noncivil Associations in the Democratization of Poland.

Landemore, Hélène. 2012. "Democratic Reason: The Mechanisms of Collective Intelligence." In *Collective Wisdom: Principles and Mechanisms*, edited by Helene Landemore and Jon Elster, 251–89. Cambridge: Cambridge University Press.

  2013. *Democratic Reason: Politics, Collective Intelligence, and the Rule of the Many*. Princeton; Oxford: Princeton University Press.

  2017. "What is a Good Constitution? Assessing the Constitutional Proposal in the Icelandic Experiment." In *Assessing Constitutional Performance*, edited by Tom Ginsburg and Aziz Z. Huq, 71–98. New York: Cambridge University Press.

Landemore, Hélène and Jon Elster. 2012. *Collective Wisdom: Principles and Mechanisms*. Cambridge; New York: Cambridge University Press.

Lange, Matthew. 2009. *Lineages of Despotism and Development: British Colonialism and State Power*. Chicago: University of Chicago Press.

Lebas, Adrienne. 2011. *From Protest to Parties: Party-Building and Democratization in Africa*. Oxford: Oxford University Press.

Lederman, Daniel, Norman V. Loayza, and Rodrigo R. Soares. 2005. "Accountability and Corruption: Political Institutions Matter." *Economics & Politics* 17 (1):1–35.

LeDuc, Lawrence. 2003. *The Politics of Direct Democracy: Referendums in Global Perspective*. Peterborough, ON; Orchard Park, NY: Broadview Press.

Lerner, Daniel. 1954. *The Passing of Traditional Society*. New York: The Free Press. Reprint, In File.

LeVan, A. Carl. 2011a. "Power Sharing and Inclusive Politics in Africa's Uncertain Democracies." *Governance: A Journal of Policy, Administration, and Institutions* 24 (1):31–53.

2011b. "Questioning Tocqueville in Africa: Continuity and Change in Nigeria's Civil Society during Democratization." *Democratization* 18 (1):135–59.

2014. "Analytic Authoritarianism and Nigeria." *Commonwealth and Comparative Politics* 52 (2):1–20.

2015. *Dictators and Democracy in African Development: The Political Economy of Good Governance in Nigeria*. New York, NY: Cambridge University Press.

LeVine, Victor T. 1997. "The Rise and Fall of Constitutionalism in West Africa." *Journal of Modern African Studies* 35 (2):181–206.

Levitsky, Steven and James Loxton. 2013. Populism and Competitive Authoritarianism in the Andes. *Democratization* 20 (1):107–36.

Levitsky, Steven and Kenneth M. Roberts. 2011. *The Resurgence of the Latin American Left*. Baltimore: Johns Hopkins University Press.

Levitsky, Steven and Lucan Way. 2010. *Competitive Authoritarianism: Hybrid Regimes After the Cold War, Problems of International Politics*. Cambridge and New York: Cambridge University Press.

Lewis, Peter M., Pearl T. Robinson, and Barnett Rubin. 1998. *Stabilizing Nigeria: Sanctions, Incentives, and Support for Civil Society*. New York: Century Foundation Press.

Lijphart, Arend. 1971. "Comparative Politics and the Comparative Method." *American Political Science Review* 65:682–93.

1999. *Patterns of Democracy: Government Forms and Performance in Thirty-Six Countries*. New Haven: Yale University Press.

2012. *Patterns of Democracy: Government Forms and Performance in Thirty-Six Countries*, 2nd edn. New Haven: Yale University Press.

Lindberg, Staffan I. 2009. *Democratization by Elections: A New Mode of Transition*. Baltimore: Johns Hopkins University Press.

Linz, Juan J. 1990. "The Perils of Presidentialism." *Journal of Democracy* 1 (1):51–69.

2000. *Totalitarianism and Authoritarian Regimes*. Bolder and London: Lynne Rienner.

Linz, Juan J. and Alfred Stepan. 1991. "Democratic Transition and Consolidation: Eastern Europe, Southern Europe and Latin America." *Unpublished Draft*.

1996. *Problems of Democratic Transition and Consolidation*. Baltimore: Johns Hopkins University Press.

Linz, Juan J. and Arturo Valenzuela. 1994. *The Failure of Presidential Democracy: Comparative Perspectives*. Baltimore: Johns Hopkins University.

Lipset, Seymour Martin. 1959. "Some Social Requisites of Democracy: Economic Development and Political Legitimacy." *American Political Science Review* 53 (1):69–105.

1998. "George Washington and the Founding of Democracy." *Journal of Democracy* 9 (4):24–38.

Liss, Sheldon B. and Peggy K. Liss. 1972. *Man, State, and Society in Latin American History*: New York: Praeger.

Loveman, Brian. 1993. *The Constitution of Tyranny: Regimes of Exception in Spanish America, Pitt Latin American Series*. Pittsburgh: University of Pittsburgh Press.

Lupia, Arthur and Richard Johnston. 2001. "Are Voters to Blame? Voter Competence and Elite Maneuvers in Referendums." In *Referendum Democracy: Citizens, Elites, and Deliberation in Referendum Campaigns*, edited by Matthew Mendelsohn and Andrew Parkin, 191–201. Houndmills, Basingstoke, Hampshire; New York: Palgrave.

Lynch, Gabrielle. 2006. "The Fruits of Perception: 'Ethnic Politics' and the Case of Kenya's Constitutional Referendum." *African Studies* 65 (2):233–70.

Maboudi, Tofigh. 2016. *Constitution-Making in the Arab Spring Era: Unpacking Citizen Participation and Constitutional Outcomes, Ph.D. Dissertation*. Washington, DC: American University.

Maboudi, Tofigh and Ghazal P. Nadi. 2016. "Crowdsourcing the Egyptian Constitution: Social Media, Elites, and the Populace." *Political Research Quarterly* 69 (4):716–31.

Mackenzie, Michael K. and Mark E. Warren. 2012. "Two Trust-based Uses of Minipublics in Democratic Systems." In *Deliberative Systems: Deliberative Democracy at the Large Scale*, edited by John Parkinson and Jane J. Mansbridge, 95–124. Cambridge: Cambridge University Press.

Mackie, Gerry. 2003. *Democracy Defended, Contemporary Political Theory*. Cambridge: Cambridge University Press.

2012. "Rational Ignorance and Beyond." In *Collective Wisdom: Principles and Mechanisms*, edited by Helene Landemore and Jon Elster, 290–318. Cambridge: Cambridge University Press.

Madison, James. 2006a. "Federalist No. 10: The Union as a Safeguard against Faction." In *Selected Writings of James Madison*, edited by Ralph Ketcham, 83–9. Indianapolis and Cambridge: Hackett Publishing. Original edition, 1788.

2006b. "Federalist No. 49: Reason, Not Passion, Necessary for Good Government." In *Selected Writings of James Madison*, edited by Ralph Ketcham, 117–20. Indianapolis and Cambridge: Hackett Publishing. Original edition, 1788.

Magaloni, Beatriz. 2006. *Voting for Autocracy: Hegemonic Party Survival and Its Demise in Mexico, Cambridge Studies in Comparative Politics*. Cambridge; New York: Cambridge University Press.

Manin, Bernard. 1997. *The Principles of Representative Government*. Cambridge: Cambridge University Press.

Mansbridge, Jane, James Bohman, Simone Chambers, Thomas Christiano, Archon Fung, John Parkinson, Dennis F. Thompson, and Mark E. Warren. 2012. "A Systemic Approach to Deliberative Democracy." In *Deliberative Systems: Deliberative Democracy at the Large Scale*, edited by John Parkinson and Jane J. Mansbridge, 1–26. Cambridge: Cambridge University Press.

March, James G. and Johan P. Olsen. 1996. "Institutional Perspectives on Political Institutions." *Governance* 9 (3):247–64.

Martínez Novo, Carmen. 2013. "The Backlash against Indigenous Rights in Ecuador's Citizen Revolution.'" *Latin America's Multicultural Movements*: 111–31.

Masud, Harika and Jason M. Lakin. 2011. "Documents You Can Use: What the Open Budget Survey 2010 Tells Us about the Global State of Transparency." *Yale Journal of International Affairs* 64 (6):64–80.

Matsusaka, Jonh G. 2005. "The Eclipse of Legislatures: Direct Democracy in the 21st Century." *Public Choice* 124 (1/2):157–77.

McAdam, Doug, John D McCarthy, and Mayer Zald, N. 1996. *Comparative Perspectives on Social Movements Political Opportunities, Mobilizing Structures, and Cultural Framings: Cambridge Studies in Comparative Politics*. Cambridge, England, New York: Cambridge University Press.

McAdam, Doug, Sidney Tarrow, and Charles Tilly. 2009. "Comparative Perspectives on Contentious Politics." In *Comparative Politics: Rationality, Culture, and Structure*, 2nd edn, edited by Mark Lichbach and Alan Zukerman, 260–90. New York: Cambridge University Press.

McCaa, Robert. 2003. "Missing Millions: The Demographic Costs of the Mexican Revolution." *Mexican Studies/Estudios Mexicanos* 19 (2):367–400.

McCarthy, Michael M. 2012. "The Possibilities and Limits of Politicized Participation: Community Councils, Coproduction, and Poder Popular in Chávez's Venezuela." In *New Institutions for Participatory Democracy in Latin America: Voice and Consequence*, edited by Maxwell A. Cameron, Eric Hershberg, and Kenneth Evan Sharpe, 123–48. New York: Palgrave Macmillan.

McCool, Carolyn. 2004. *"The Role of Constitution-Building Processes in Democratization. Case Study: Afghanistan."* Stockholm: International IDEA.

Mecham, Quinn. 2014. "Bahrain's Fractured Ruling Bargain: Political Mobilization, Regime Responses, and the New Sectarianism." In *Beyond the Arab Spring: The Evolving Ruling Bargain in the Middle East*, edited by Mehran Kamrava, 341–72. London: Hurst & Company.

Meisburger, Timothy M. 2012. "Getting Majoritarianism Right." *Journal of Democracy* 23 (1):155–63.

Mill, John Stuart. 1888. "Two Methods of Comparison." In *Comparative Perspectives: Theory and Methods*, edited by Amitai Etzioni and Fredric Dubow, 205–13. Boston: Little, Brown.

Miller, Laurel and Louis Aucoin. 2010. *Framing the State in Times of Transition: Case Studies in Constitution Making, Peacebuilding and the Rule of Law*. Washington, DC: United States Institute of Peace Press.

Moehler, Devra C. 2008. *Distrusting Democrats: Outcomes of Participatory Constitution Making*. Ann Arbor: University of Michigan Press.

Moore, Ryan A. and Donald L. Robinson. 2004. *Partners for Democracy: Crafting the New Japanese State under MacArthur*. New York: Oxford University Press.

Morel, Laurence. 2001. "The Rise of Government-Initiated Referendums in Consolidated Democracies." In *Referendum Democracy: Citizens, Elites, and Deliberation in Referendum Campaigns*, edited by Matthew Mendelsohn and Andrew Parkin, 47–64. Houndmills, Basingstoke, Hampshire; New York: Palgrave.

Morlino, Leonardo. 2009. "Are There Hybrid Regimes? Or Are They Just an Optical Illusion?" *European Political Science Review* 1 (2):273–96.

Mumuni, Mikail. 1998. "New Bottle, Old Wine." *TELL*: 22–4.

Murphy, Walter F. 1993. *Constitutionalism and Democracy: Transitions in the Contemporary World*. Oxford University Press.

Nadi, Ghazal P. 2017. *Transparent they Endure: Institutional Determinants of Fiscal Transparency in Hybrid Regimes*, Doctoral dissertation. Department of Government, American University, Washington, DC.

Negretto, Gabriel L. 2013. *Making Constitutions: Presidents, Parties, and Institutional Choice in Latin America*. Cambridge; New York: Cambridge University Press.

Niboro, Ima. 1998. Walking a Tightrope. *TELL*, June 29, 12–19.

Norris, Pippa. 2008. *Driving Democracy: Do Power-Sharing Institutions Work?* Cambridge and New York: Cambridge University Press.

O'Donnell, Guillermo A. 2007. *Dissonances: Democratic Critiques of Democracy, Helen Kellogg Institute for International Studies*. Notre Dame, Ind.: University of Notre Dame Press.

O'Donnell, Guillermo and Philippe C. Schmitter. 1986. "Negotiating (and Renegotiating) Pacts." In *Transitions from Authoritarian Rule: Prospects for Democracy*, edited by Guillermo O'Donnell, Philippe C. Schmitter, and Lawrence Whitehead, 37–47. Baltimore and London: Johns Hopkins University Press.

O'Donnell, Guillermo, Philippe C. Schmitter, and Lawrence Whitehead. 1986. *Transitions from Authoritarian Rule: Prospects for Democracy*. Baltimore and London: Johns Hopkins University Press.

Ober, Josiah. 2012. "Epistemic Democracy in Classical Athens." In *Collective Wisdom: Principles and Mechanisms*, edited by Helene Landemore and Jon Elster, 118–47. Cambridge: Cambridge University Press.

Olorunfewa, Ade. 1998. Coup Scare. *TELL*, February 16, 1998, 12–18.

Onwudiwe, Ebere. 1999. "On the Sovereign National Conference." *Issue: A Journal of Opinion* 27 (1):66–8.

Ottaway, Marina. 2003. *Democracy Challenged: The Rise of Semi-Authoritarianism*. Boulder: Lynne Rienner.

Parkinson, John and Jane J. Mansbridge. 2012. *Deliberative Systems: Deliberative Democracy at the Large Scale, Theories of Institutional Design*. Cambridge: Cambridge University Press.

Pateman, Carole. 1970. *Participation and Democratic Theory*. Cambridge: Cambridge University Press.

  2012. "Participatory Democracy Revisited." *Perspectives on Politics* 10 (1):7–19.

Pemstein, Daniel, Stephen A. Meserve, and James Melton. 2010. "Democratic Compromise: A Latent Variable Analysis of Ten Measures of Regime Type." *Political Analysis* 18 (4):426–49.

Pildes, Richard H. 2011. "Political Parties and Constitutionalism." In *Comparative Constitutional Law*, edited by Tom Ginsburg and Rosalind Dixon, 254–64. Cheltenham, UK; Northampton, MA: Edward Elgar.

Podolnjak, Robert. 2007. "'The Assent of the People Is Not Necessary to the Formation of a Confederation': Notes on the Failure of the European Constitutional Referendums." *Politička misao* 43 (5):99–120.

Przeworski, Adam. 1988. "Democracy as a Contingent Outcome of Conflicts." *Constitutionalism and Democracy* 59:63–4.

  1991. *Democracy and the Market: Political and Economic Reforms in Eastern Europe and Latin America, Studies in Rationality and Social Change*. Cambridge, New York: Cambridge University Press. Reprint, Not in File.

2003. "Minimalist Conception of Democracy: A Defense." In *The Democracy Sourcebook*, edited by Robert A. Dahl, Ian Shapiro and Jose Antonio Cheibub, 12–17. Cambridge, MA: MIT Press.

2010. *Democracy and the Limits of Self-Government*. Cambridge: Cambridge University Press.

Puddington, Arch. 2013. "Introduction." In *Freedom in the World 2012: Democratic Breakthroughs in the Balance*, edited by Freedom House, 1–13. New York: Freedom House.

Qvortrup, Matt. 2006. *A Comparative Study of Referendums: Government by the People*. Manchester: Manchester University Press.

2014. "Introduction: Theory, Practice and History." In *Referendums around the World: The Continued Growth of Direct Democracy*, edited by Matt Qvortrup, 1–16. Houndmills, Basingstoke, Hampshire: Palgrave Macmillan.

Raftopoulos, Brian. 2013. "The 2013 Elections in Zimbabwe: The End of an Era." *Journal of Southern African Studies* 39 (4):971–88.

Rahat, Gideon. 2009. "Elite Motives for Initiating Referendums: Avoidance, Addition, and Contradiction." In *Referendums and Representative Democracy: Responsiveness, Accountability and Deliberation*, edited by Maija Setälä and Theo Schiller, 98–116. London; New York: Routledge.

"Rawlings, Jammeh, Jawara, The International Community." 1995. *Foroyaa*, August 2, 1–2.

Recasens, Andreu Viola. 2014. "Discursos 'pachamamistas' versus políticas desarrollistas: el debate sobre el sumak kawsay en los Andes." *Íconos-Revista de Ciencias Sociales* 48:55–72.

Reynolds, Andrew. 2011. *Designing Democracy in a Dangerous World*. Oxford: Oxford University Press.

Riker, William H. 1962. *The Theory of Political Coalitions*. Westport, CT: Greenwood Press.

Roberts, Kenneth M. 2006. "Populism, Political Conflict, and Grass-Roots Organization in Latin America." *Comparative Politics* 38 (2):27–148.

Roeder, Philip G. 1993. *Red Sunset*. Princeton: Princeton University Press. Reprint, In File.

Rosen, Lawrence. 2006. "Expecting the Unexpected: Cultural Components of Arab Governance." *Annals of the American Academy of Political and Social Science* 603:163–80.

Rosenthal, Albert J. 1990. "Afterward." In *Constitutionalism and Rights: The Influence of the United States Constitution Abroad*, edited by Louis Henkin and Albert J. Rosenthal, 397–404. New York: Columbia University Press.

Rueschemeyer, Dietrich, Evelyne Huber Stephens, and John D. Stephens. 1992. *Capitalist Development and Democracy*. Chicago: University of Chicago Press.

Saine, Abdoulaye and Ebrima Jogomai Ceesay. 2012. "Post-Coup Politics and Authoritarianism in the Gambia: 1994–2012." In *State and Society in the Gambia since Independence*, edited by Abdoulaye S. Saine, Ebrima Jogomai Ceesay, and Ebrima Sall, 151–86. Trenton, NJ: Africa World Press.

Samuels, K. 2006. *Constitution Building Processes and Democratization: A Discussion of Twelve Case Studies*. Geneva: IDEA.

Sartori, Giovanni. 1962. "Constitutionalism: A Preliminary Discussion." *American Political Science Review* 56 (4):853–64.

Schedler, Andreas. 2006. *Electoral Authoritarianism: The Dynamics of Unfree Competition*. Boulder and London: Lynne Rienner.

Schiller, Theo. 2009. "Conclusions." In *Referendums and Representative Democracy: Responsiveness, Accountability and Deliberation*, edited by Maija Setälä and Theo Schiller, 207–19. London; New York: Routledge.

Schmidt, Vivien A. 2010. "Taking Ideas and Discourse Seriously: Explaining Change through Discursive Institutionalism as the Fourth 'New Institutionalism.'" *European Political Science Review* 2 (1):1–25.

Schmitter, Philippe C. 1977. "Modes of Interest Intermediation and Models of Societal Change in Western Europe." *Comparative Political Studies* 10 (1):7–38.

2010. "Twenty-Five Years, Fifteen Findings." *Journal of Democracy* 21 (1):17–28.

Schneider, Cathy Lisa. 1995. *Shantytown Protest in Pinochet's Chile*. Philadelphia: Temple University Press.

Secrest, A. and G. Norquist. 1995. "Direct Democracy: Good or Bad?" *Campaigns and Elections* 16 (8):47.

Segura, Renata and Ana María Bejarano. 2004. "¡ Ni una asamblea más sin nosotros! Exclusion, Inclusion, and the Politics of Constitution-Making in the Andes." *Constellations* 11 (2):217–36.

Segura, Renata and Ana Maria Bejarano. 2013. The Difference a Constituent Assembly Makes: Explaining Divergent Constitutional Outcomes in Colombia and Venezuela. In *The Gap from Parchment to Practice: Ambivalent Effects of Constitutions in Democratizing Countries*. American University, Washington, DC.

Seiwald, Markus. 2011. REDD and Indigenous Peoples: The Programme Socio Bosque by the Ecuadorian Ministry of Environment in the Context of the Debates around Development and Climate Change, University of Salzburg.

Selassie, Bereket Habte. 2010. "Constitution Making in Eritrea: A Process-Driven Approach." *Framing the State in Times of Transition: Case Studies in Constitution Making*: 57–80.

Sheahan, John. 1987. *Patterns of Development in Latin America*. Princeton: Princeton University Press.

Shirk, Susan L. 1993. *The Political Logic of Economic Reform in China, California Series on Social Choice and Political Economy*. Berkeley: University of California Press.

Shugart, Matthew S. and John Carey. 1992. *Presidents and Assemblies*. Cambridge: Cambridge University Press.

Skidmore, Thomas E. 1990. *The Politics of Military Rule in Brazil, 1964–1985*. New York: Oxford University Press.

Smith, Graham. 2009. *Democratic Innovations: Designing Institutions for Citizen Participation, Theories of Institutional Design*. Cambridge, UK; New York: Cambridge University Press.

Steiner, Jürg. 2012. *The Foundations of Deliberative Democracy: Empirical Research and Normative Implications*. Cambridge: Cambridge University Press.

Stepan, Alfred. 1988. *Rethinking Military Politics: Brazil and the Southern Cone*. Princeton: Princeton University Press. Reprint, Not in File.

Stepan, Alfred and Juan J. Linz. 2013. "Democratization Theory and the 'Arab Spring.'" *Journal of Democracy* 24 (2):15–30.

Stoner, Kathryn and Michael McFaul. 2013. *Transitions to Democracy: A Comparative Perspective*. Baltimore, MD: Johns Hopkins University Press.

Suberu, Rotimi T. 1997. "Crisis and Collapse: June-November 1993." In *Transition without End: Nigerian Politics and Civil Society under Babangida*, edited by Larry Diamond, Anthony Kirk-Greene, and Oyeleye Oyediran, 281–99. Boulder and London: Lynne Rienner Publishers.

Sunstein, Cass R. 2001. *Designing Democracy: What Constitutions Do*. New York: Oxford University Press.

Surowiecki, James. 2004. *The Wisdom of Crowds: Why the Many Are Smarter than the Few and How Collective Wisdom Shapes Business, Economies, Societies, and Nations*, 1st edn. New York: Doubleday.

Svolik, Milan W. 2012. *The Politics of Authoritarian Rule*. New York: Cambridge University Press.

Tarrow, Sidney. 1994. *Power in Movement: Social Movements, Collective Action, and Politics*. New York: Cambridge University Press. Reprint, In File.

Teorell, Jan. 2010. *Determinants of Democratization: Explaining Regime Change in the World, 1972–2006*. Cambridge: Cambridge University Press.

"The Citizens and the Constitutional Review Commission." 1995. *Foroyaa*, April 26, 1–3.

Thompson, Bankole. 1997. *The Constitutional History and Law of Sierra Leone (1961–1995)*. Lanham, MD: University Press of America.

Tierney, Stephen. 2012. *Constitutional Referendums: The Theory and Practice of Republican Deliberation*, 1st edn. Oxford constitutional theory. Oxford, UK: Oxford University Press.

Tilly, Charles and Sidney Tarrow. 2007. *Contentious Politics*. Boulder: Paradigm Publishers.

Tinker Salas, Miguel. 2015. *Venezuela: What Everyone Needs to Know*. New York: Oxford University Press.

Tocqueville, Alexis de, Harvey Claflin Mansfield, and Delba Winthrop. 2000. *Democracy in America*. Translated by Harvey C. Mansfield. Chicago: University of Chicago Press.

Touchton, Michael, and Brian Wampler. 2013. "Improving Social Well-Being through New Democratic Institutions." *Comparative Political Studies*.

Tsebelis, George. 2002. *Veto Players: How Political Institutions Work*. New York and Princeton: Russell Sage Foundation with Princeton University Press.

United Nations Office of the High Commission on Human Rights. 2010. *National Human Rights Institutions History: Principles, Roles and Responsibilities*. New York: United Nations.

United Nations Secretary-General. 2009. *United Nations Assistance to Constitution-Making Processes*. New York: United Nations.

Valenzuela, J. Samuel. 1989. "Labor Movements in Transitions to Democracy: A Framework for Analysis." *Comparative Politics* 21 (4):445–72.

Veja. 1980. "Documento: A Conferencia Secreta da ESG – A Abertura por Golbery." 6.

von Beyme, Klaus. 2011. "Representative Democracy and the Populist Temptation." In *The Future of Representative Democracy*, edited by Sonia Alonso, John Keane, Wolfgang Merkel, and Maria Fotou, 50–73. Cambridge; New York: Cambridge University Press.

Walker, Lee Demetrius, and Philip J. Williams. 2010. "The Nicaraguan Constitutional Experience: Process, Conflict, Contradictions, and Change." In *Framing the State in Times of Transition: Case Studies in Constitution Making*, edited by Laurel E. Miller and Louis Aucoin, 483–504. Washington, DC: United States Institute of Peace.

Walker, Mark Clarence. 2003. *The Strategic Use of Referendums: Power, Legitimacy, and Democracy*. New York, NY: Palgrave Macmillan.

Wampler, Brian. 2012. "Participation, Representation, and Social Justice: Using Participatory Governance to Transform Representative Democracy." *Polity* 44:666–82.

Way, Lucan. 2005. "Kuchma's Failed Authoritarianism." *Journal of Democracy* 16 (2): 131–45.

Weeks, Jessica L. 2008. "Autocratic Audience Costs: Regime Type and Signaling Resolve." *International Organization* 62 (1):35–64.

Weingast, Barry R. 2008. "The Performance and Stability of Federalism: An Institutional Perspective." In *Handbook of New Institutional Economics*, edited by Claude Ménard and Mary M. Shirley, 149–72. Heidelberg: Springer.

Weldon, Jeffrey. 1997. "Political Sources of Presidencialismo in Mexico." In *Presidentialism and Democracy in Latin America*, edited by Scott Mainwaring and Matthew Soberg Shugart. New York: Cambridge University Press. Reprint, In File.

Weller, Nicholas and Jeb Barnes. 2014. *Finding Pathways: Mixed-Method Research for Studying Causal Mechanisms, Strategies for Social Inquiry*. Cambridge: Cambridge University Press.

Welzel, Christian. 2013. *Freedom Rising: Human Empowerment and the Quest for Emancipation*. New York: Cambridge University Press.

Widner, Jennifer A. 2004. *Constitution Writing and Conflict Resolution Dataset Parts 1 and 2*. Princeton, NJ.

2007. "Proceedings." In *Workshop on Constitution Building Processes*. Princeton: Princeton University.

2008. "Constitution Drafting in Post-Conflict States Symposium." *William and Mary Law Review* 49:1513–41.

Wilentz, Sean. 2005. *The Rise of American Democracy: Jefferson to Lincoln*, 1st edn. New York: Norton.

William S. Hein & Company. 2012. "Hein Online." In. Buffalo, NY: W.S. Hein. http://www.heinonline.org.

Wing, Susanna D. 2008. *Constructing Democracy in Transitioning Societies of Africa: Constitutionalism and Deliberation in Mali*. New York: Palgrave Macmillan.

Wood, Elisabeth Jean. 2000. *Forging Democracy from Below: Insurgent Transitions in South Africa and El Salvador, Cambridge Studies in Comparative Politics*. Cambridge and New York: Cambridge University Press.

World Bank. 2013. *World Development Indicators*. Washington, DC: World Bank.

Index

Tahrir Square, 135
Tarrow, Sidney, 123
term limits, 18, 65, 85, 103, 105, 111, 124, 135, 145
The Gambia, 13, 21, 66, 80, 86, 98, 101, 103–4,
    110–13, 122, 146
Tierney, Stephan, 11, 15, 95, 152, 160
Tilly, Charles, 61, 123
Tocqueville, Alexis de, 59, 120, 154
transitions (regime), 2, 6, 9–10, 12–14, 21, 27,
    29, 38, 39, 46, 47, 55, 58, 60, 74, 78, 87–9,
    91–4, 97, 99, 103, 105–11, 115, 122–3, 128–9,
    135–6, 138–9, 155–6
transparency, 2–3, 5, 8, 11, 13, 16–17, 28–9, 55,
    63, 85, 92, 97, 102, 137, 143–5, 153, 157
Tunisia, 1–3, 21, 23–4, 46, 50, 55–8, 81, 83, 87,
    98, 112, 114, 118–19, 122–5, 128–31, 135–6,
    138–41, 146–8, 151, 155–6, 162
Turkey, 18, 73, 83, 96

Uganda, 12, 46, 67, 84, 88, 91, 113, 116
United Nations, 11, 158
United States, 7, 15, 41, 93–4, 160
United States Agency for International
    Development, 78

Venezuela, 21, 26, 46, 79–80, 85–6,
    98–101, 103, 110–13, 122, 132,
    134, 146
veto players, 27, 55, 58
Villa, Francisco "Pancho", 48, 83, 140

Washington, George, 7
Widner, Jennifer, 10, 26–7, 33, 55
Wilson, Kenneth A., 26, 39, 62,
    64, 122
Wing, Susanna, 12
wisdom of crowds, 120
Woods, Elisabeth, 139
World Bank, 11, 33, 70
World War I, 50

Yasuní Reserve, 134
Yeltsin, Boris, 13

Zambia, 26, 84
Zapata, Emiliano, 48, 140, 161
Zimbabwe, 65, 76